Another Heart in His Hand

ANOTHER HEART
IN
HIS HAND

A SPIRITUAL ANOMALY

**Adventures and Conversations
with a Poker Playing Master of Life**

J. Jaye Gold

♦

PERADAM PRESS

Mountain View, Arkansas & Santa Barbara, California

PERADAM PRESS
P.O. BOX 2035
MOUNTAIN VIEW, ARKANSAS 72560

A DIVISION OF THE CENTER FOR CULTURAL AND NATURALIST STUDIES

© 1994 J. Jaye Gold
HOUSTON PUBLIC LIBRARY
Printed in the United States of America

Owing to limitations of space, all permissions and
acknowledgments appear in the back of this book.

First Printing
Book design and cover by Amalthea Birkholz.

Library of Congress Cataloging-in-Publication Data

Gold, J. Jaye,   date.
    Another heart in his hand : a spiritual anomaly : adventures and
conversations with a poker playing master of life / J. Jaye Gold.
        p.   cm.
    Includes bibliographical references and index.
    ISBN 1-885420-11-0
    1. Life. 2. Self-realization 3. Quality of life--Psychological
aspects. I. Gold, J. Jaye,   date. II. Title.
BD431.G52   1994
128--dc20   94-26239
                                                CIP

For Adam, Lara, and Demian, and for all the other children and their children as well. This book is for you, when and if you ever need it.

From a conversation between Carl Jung and Hermann Hesse:

Why would I want to read this new book of yours?

It might get you hoping, wishing, questioning again.
It might get you moving.
It might remind you that you've forgotten your road.

If all that happens, and I remember my road, how far can I walk on that road?

Get up, get on it, start walking, and find out.

Contents

CONTENTS

Author's Note on Gender Usage

The subject matter of this book is equally relevant to both women and men. Since historically women have had more inclination toward nurturing peace and love in our world, one might even surmise that a book of this kind could be more relevant to female readers than to male ones. In these times, the exploration for women's identity has subjected all our previous assumptions of strength and weakness to re-evaluation. I am sincerely sensitive to this issue and although this re-evaluation is not the focus of this book, I wish to do my part to assist in recognizing mistakes of the past, for which we all have suffered, and try to correct them in the present.

For that reason, I would have preferred to use the feminine (woman, she) as a synonym for human, rather than the conventional usage (man, he). It is my assessment, unfortunately, that males have not yet attained the flexibility to absorb the content of prose containing that gender usage.

Recognizing that women, through their present struggle, have become more resilient than men (perhaps they always were), I will burden them once more with the use of the masculine gender. I apologize to my female readers for the pace at which these needed changes are proceeding.

I hope that these statements don't alienate prospective male readers, but I can assume that anyone who would be offended by these words, would have a hard time appreciating this book anyway.

Preface

It rained most of last night and it's still raining this morning. I live in a mobile home, so the sounds of the rain reach me in a less insulated way than if I lived in a house. Sometimes I wonder why people like to be so insulated from the outside. If you don't hear the rain, then it can't awaken you and you can't go into the living room and stare out of the window at the drops falling on the porch.

Well my roof is metal, so that's what happened to me. And as I sat, eyes fixed on the falling of the droplets into a puddle on the top of an upside down plastic bucket, my mind wandered actively to the subject that had been occupying me for the last few weeks.

I had recently completed, with the aid of a computer, the editing of about three hundred pages of precious stories and conversations, each conveying incredibly unique wisdom, either told to me by a certain remarkable person over the last three years, or lived out by me in the company of that person.

The challenge I was facing was this: How was I going to follow the only instructions that I was given in relation to all this material and the only price I was asked to pay for it -- *Pass it on as best you can.*

Through the good fortune of living under a noisy metal roof, I believe now that I have the answer to how to go about my task. My intention is to pass on, unaltered, all the knowledge and wisdom that was given to me. I will tell only as much of the circumstances in which I acquired this knowledge, as necessary to assist the reader in assimilating it.

In other words, this will be no adventure story; it will probably not entertain you, and if eventually you put it down because it requires too much of you, I won't be at all surprised.

1

IT'S HARD TO PLANT FRUIT TREES

Through what may have been mistakes in my upbringing and a series of both fortunate and misfortunate circumstances, I developed, as a young man, the questionable skills of a reasonably proficient poker player. Which means, if I played with average players, I usually won, but if I played with professionals, I usually lost. I eventually moved to California because public poker casinos had recently become legal there, and I figured it was time for me to try my hand at becoming a full time player. I don't use the word gambler, because gambling means maybe you win and maybe you lose, and this was not my intention.

When I first arrived in California, I did some traveling around to find the best spot to "make my stand." Or perhaps I would discover that I fit better into the category of a roving poker player. My travels eventually took me to a small card casino near San Diego, and this is where my story begins.

The game that I prefer to play is called seven card stud. It's the game that I'm most familiar with because I've been playing it since childhood. Recently I've had to learn other poker games

5

because stud isn't as popular as it used to be. These days, a game called Texas hold-em is what most people play. So for the last couple of years, that's the game that I've been playing.

In hold-em, each player gets two cards that are known only to the player himself (it could also be herself, because there are numerous women hold-em players, some, much better players than I), and there are five cards that are dealt facing up in the middle of the table. Everyone shares those five in common. The idea is to make the best poker hand out of the seven cards available. The game is very fast and lends itself to a lot of gambling. That's why it has become more popular than stud, which is much more conservative.

Most, if not all casino poker rooms operate similarly, taking their example from the Las Vegas model. So wherever you are, you pretty much know what the routine is when you walk in the door. Walk around and scope out the games, go up to the man in charge (the floor man) and tell him you want the next available seat in the game of your choice. That's what I did as I wandered around California looking to find the best spot for me to turn pro, and that's what I did one October evening near San Diego.

Nine or ten people can sit around a hold-em table, so it's not so easy to get to know the style of the competition, unless you really put in some extensive time with the same people. I was the only non-local at the table, but as far as I could tell, nobody took much notice when I sat down. Time passed as it usually did for me in the early hours of playing at a new game, conservative play, don't attract attention, exude an air of confidence but don't neglect to scope out the other players.

It was during that scoping out that I noticed, amongst my unremarkably appearing opponents, a man sitting directly opposite me at the table, in what is known in poker table jargon, as the "eight seat." I was sitting at the "two seat," which is the second seat to the left of the dealer, and the rest of the seats are numbered accordingly around the table.

Mr."eight seat" was in his middle years though not yet graying and he wore the narrow type of reading glasses that you can peer over if you want to let someone know that you're looking at them. It may have been my imagination, but he seemed inordinately interested in my style of play, paying special attention to the "hands" that I was involved in. Of course, this could simply have been because I was a new player.

Since my aim was to assess if I could make money at this game, in addition to, of course, making money while I assessed, there wasn't much time for theorizing about this man who occasionally gazed over his glasses at me.

I played a couple of hours of uninspired poker in what seemed to me to be an uninspiring game. Then I took my minimal winnings, enough to pay my living expenses for the day, and retired to a nearby motel.

The next morning, I awoke expecting that I would be hitting the road, resuming my search for my poker place on the planet. My thoughts of where to drive were repeatedly interrupted by subliminal flashes of curiosity about seat #8 and its inhabitant. Being a more than less practically thinking person and not normally given to thoughts of destiny and fate, made it all the more unusual for me to forgo my departure and sign up for another night at the Motel 6 so I could hang around until it was an appropriate time to hit the tables. I pacified my practical beast with the rationale that I had indeed won money the day before.

A similar collection of regulars were present on my second visit. Although not a regular myself, I was now not a stranger, at least to the floor man who asked me if I wanted a seat. I scanned the game, noticing the vacant seat which was, according to the floor man, "waiting for me," and agreed to sit.

One of the few remaining bastions of cigarette smoking is the Poker Parlor. Some casinos have sophisticated exhaust equipment to help create tolerable environments for the non-smoker, but in some of the casinos, mostly the smaller ones on the smaller budgets, you're on your own. Being an ex-smoker anti-smoking fascist, one of the criteria with which I measure the appeal of any potential game, is will I have to sit down-wind from someone smoking. I used to carry one of those little battery operated fans that I would set in front of me and blow away the "incoming," but now I just pick and choose.

Now that you know the jargon, you'll know where I sat if I tell you that I occupied the "five seat." Once I walked into the card room and entered my poker playing world, I entirely forgot my unexpected curiosity about the man in the narrow glasses. I didn't even realize that he wasn't at the table until more than an hour had passed and the game started to lose some of its interest for me.

I looked around to see if he was in some other part of the place and spotted him sitting facing me from a corner booth in the small casino restaurant. I had to turn deliberately halfway around to spot him again, and this made me uneasy. As I did, he looked at me over his glasses and gave me a slight nod of the head, which I returned. My preoccupation with this man at my back, added to the fact that I wasn't much into playing, got me to wondering if I should go into the restaurant and say hello.

Since sometimes people play for hours and hours in games of this kind, you can take a break whenever you want to. If people are waiting, the floor man will probably remind you after a half an hour or so, but sometimes not even then. I stacked up my chips, got up and walked toward the rear booth in the casino coffee shop.

He gestured that it was okay to sit down opposite him. I didn't really know what, if anything, I wanted from him. So after we exchanged a few "pokerisms" about the game that I had just gotten up from, I figured I'd try a little small talk.

"You lived around here long?" I asked.

Rather than look at me over the top of his glasses, which was the only eye contact that I had made with him thus far, he took them off and put them on the table in front of him. In the years to follow, ones in which we became friends, this would become a cue to me that he was about to say something to which I should give my maximum attention. At that moment, I just thought he was going to pick up the thread of the small talk that I had initiated.

"I've lived here for a few years. I came down from Oregon."

Oregon seemed like a curious place for a gambler to live, so I probed further by asking him what part of Oregon and what he did there.

"...on a farm in the Willamette Valley with a group of friends," he said.

He spoke with a casual deliberateness that gave me the impression that there was a lot more to him than these one line answers indicated. I was becoming genuinely curious, so after chatting awhile about the climate there and where exactly this valley was, I asked him if he would tell me a little about how he came to do what he does, having come from where he came. He accepted my request graciously and responded with this story.

"After we first moved to the farm and got our housing set up, one of the first things that we tried to figure out was what we could plant as a major crop. We had a lot of discussions about what to plant. I say 'we,' not only because there were several of us there, but also because the local deer population, unbeknownst to us, had a major interest in our decision. The deer managed to get their input included, because we took very good care of deer nutrition in that part of Oregon that year."

I was more interested in his manner of speaking than I was in Oregon farming, but since I wanted to appear like I was into his story, I contributed the appropriate question.

"So what did you plant?" I asked.

"When we met to make the final decision," he continued, "there were a lot of suggestions -- strawberries, vegetables, mushrooms, lawn seed..., then somebody said, 'How about planting a whole bunch of fruit trees?'

"Being a city boy, I didn't know anything about any of it, so I asked, 'How long do they take to have babies? You know, how long do they take to do their thing, make fruit?' And somebody said, 'I think five years, six years, whatever it is, seven years. It takes a while.'

"So we looked at each other, there were a few moments of awkward silence, then somebody said, 'Let's do strawberries.'"

He stopped talking to take a sip of whatever was in the cup in front of him, I think it was tea. I liked his story telling style even though I had no idea where this particular one was leading, if anywhere.

"I don't want to bore you -- are you interested in this? Should I go on?" He asked in such an exaggeratedly ingenuous manner, that I had a momentary thought that he was putting me on.

"No, go on, go on," I said, only half meaning it.

He continued, "I could tell you a lot of funny stories about the strawberries we planted and how the deer ate them all, which they did. How we put up a six foot fence, then we put up an eight foot fence, then we put out the dog. The dog made friends with the deer, the deer jumped the eight foot fence, and most of the crop got eaten. So we could just as well have planted fruit trees, but that's not my point."

His story was certainly entertaining enough, but that it had, or was going to have a point was a surprise to me. "Point?" I said confused.

"I've always remembered," he proceeded, "that we didn't plant the fruit trees, and I've always known why we didn't plant the fruit trees. Because we wanted to get the fruit for ourselves. We wanted to be the ones to get it."

"That seems pretty natural to me," I said.

"Of course in a way you're right," he said. "But because I know how difficult it would have been for us to decide to plant trees, it always impresses me when I hear that people are doing something so that their children or grandchildren will get to reap the benefits. That strikes me as really extraordinary, because we live in a world where it's even really hard to take a quick shower when water is scarce. It's easy to be critical about the oil companies, but it's hard to leave your car at home and bike or walk or share rides."

He paused and replaced his glasses.

10

Now I consider myself a pretty loose guy, but to get that kind of response from the question, "lived around here long," was a big stretch from what I was accustomed to. I knew we weren't doing small-talk anymore, but I didn't know what we actually *were* doing.

I couldn't think of any questions. So not knowing what else to do, I just looked at him like he was going to continue, and he obliged. "You like music?" he asked.

I nodded that I did.

"Remember a few years ago, Bob Dylan wrote a song called *You Gotta Serve Somebody*. Well it's so. Everyone is serving either someone or something. There are even people that serve their businesses. They give part of their life to their hobbies, part of their life is for their family. But their business, they live for that, they serve that, they take care of that. They're concerned not only with the demands of the moment, but when those people go away from their business, they still think about what can be done to improve it. They feel connected to that business. There is no separateness between that business and themselves."

I was beginning to find it a little difficult to listen to him. Having been in business just once, and then only for a short time, it was hard for me to relate to his enthusiasm for the subject. More than that though, I thought we were talking about his farm, and I guess this track jumping had me a little off balance.

He, however, proceeded like everything was going fine. "It's very magnetic for people to serve something. When people serve, they have special feelings that don't come from anything else. Serving happens where separateness stops. It's the natural behavior between two things that belong to each other and aren't seprate from each other. Like a mother and child. Do you know what I mean?"

Being called into the conversation at this time was a little awkward. I knew what he meant, mostly from what I recognized as my lack of ability to really get behind something in my own life. I was hesitant to jump in with a confession of my

11

inadequacies to a stranger, so I just told him that I understood and he went on.

"It feels great to belong, and it feels terrible to be separate. But still, look around and see peoples' actions -- most of those actions are self-consumed. People spend most of their time pushing away and being separate. It's a strange thing to do, because it's such a wonderful feeling to be part of something more expansive. Why is so much energy put into being separate?"

He posed a rhetorical question that, thank God, he didn't expect me to answer. Actually, I was beginning to become slightly interested. It was different, but it was -- I don't really know what it was.

He proceeded to tackle his own question. "If you belonged to an entity more expansive than yourself alone, that entity would engulf you and support you in the accomplishing of whatever was in its interests. If you were the team cook, for instance, and you got sick, then the other team members would bring you tea and soup and vitamin C or whatever it took for you to get better. Because there was an entity formed of which you were a necessary part."

He was silent for a moment before he added: "Do you mind if I say something rather personal?"

"Why not," I answered, thinking that he meant personal about him, not personal about me.

"Is there anybody bringing you tea and soup now? No? And how about the qualities of patience, compassion, detachment or the ability to love unconditionally? They're not being granted to you either. Why should they be? You haven't become part of something that necessitates your having those qualities."

Now hold on just one second, I said to myself.

You, the reader, have to remember that I just met this guy across a poker table the day before, and these were the first words that we had ever exchanged. So how did he know how patient or compassionate I was? I was beginning to think that it was a little pretentious of him to be making assumptions about somebody -- me, who he obviously didn't know anything about.

12

If I had fallen into my usual pattern at this point, I would prob-ably have started to merely pretend to listen to him, while actually beginning to talk to myself about how "off the wall" this guy was. But for some reason that's not what happened. Even though those last words registered as something of an insult, I could feel this halfway smile on my face and my head got into this bobbling up and down motion like I was agreeing with everything he was saying. Since no words came out of my mouth, I guess he ac-cepted my stupor as a sign that I could handle some more.

He went on. "Say that you work for some company and they give you a credit card to use for business expenses. Now, nobody has an expense account credit card from a company that they don't work for.

"If you walked into a company and said, 'Hey, I hear this is a good company, can I have one of your credit cards to use?' Or maybe you'd say, 'You gave him a credit card, what did he do?' 'Well he works for us.' 'Big deal! I want a credit card too.' Of course that sounds absurd. You probably think it's silly. It *is* silly, but the situation of working for a business and getting a credit card to pay for company expenses -- that's a normal thing."

It was time to fight back. At least that's the way I felt. I didn't think I had anything pertinent to say on the subject, but I felt that I'd better say something. It was a "salvage the ego" thing.

"What does all this have to do with your farm in Oregon?" I asked. It was the best I could do.

"Not only does it have to do with the farm, it's an analogy to the rest of our lives. The credit card we want, in this case, is the right to a beautiful experience. What's our claim to that? Is it our birthright? We don't know that it's our birthright. It doesn't appear to be our birthright. If you look around, you see millions of miser-able people -- you can't say having a beautiful experience of life appears to be *their* birthright."

The waitress passed by and he stopped talking. He asked her to bring him some dry toast with jelly on the side. He then asked me if I wanted anything and after I declined, he asked me if I was interested in this kind of stuff.

I said, obliviously, that I had just eaten. He laughed and said that he didn't mean food but was I interested in what he was talking about. I said, "Sure," without much conviction, but I guess it was enough, because he went on.

"People are into such an overwhelming state of self-serving, that there is no recognition of 'a company.' Is there a company? What is the company? Where is the company? Who represents the company? So all the credit cards have been withdrawn. They've all been canceled. There's a Leonard Cohen song that goes:

There are no letters in the mailbox,
and there are no grapes upon the vine.
And there are no chocolates in the boxes any more,
and there are no diamonds in the mine.

"The credit cards have been canceled! People are looking for substitutes for these canceled credit cards and it's not going too well. The substitutes are getting more and more complex. But these substitutes are still not replacing the original, because the original is very pure and simple."

I don't know how all this sounds to you, but at this point it started sounding like a sermon to me -- and I hate sermons. You get to meet a lot of extreme personalities around a gambling hall -- desperate people, frustrated people, lonely people, all looking for a way out.

It was appearing to me that I had unfortunately crossed paths with one of the above types and was now in the uncomfortable position of having to find some way to escape graciously from this erstwhile preacher. I couldn't just get up and walk away, so I figured that my best shot was to ask him a final question, one that would force him to reveal his religious fervor. Then I could excuse myself by saying that I wasn't interested in religion, or at least not in his. I latched onto his last sentence and asked him to define this "original credit card that was so pure and simple." He took the bait.

14

"A person is a servant of what creates him. A person is a natural employee of his creator, and that creator will issue expense account credit cards to that person -- credit cards which make accessible all the capacities necessary for a beautiful experience of life, in exchange for the dependable service of that natural employee. It doesn't take much to establish this relationship. Yes, there are obstacles, but it doesn't take any new building. We can be servants or we can resist being servants. There is no other possibility for us. Either we spend our time and energy serving, or we spend our time and energy resisting being in that service.

"Regardless of how colorful and varied the forms of this resistance, it will never be a successful substitute for the experience of being a servant of the creator and the creation. That experience cannot be simulated. So what do you think about all this?"

As our relationship progressed in the ensuing weeks, I realized that he often finished with this question and it was never rhetorical. He wanted to know what I had made of what he said. As for this time, as much as I would have liked to negate his views by questioning his sanity, I found it difficult to entirely dismiss them.

My mind was reeling and my eyes were probably rolling in my head. I had just been assaulted, without preparation, by a barrage of original ideas, only a few of which were familiar to me. I felt giddy, and although somewhat uncomfortable, not at all as displeased as I would have imagined.

The floor man came up behind me and I was saved from giving what could only have been a stupid or at any rate an inappropriate answer as to "what I thought." He informed me that if I didn't come back to my seat that I would be "picked up." Picked up means that he picks up your chips and holds them for you till you show up to claim them, but you lose your seat in the game to the next person waiting.

I acknowledged the floor man's warning, then looked over at this most unusual person across from me, whose name I didn't even know. I said, "I gotta go," with something of the aplomb of a person with a severe bladder problem.

This is how my re-education started, and it continued through three years of frequent contact with this most unusual man. Sometimes we did things, sometimes we went places, sometimes we played poker, and sometimes we just talked. As I said, I'm going to try to pass on everything he explained to me as accurately as I can, but don't expect much in terms of entertainment and adventure, because that's not the purpose of this book.

My new friend, as I discovered, could talk for extraordinary lengths of time, unprovoked. What was, perhaps, most remarkable was that he rarely repeated himself. At first his discourses were short (if you can call our introductory talk short), but as I developed the ability to listen better, he would sometimes go on uninterrupted for an hour or more.

When the idea of writing down this wealth of knowledge and wisdom, of which I was the beneficiary, first occurred to me, I realized that there were some gaping holes in my writing plan. First, I don't have any talent for writing, and second, I have a shitty memory when it comes to anything other than playing poker.

My eventual remedy or, more accurately, patch for those holes was the following strategy: (1) Don't try to tell a chronological story. (2) Arrange the information according to my own understanding of how it fits together. (3) Don't add or subtract anything. (4) Don't exaggerate and don't be clever. What you're about to read (I hope you continue) is my attempt to adhere to these self-imposed rules.

I returned to the poker parlor in pursuit of something which was extremely indefinite to me and someone whose name I didn't even know, but who was most definitely, definite. My re-education continued immediately upon locating him and lasted, as I said, for three years.

Some of the stories that follow are ones that he told to me, but most are the recounting of events at which I was present. The chapter divisions are included for the purpose of organizing the material into manageable sections. As he used to say to me, so I'll say to you, "Take what you can and leave the rest."

Although he was in the card room on my next visit, he made no attempt to make contact with me. It was actually I who tried several times, with no results, to establish eye contact with him. Being ignored in this way resulted in my feeling extremely distracted and not at all interested in playing poker.

I eventually went back to my motel to get some perspective on what was going on with this unusual mood of mine. It was only after soaking in a hot bath for fifteen minutes that I began to realize that whatever had been on my list of priorities, before this introductory conversation of ours, had fallen from recognition. All my inner conversations were occupied with my imaginary responses to his presumptuous sermon, of which, by the way, I had curiously retained almost every word.

I returned to the card room intending to make a clean break of this bad situation. Almost immediately upon entering, he approached me with a "where have you been" smile, adding that he had just had a "bad beat" (lost a tough hand) and was on his way out to get some air. He asked if would I care to take a walk with him around the block.

To this day, I never have gotten the upper hand with this man, and I certainly didn't that time. I found myself acquiescing instantly, and before I knew it, we were strolling down the street, and he was taking up where he left off with his ideas of creators and creations and credit cards.

"Basically all we've learned, is to see ourselves in relation to ourselves. Of course people get married or go into a business that they really care about, or get to own some property of some kind, some possession that they really like, and then their world expands. They become me-and-my-car or me-and-my-house, me-and-my-family, me-and-my-business.

"I'll tell you something interesting. The amount of your capacity is directly proportional to what you identify yourself with, or as I said before, what you see yourself in relation to. So if you're identified with your family, you have a family's worth of capacity. If you're identified with your city, you have a city's worth of capacity. If you're identified only with yourself, then you have one person's worth of capacity."

I figured if I was going to listen to what he had to say, I might as well get something out of it. So I told him that since I was real weak with absorbing theoretical stuff, maybe he could give me an example of what he was talking about.

"Take a situation that has always been extraordinary to me," he responded, "the situation of the politician. An ordinary person, a hard worker maybe, a diligent person, also probably a jerk, all of those things. You know, some of these guys read fifteen newspapers a day. Now you and I don't read fifteen newspapers a day! You understand? The energy for all that reading comes from their identification with their job. For whatever reason, positive or negative, they are identified with their constituency, which is a bigger entity than themselves. That identification energizes them to do all this newspaper reading. So, the more encompassing one's identification is, the larger the energy pool that one has to draw from.

"Some people think it's good to lose all identification, but really there's something not quite right about that. Because if, in actuality, we are part of the whole creation, then our natural identification is with that whole. The greatest amount of capacity comes from identification with the greatest entity. If we're identified with being part of the human race, we root for circumstances that will improve the lot of that race, and we feel concern about the circumstances that degrade the conditions of the race."

We concluded our walk and re-entered the poker room through the rear door. The sounds of pro-football on the T.V. that hung over the bar made it difficult to continue our conversation. He urged me over to some tables and chairs at the far end of the room where the noise was more moderate.

I discovered, not necessarily on that particular walk around the block, but more as our relationship continued, that this guy not only had a huge view of the world, but he had the incredible capacity to pull spontaneous examples out of everyday life that could clarify and simplify the bigness of his vision.

"How about football, you like football don't you?" he asked.

I actually liked football quite a bit, and what's more I knew a lot about it (mostly from betting on games). I thought that I would have a chance to display some of my prowess, but after nodding my head in the affirmative, he took off in an uncharted direction.

"Take the example," he said, "of a person who's identified with the entire sport of football, like Pete Rosell, the football commissioner. He's hoping to have great football games with exciting plays, the kind of games that guys like us love to watch. He's not identified with this team or that team. He says, 'Let's have a great game.' But the guy who's on one side or the other, says, 'Let's *our* team have a great game.'

"So, the way it goes is, the more encompassing your identification, the greater the game you wish for. The greater the entity that you serve, the more energy that you have. There is no other source of energy. There is no personal energy. If a person is identified with the entire creation, they are given incredible wisdom, incredible magic, incredible compassion, incredible strength, incredible endurance -- and incredible patience."

I was beginning to see the thread in his discourse. Some years back, I had gone through a stage of reading whatever I could get my hands on relating to different philosophies. Even though I had never thought about these ideas in an organized way, I remembered flashes of insight that seemed parallel. A genuine question popped into my thoughts. "How do you explain the great things that people do who are not connected to anything bigger than themselves?"

He seemed pleased that I had hooked into his idea. He answered thoughtfully, "Very difficult circumstances sometimes thrust people into situations where they become temporarily identified with something greater. If all the lights blacked out here in the city, there would, all of a sudden, be no more *my* house and *your* house. There would be no *our* problem and *their* problem. We would become one against a common foe, like the power outage or some such thing. Everyone would come out into the streets. These streets that are normally used for going "to and from," would suddenly become the congregating place for all.

"When these kinds of things happen, they create entities that can work together, do great things together, lift things, move things, raise money, save lives, even drink coffee together. But when that external crisis subsides, that is no longer the case, no permanent basic change has taken place. The only identification that causes permanent change is an identification that isn't maintained by external forces or factors. Only something that *is*, doesn't change.

"There are entities to serve far greater than yourself, and that greater service that I'm talking about is a natural thing. Not a thing that you have to work toward, but one that you have to relax into. We are all born as servants, and no struggle is needed to become one."

2

PROBLEMS, PLANS & RELATIONSHIPS

We asked Canopus how things were on other planets.
And suddenly our minds seemed filled with newness...
we were stretched...we were much larger than we had been.

Doris Lessing

I didn't see my new friend for a few days, and it felt good to get down to the normality of playing poker and putting philosophy aside.

Our next encounter was at the poker tables. It was getting close to midnight and I had been playing since late afternoon. He came in and we were soon sitting across from each other. Poker is a game of win and lose, beat your opponent or get beaten yourself. So it was somewhat awkward for me to have him as an adversary, and I could tell that he knew it. Whenever we came close to going up against each other, he would smile or laugh or tell a joke, which I knew was for the purpose of lightening things up.

After about an hour of playing, we both took a break and met over some hot drinks in the restaurant. We joked a little about who was the better player, and then I mentioned that I had done something that was unusual for me. I had written down several questions for him on the subject of serving. He seemed very

21

pleased by my interest, and suggested that since he was getting tired and in need of some quiet time, maybe we could meet the next day and talk about my questions.

One of his favorite places to walk in San Diego was through the rows of sailboats down by the marina. He mentioned the place and we set a time to meet there.

We spotted each other around noon, and as we walked I read him the four questions that I had written down: (1) Why is it that we seek out such separateness? (2) Why do we identify with such a personal view of the world? (3) Why aren't we the agents of a more giving force? (4) If that greater service is indeed our natural capacity, then something unnatural must be in the way. How did that something unnatural get in the way, and what keeps it there?

His answers were unexpected, unique, and challenging to understand.

"In ordinary life there are only a few subjects that people generally talk about with each other. Mostly, it's the things that happen to them and the things that happen to others. It would be unusual that a subject of conversation between people would be the atmospheric conditions on Jupiter, or any other subject not related to the things that people do.

"That's basically how it goes. People are interested in people stuff. I call it the problems, plans, and relationships of life. You spend all of your time dealing with these three concerns, and all the people that you know also spend their time dealing with similar problems, plans, and relationships. After a while the world becomes a place where the only things that exist are people and their P.P.& R."

As much as I would have liked to interrupt him and claim an exemption from that particular club, I knew enough about myself to know that he was right. After chewing on my pride long enough to get it into small pieces, I swallowed it.

"So the total picture that we draw," he continued, "through our focus on our own P.P.& R. is that we humans are the central focus of the earth, the essence of life on earth. Everything else circulates around us.

"Certainly, we couldn't feel and think anything else because such a huge portion of our energy goes into thinking about our own personal problems, plans, and relationships. We also think, in decreasing amounts, about the P.P.& R. of those that we know and sometimes even those that we don't know, with a teeny bit left over for the other world, the one that doesn't have to do with people."

I asked him if he could be a little more specific about how this P.P.& R. business actually caused trouble for us.

"Good idea!" he said. "Since we're exploring obstacles to being a servant of the creation, I'll tell you about a specific manifestation, one which is encouraged by our excessive attention to our problems, etc. I call it self-importance.

"It's neither a quality that we sought to have nor is it one that we are meant to have. It's something that came about mostly because we were always pushed into this position."

"What position do you mean?" I interrupted.

He did a three-sixty pirouette and said, "The position of looking at ourselves like we are at the center of things. Even the most progressive of us has been taught that we are ruining *our* environment.

"I'll tell you a little about this idea of self-importance, and I want you to try to understand it in a really impersonal way, because it is a really impersonal idea. It's not an accusatory idea. It's not like you've got it and somebody else doesn't. Everybody's got it, they couldn't have avoided it. The fact that you see fit to listen to me means that you have it. The fact that you saw fit to take care of yourself today says that you have it."

My attention shuttled between noticing the lush sailboats parked along the pier and listening to his responses to my questions. It was curious, shifting back and forth between looking at these sailboats, the symbols of freedom's fantasy in the western world, and listening to a description of some unavoidable limitation called self-importance that we drag around with us.

23

After a while, we stopped next to a long sleek cruising boat --
the kind that had probably sailed into most of the exotic ports of
the world. Its name was "Impossible," and it was from The
Bahamas. My friend laughed at some private joke and then asked
me if I ever did any sailing. We exchanged a few stories of our
minor attempts at learning to sail, and soon he finessed his remarks about sailing into a continuation of our conversation about
self-importance.

"What happens when this life of ours starts to go off course?
When does it start? When you're very small you have some sense
of your own importance, and then slowly you develop and develop
and develop. Not all that develops is informational, physical or
emotional. What also develops, through external influences on
you, is this incredibly distorted sense of your own importance."

"Are you saying," I asked, "that all self-importance is bad, or
is it okay to have some?"

"Good question," he said. "There's a saying from a story about
mountain climbing called *Mount Analogue:*

> *Your life depends to some extent on your shoes;*
> *care for them properly. But a quarter of an hour*
> *each day is enough, for your life depends*
> *on several other things as well.*

"We are the shoes. We are what walks on the Earth. Not only
in a poetic sense, but we actually are the shoes. Our bodies, our
ideas, our feelings, our personal property, all walk the earth -- not
our possessions, but our personal property in the form of our
concept of ourselves, which is very personal property.

"We're very important, we need attention, we need astute attention. We need to be taken care of, and fifteen minutes a day is
enough. Well when I first read that, it shocked me, but somehow I
really believed it. I couldn't say that I was ready to act on what I
believed, because I was one of those people who had fifteen
minutes a day left for everything else, but still it rang true to me."

I suspected he was going to talk about his own personal experience. My ears perked up and my attention increased, partly, as I later found out, because of the additional entertainment value, but also because I thought that perhaps I would hear something that might inform me as to some course of action that was connected to all this theory. I also suspect that he threw me these tidbits when he noticed that my ability to concentrate was waning.

"I was a reasonably okay person," he continued, "but still, this tremendous incongruity. So I spent some time checking out what was going on. How was I taking care of myself? How much time was it taking? Was I over caring for myself? How much was I over caring for myself? In what ways was I over caring for myself? How much care did I really need?

"I discovered that not only was fifteen minutes a day enough, but some days I only needed to make sure that yesterday's fifteen minutes had me covered. What I started to see was that the rest of my time was occupied with thinking about my situation -- problems, plans, and relationships. Are you familiar with thinking about your situation?"

I nodded that I was familiar, and he went on.

"I was constantly thinking about how my situation had been, thinking about how my situation is, and thinking about how it could and should be. And since I was so occupied with these self-serving thoughts, how could I possibly feel anything other than separate from everything and everyone?

"If somebody had told me that I spent ninety percent of my time thinking about my situation, I would have thought their observation ridiculous and inaccurate. After checking it out, there was no doubt. They *were* inaccurate. I discovered that I was thinking about my situation one hundred percent of the time. No, not always thinking about my job, friends, or family, but more like in each moment thinking about my situation. It might be like thinking about my physical comfort, or thinking, 'I wonder how long he's going to go on talking?'"

When he said this, he glanced over at me with a twinkle in his eye, knowing that he had caught me. We both had a good laugh.

25

His laugh, in the early stages of our relationship, was infinitely superior to my own, but as time passed, I caught up. He asked if he should go on talking. I said that I was following really well most of the time, but that I was subject to having a wandering mind. He continued in mid-sentence.

"...thinking about the temperature out here, thinking about things I might have to do later, things I did before. Thinking, 'I wonder what he's thinking, why is he looking at me?' All these things that occupy the little moments that are in between situations, all sewed together as a non-stop endeavor called *thinking about my situation*. Problems, plans, relationships, all joined together by a million moments of general awkwardness which always seem to demand consideration, or some sort of massage at the very least, either physical, emotional, mental, sexual, intellectual, spiritual, mechanical -- something.

"In other words, it's never quite right. Something additional is always needed. I discovered that the greatest and most encompassing identification that I felt was with myself. The only credit card that I was getting the benefit of was the one that I issued to myself."

We had been walking and talking for almost an hour. My view of this man's knowledge was definitely being altered. He was, I realized, no fanatic, religious or otherwise. The way he was beginning to appear to me was as a man who had taken life as an opportunity to learn, rather than as an opportunity to enhance his position.

For the first time that I could remember, maybe even since childhood, I felt a little humble, because I knew that my life had taken the opposite course.

He looked over at me, probably because I was looking down and distant. We sat quietly on a bench for a while. It was a beautiful California day, and we were facing the ocean. After a while I returned from my past, and he returned to where he left off.

"I know this is an extremely volatile, revolutionary, and controversial point of view to bring up here in the U.S.A. where we

26

have so finely developed the art of dealing with problems, plans, and relationships. You know there are actually living masters in this art among us here in this country. There are people with great amounts of knowledge and experience who can advise and teach others how to take care of themselves. We live in the mecca, we are the mecca of self-serving.

"Life has become nothing but dealing with, 'How can I improve my lot at this moment?' or, 'How can I improve my lot in the next moment?' And that's not where it's at -- that is definitely off-course. Maybe the title of that song *You Gotta Serve Somebody* could be *You Gotta Serve Somebody Other Than Yourself.*"

I was, for some reason, starting to become depressed. Feeling the need to re-establish myself as a credible human being, I snatched a little doubt from my pocket and said, "It's hard for me to picture anybody, except maybe Mother Theresa, who spends only fifteen minutes on themselves. It doesn't even sound possible."

He smiled at me like he knew where I was coming from and said, "Let me give you an example. You know this word, 'comfortable'? It has always been in the dictionary, but never has it gotten as much use as in this last period of years. I doubt that hundreds of years ago a host would greet his guests by saying, 'Well, I hope everyone is comfortable?' These days, the demand for comfort is everything and everywhere. So much so that you might think, 'So what's wrong with that?'"

I wasn't thinking that right then, but since I certainly knew tons of people who would have, including myself at some other time, I saw no reason to interrupt.

"It takes a lot to convince people that they don't have to be concerned about all those moment-to-moment minuscule ill-at-easenesses. The ones that they spend so much time and energy dealing with, desperately trying to bring themselves to the level of okayness that they're used to. Could it be possible that fifteen minutes a day is enough to deal with all our needs, and the rest of the time we're okay to proceed on?"

The interactions that I've described so far have been exceedingly impersonal and not at all personally confronting. In the beginning, that was indeed the case. As my ability to understand both the content of his words and the goodness of his motivation increased, he became personally challenging and confronting more often -- and some few times even terrifying.

He was truly adept at scaring the shit out of me, but he always followed a harangue with a lot of good-natured laughing -- laughing that I was not always able to partake in, but at least I got the idea that for him, what was going on was light as opposed to heavy.

I thought I understood his point and was ready to go on to some other subject when he raised his eyebrows inquisitively.

"Maybe you think that I'm being repetitious," he said, "and you're beginning to get a little uncomfortable. I've told you this three times, and now you're getting a little antsy. So now you want me to go on to something else. But why? Why should I go on? Maybe I should tell it to you all over again. Do you really understand this idea already? Do you know it so well that you'll never forget it?

"That's not why you want me to go on. You want me to go on because you're getting uncomfortable, and you're not used to being uncomfortable. Soon you'll get fidgety. Then you'll start having opinions. Right? All because you have this idea that you're supposed to be comfortable.

"But haven't you already taken your fifteen minutes? It's late in the day. I'll bet you have, and more. If you took your fifteen minutes, then you don't have any time left. Your clock has run out. You have to suffer now. And how much are you willing to suffer? You understand what I'm saying? Basically you're unwilling -- not at all.

"Feel the level of your tolerance in this moment for this little grain of abrasion and how it demands to be taken care of. You say to yourself, 'Don't tell me that one more time or that'll be it. If he tells that story once more about the shoes, I'm outta here.'"

It felt like he was teasing me, but that didn't bother me. What gave me the most trouble was that he knew, without me saying anything, exactly what I was going through. I didn't know to what I should attribute his intuitive powers, but the possibilities made me even more uncomfortable than his repetition or teasing. It was that discomfort that moved me to inquire, "How did you know that?"

He shook his head like I'd missed the point. "That's not what's important right now," he said. "What I'm trying to explain to you is that this distorted sense of our own importance, this self-importance of ours which manifests in our always thinking that we need something additional, keeps us removed, moment to moment and day to day, from our natural capacity to serve.

"This natural capacity for service requires less separateness and the identification with something greater than our own needs. This obstacle of self-importance that we're talking about is kept in place by our daily self serving-actions, and since those actions are continuous, this obstacle never seems to let up."

I noticed that we had almost arrived back at the point where our promenade through the sailboats began. I was entertaining the possibility of going around again, when I felt this strong counter urge arise with the suggestion of flight. Interestingly though, along with this urge came a completely different reaction -- the calm observation that my capacity for this kind of input seemed extremely limited and that this didn't match up with my picture of myself.

In the middle of his last sentence about "daily self-serving actions" he looked over at me, obviously noticing that my thoughts were elsewhere. Right at the point of commitment whether to make the circuit again or not, he dropped the subject of self-importance and engaged me in a conversation that took me through the turnstile. Before I knew it we were passing the "Impossible" again and he was asking me why I played poker.

I appreciated the inclusion of a more benign subject. I told him about my monetary aspirations and how I thought I had a gift for playing the game that if nurtured could make me into a top flight professional. I went rambling on for awhile until I noticed that he was actually listening to what I was saying more conscientiously than I was listening to myself. At that point, probably brought about by embarrassment, I asked him why *he* played.

He told me a little about his poker history and then he said something that I still clearly remember. He explained that much of what he understood about human nature was learned at the poker tables because there, people behaved "as they were" (one of his favorite expressions). At the poker table, he explained, everyone, by the fact of their presence, is declaring that they want to win and that they want you to lose -- a situation which exists in ordinary life, but is always concealed behind politeness and subtle dishonesty.

3

LAUNCHING-PADS AND ROCKETSHIPS

The nearer your destination
The more you're slip slidin' away.
Paul Simon

His explanations were so precise and full of common sense, I can honestly say that I rarely out and out disagreed with him. The way I most often reacted to the revelations that I was being presented with, was by wondering how the conditions that he was describing came about, and what could be done to set them right. In the early times, he sternly brushed off any inquiry on my part that would lead our conversation in the direction of "what to do about it," but he always responded to my questions about "how did this come about" by taking the question at hand to the next deeper level.

The next deeper level, in the case of this subject of serving, involved an analogy which was one of his favorites and one to which he referred often. Because of the importance of the following, what he called, "point of view," I will recount that analogy in its entirety, without any description of the scene in which it took place or any comments or questions that I may have interjected.

I will however, before I begin, mention that my memory of his presentation of this point of view was enhanced by the fact that he explained it to me while passing Edward's Air Force Base, the place where the space shuttles land, on one of the trips that we took together to Las Vegas.

He began, "I'm from the East coast originally, so when I think of rocket ships, I think in terms of Cape Canaveral. It's a little bit different out here on the West coast -- here it's Vandenberg or Edwards. Wherever it is, they launch rockets there.

"One basic principle of launching a rocket is that you gotta have something that's really solid on the ground from which this huge craft can begin its flight. So they build these launching pads that hold the rocket securely in place, facing them in the right direction. They gotta be real sturdy so the force going down will shoot the rocket up.

"The flight that we call our lives also begins on a launching pad. We need to have something relatively stable set up for us, some dependable food source, someone to respond to our cries for assistance, basic stuff. Of course our parents don't see it as a launching pad. They see it as supplying the basic necessities of life.

"Then eventually, you go off to school and learn what your skills are, what your talents are. You learn how to relate to people and how to be okay. A little later on, you learn how to make money, how to prepare food, how to get clothes, and how to lie to the extent necessary to feel okay in this world. You also learn how to 'look' the way that's expected of you, and in your case, you learn how to be a card-shark.

"You gather up this whole package around you, under you, and that's what I call a launching pad. It's all the grounding that allows a person to feel okay about life. It takes most people twenty or twenty-five years to develop, but I think it's realistic to say that all of us have put in a good chunk of time working on our grounding and have successfully developed some kind of launching pad.

"Most of us have worked it out so we don't miss many meals. Maybe we have to live with our folks, or be on social security or whatever, but we've worked it out somehow. That's pretty basic and not too difficult to come by for the people in this culture.

"Then there are also other things that are connected with this grounding. You learn how to get people to like you, and are

32

somewhat successful at it. You learn how to like a few people, and are somewhat successful at that. You learn how to buy things -- on sale. You learn a little about sex, how to get from one place to the other, maybe drive a car. So we're basically describing what it takes to be relatively okay.

"Think about those guys over there at Edwards, they also spend plenty of time building their launching pads. I'm sure they're considerable and very technological structures -- they cost a lot of money, and building them takes a long time. It's not just a few sheets of plywood with cinder blocks underneath.

"So once they've built a launching pad, they start building the next step, which is the rocket ship, because they know when they're building the launching pad that it isn't the end product of their project. They're building the launching pad so that they can then build the rocket ship, and eventually it can take off. Otherwise, I doubt that they would build the launching pad.

"Now, this is where things get complicated and where we go off course. Because from the beginning, we're not informed in any way that we're building a launching pad. What we're told, and what our teachers and forebears understand, is that we're building *something*. But they've actually lost touch with what it is that we're building.

"They know how to build it. They know what it's supposed to look like and how to make it really strong and stable. But they don't know what it's for, so they can't tell us what it's for. Once it gets set up and there it is, we don't know what then to do with this launching pad.

"So, here's the situation. The guys at Edwards know what to do with their launching pads, but unlike them, even though we've taken years and years to build this structure of our lives, all our abilities, our possessions, our talents, we have no idea whatsoever of the purpose for this humongous structure that we've built. No idea! None whatsoever!

"I want to make that really clear, because I remember that *I* had no idea what to do with it. All I knew was 'Hmmm, this looks good,' or 'This doesn't look so good.' Then maybe I took a couple of breaths waiting to find out what to do with this thing.

"When nothing happened, I started to check it out again. 'Wow, this platform is pretty nice, but I think if it had a couple of windows it would be a little nicer. I think if it were another color it would be a little better. I think if I picked up the whole thing and moved it to Southern California it would be even better. I think if it were at a higher altitude, if it were a different shape, blah, blah, blah, blah...' But everything that I thought of was in relation to improving this launching pad, *never having any idea of its purpose.*

"Now I certainly couldn't be faulted for that, because what's a person to do? If you get together this substantial infrastructure and you have no idea what to do with it, the only thing you *can* do is try to improve it. Of course, improve it toward what end? Certainly not improve it toward being better for launching our-selves -- our rocket ships. It couldn't be, because we don't know that's what it's for. And even if we do suspect, we don't know where that flight is bound for. So we improve it for the only reason that occurs to us -- for our own comfort, for our own con-venience, for our own improvement, for our own benefit, and we do that again and again and again.

"You can see how we've lost touch with the possibility that fifteen minutes a day might be enough for taking care of our-selves. After a few of these cycles, we become creatures dedicated to the full-time improvement of our conditions. We see the world as a drama in which we are the central figures and our problems, plans and relationships the principal story. The possibility of feeling less separate, of being part of and serving something greater than ourselves, along with identifying with a more encom-passing entity has become remote to us because of our non-stop efforts to revamp our launching pad.

"A lot of people know, by the time they're your age, that repeating yesterday with a new twist isn't the key. Maybe they don't know what to do about it, but they know that it's not the key. They may even be saving up for the next alteration. They may be ready and even working at this very moment to get the next one rolling, but in their heart they have a very deep suspicion that it's not going to be the answer to anything.

"And of course, how could it be? Because all it is, is a launching pad. All it is, is the grounding of life, from which the next stage must then take place. All it is, is the foundation that the building is built on. And if you keep working on improving the foundation, sooner or later you're going to get the idea that you aren't getting anywhere. But as you look around, you see that everyone else is also working on the foundation, so you really don't know what else to do. So you go back and try to get another idea to improve your own launching pad.

"Wouldn't the engineers that build these launching pads feel very stale if sooner or later they didn't get to work on building a rocket ship, and then didn't eventually get to launch one? It would start to feel like, 'Hey, let's do something with this thing.'

"Wouldn't it be interesting if this analogy was a parallel to human life and we didn't know it. What if we actually were presented with some extraordinary possibilities which started with -- set up your grounding, get a few skills, meet a few people, learn a little language, get a few bucks -- basically get what most everybody in the western world already has -- then okay, next!

"From my perspective so many of the problems of this culture are connected to this one off-courseness of re-working, re-designing and relocating launching pads. That's why people get into things like, 'Everything's great but I've got a little twitch in my shoulder, a little tightness in my neck. I need something for it.' *No you don't!* Or, 'I have a lot of energy, but sometimes between three and four in the afternoon, I don't feel quite right.' *There's no problem!* You don't need anything between three and four in the afternoon. You don't need anything for any of the things that you have set up as problems -- you don't need!

"Your relationships are okay, your jobs are okay, your living space is okay. It's all okay. The problem is, it's all been set up, and you don't feel okay because you don't know what to do with it. You're over-ripe. You've been all set to go for years, some

35

people for years and years, but everyone for a bunch of time. You're hanging out there with this launching pad wondering what the fuck you're supposed to do with it. You don't know what you're supposed to do and you don't feel so good about it.

"You're ready to start on that rocket ship, and until you start on it, you're not going to feel okay. When you're due, you're due. Nothing else you do is going to feel right. You'll win some and you'll lose some, but it's going to be basically downhill.

"It doesn't take all that much energy to maintain the grounding that we need -- fifteen minutes a day may even be enough. Most of your energy, whether you know it or not, doesn't even go into the actual maintaining of grounding. It goes into your thoughts and efforts of how to improve it.

"It's hard for people to believe that the job that they have now is sufficient, *but it is sufficient.* There may be somebody else over there that has a better job, but what's the purpose of a job anyway? What's the purpose of a place to live anyway? What's the purpose of food on the table anyway? It's only to supply you with this launching pad from which you can take off.

"Think how ridiculous it would look, if these guys at this rocket base built these launching pads, and then started carving designs on the edges or putting little stained glass panels in the side. Would you say, 'Wow, that's really far out, that's really artistic'? No! You'd say, 'Why would you need these on a launching pad? What do they have to do with rockets taking off?'

"But go around to peoples' houses, you understand, go around to their lives, and you'll see all these extras. Their experience of life is not going to change from any of the alterations that they're planning to make, because it's disharmonious that they continue to work on their launching pad. It is only harmonious when you proceed and start to work on the next step -- the step that begins to face you in the direction of losing some of this self-importance and separateness, and starts you on the road to identifying with and serving something greater than yourself."

For a person who made frequent trips to Las Vegas, this was an invaluable analogy. At least twice each trip, going there and returning, these flat and barren miles often flown over by supersonic jets served to remind me of the possibilities and their adversaries.

4

BREAKING THE BOTTLE

Yes you who must leave everything that you cannot control.
It begins with your family but soon it comes round to your soul.

Leonard Cohen

Describing the analogy of the launching pad and the rocketship brings back a flood of memories relating to that particular trip to Las Vegas. It was not my original intention to do so, but since those memories are close at hand, I'll attempt to tell you about the rest of the trip.

I had heard that there was a small card room in the high desert on the way to Las Vegas. The games there were supposed to be really "loose" (people play more hands with worse cards thereby improving a good player's chances of winning). So at my suggestion, we made the turn to Adelanto. My friend had been there before, having stopped for a rest on a previous trip to Nevada. He drank some tea in the restaurant, while I sat down in the Omaha poker game.

Omaha is a relatively new game which has become fairly popular. It takes a lot of thinking because you get a lot of cards, but since you get so many cards the possibility of improving your hand is increased. People stay in the pots longer, hoping for something good to happen. The result is that there can be a lot of money on the table. I played for an hour and then joined him in the coffee shop where he was reading the newspaper.

He put the paper aside when I sat down and said, "See that young guy sitting in the #3 seat. I think his name is Barry." He pointed with his chin to the table where I'd been sitting. "I've known him for a while, he's a little daffy. He appears to be okay on the outside, but after you get to know him, you get the idea that not all the nuts and bolts are there, or both oars aren't in the water. I've always liked that expression, 'only one of his oars is in the water.'"

"What's wrong with him?" I asked.

"One time," he proceeded, "he spotted me in the parking lot of Harrah's up in Reno. I was working on my car and had all my tools spread around. He came up and asked me if I had a hacksaw that he could borrow.

"With a person like that, you wonder what he has in mind. So I said casually, 'Oh, what are you going to do with a hacksaw?'

"Now this guy is not retarded, although sometimes you might wonder. I think he's even some kind of computer engineer. Anyway, he proceeded to explain to me about this padlock that he was holding in his hand. He told me that he found this lock but there was no key in it. He explained that if you get a key from a similar lock and you saw off the two nubs on both sides nearest to the part that you hold, it will open any padlock."

My friend folded the newspaper he had been reading and put it more permanently in his carrying case. I guess he was getting into telling me this story and decided to postpone whatever he was reading about when I sat down.

"I've done a lot of handyman things," I interjected, "but I never heard that one before."

"Neither had I," he laughed in agreement, "and I've even built houses. Well anyway, I gave him my hacksaw. He sawed and sawed and eventually the nubs came off on both sides. Then he put it in the lock and when it worked, he got this really big grin on his face.

"I told Barry that I really appreciated his keymaking demon-stration. I said that it was clearly an example of somebody not knowing something learning from somebody who knows that something. Here was this very goofy guy, someone you would never think that you could learn something from. But there it was!"

He paused as though his story was over. I wondered if there was anything that I should be reading into it. When I decided there wasn't and was about to change the subject, he continued.

"I looked at Barry. He had this big smile, I had a big smile, and for that moment there wasn't any separation between us. We were the teacher and the student in this one circumstance.

"Afterwards, I went off into my opinions about him and he went off into his daffiness. But for that moment, we had some-thing that was really intimate -- an example of the possibilities of what has been created here on Earth.

"The capacity for people to take care of each other is really something very miraculous. For a random person to take care of another random person is an extraordinary happening. It's similar to the way that the hand takes care of the nose by itching it or the way the tongue takes care of the teeth by picking stuff out of them. I won't get any more gross."

This wonderful story that he had just told me made me feel a little giddy. I had completely forgotten about my surroundings which were actually somewhat drab, a little dirty, and had known better days. We joked about different parts of the body taking care of each other, and made a contest of coming up with more and more absurd examples, most of which were obscene. When our game ran its course he got back to his theme.

"When you sat down, I was reading about some of this govern-ment changing going on in Eastern Europe. I don't know what your political leanings are, but whatever they are, when you read about people that have really fought for something, you probably feel a certain supportiveness for them. Now of course, changes in government have happened before, and a lot of times it gets just as bad as last time. But aside from that, their really positive outlook evokes the same in us."

I knew exactly what he meant, because when I happened to hear on T.V. that the people of Rumania got their freedom, I got really excited. I don't even know exactly where Rumania is, but it felt like something really special had happened. I was rooting for them like they were the underdog in some sporting event.

"It's like being a football fan," was my less than brilliant contribution to the conversation.

He could tell that I was interested in this idea, so he continued. "Who really cares about Eastern Europe anyway? But still, there's this element of rooting for people that we've never seen. Like that feeling that we're in some way connected. What is a football fan? What is that anyway? Somebody who's rooting for something that he feels connected to. You want it to go well for them. You want them to have success. You want them to beat the odds."

"I guess that's just like the hand wanting to take care of the nose because it recognizes the connection," I said, feeling that I had now made a clever contribution.

"Exactly!" he agreed. "There are so many subtle manifestations of the wonderful connection that we have with each other. This connection that really isn't a connection at all, but is the actuality that we aren't separate. We're not separate!"

It was getting to be late afternoon, and since we both wanted to get into Vegas before we were too tired to look around, we decided to split. I've never stopped in Adelanto again, but their highway sign, which I have passed many times, always reminds me (with a smile) of our body parts and how well they seem to cooperate.

I went to the bathroom, and when I came out my friend was by the exit door talking to Barry. Both of them were smiling. As we walked to the car my friend said, "Sometimes people rise above their pettiness -- their pettiness of being afraid to spend money on others, pettiness of being afraid of looking corny, to be soft when it's more insulating to be tough, their fear of being vulnerable. To me, it is so inspirational to see someone take the chance to take care of something other than themselves. It really means that the seed has already been sewn."

I didn't follow his last jump, so I asked him what he meant by "the seed being sewn."

"It's hard to plant fruit trees," he answered. "It's even hard to carpool, so it's really hard to plant fruit trees. But you know something, it really is within a human's capacity to sew seeds for others. It really is within a human's capacity to serve.

"Maybe in parenthood, you get to feel that a little bit. Probably not so much in the beginning, as when you get to be near the end of your years. I'm sure you've heard stories of people who found out that their time was running out. Maybe they had a few months to live and they're doing something called 'getting their affairs in order.' You wonder why they are trying to get their affairs in order. What's the difference if their affairs are in order or not?"

By this time, we were already sitting in the car. He deliberately shifted his body position in order to face me straight on, and looking directly into my eyes with a deep and profound stare, as though directing all the energy in the creation just to me, he said:

"But some people get the feeling that life is going to go on even though 'I' am not going to go on. Needless to say, there's something scary about that feeling and that situation, but there is also something very, very beautiful and divine about that feeling and situation. Because really, we are seeds, or we are fruit, or we are trees, or we are branches -- but at most, we are part of something. And that something isn't all alive now. Part of it has lived, part of it is living, and part of it has yet to live. We are a little segment in this continuity of things. We don't usually feel like that and we certainly don't act like that. But I think that there are very few people who are what you might call thoughtful that don't in their hearts believe that. Wouldn't it be incredible if we could actually feel and live our lives more like those seeds."

I looked down, deeply touched by what I had heard. We sat in silence for a few minutes, then he started the car. When we were on the road again, he started talking about a movie he had seen. I thought that he was trying to lighten things up, but I was wrong.

"There's a really wonderful French film called *The Valley Obscured by Clouds*. It's the story of a group of people on an expedition in the remote highlands of New Guinea.

"At some point in the story, one of the travelers is having a really hard time and another of the women is trying to help her out. She is trying to explain separateness to her friend and uses this analogy: *There is the ocean, the ocean is Love. And there is a bottle floating in the ocean, full of water. The bottle is you. And if you break it, there's no bottle alone -- there's the ocean* ."

I told him that I had seen the movie years before and thought, at the time, that it was an interesting travelogue. It was curious that I had actually missed not only the scene to which he referred but probably the meaning behind the movie as well.

"It's so traumatic," he went on, "for us to feel the cap on our bottle loosening even one-sixteenth of an inch. We feel like it's all falling apart, and in a way that *is* what's happening. All the water in us is ocean water and all the water outside of us is ocean water. It's all ocean water. Then there's this bottle. There's this 'I', 'me', 'you'. What 'I' want, and 'I' need, what 'I' like, what 'I' don't like and 'I' think and 'I' don't think, all this separate bottle business. The bottle breaks and the water goes into the ocean. That breaking of the bottle is not only this physical death that we arrive at after some number of years. That breaking also happens in moments -- and I would be surprised if you haven't experienced, to some degree, a small breaking of that bottle. Am I right?"

The I-15 freeway between Victorville and Las Vegas runs through some of the most desolate parts of the Mohave Dessert. You can look out the window and try to find something to help pass the time, but all you'll come up with, in the late afternoon, is the muted colors of sand and creosote bushes.

The starkness of the landscape accentuated the accuracy of his analogy. I found it all too confronting and felt the need to soften the edges a little. I asked if it was okay if I drove for awhile. He pulled over and we switched places.

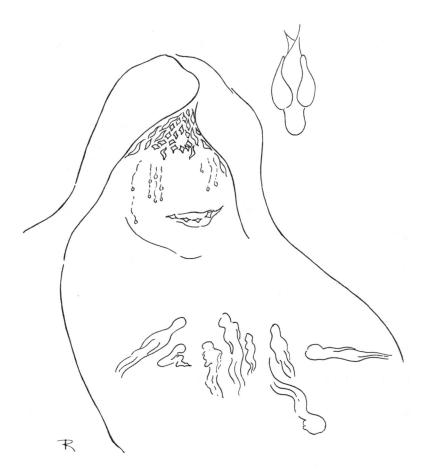

We rode along in silence for awhile, till he asked me why I was interested in what he had to say. I told him that I wasn't sure, and asked why *he* thought I was interested.

"I assume that you're interested in what I have to say because you recognize that you need help to loosen the top on this bottle, help to become less separate, help to become part of something more expansive. You know somewhere deep, deep inside you that it's gotta be opened and that your feeling of being separate is your enemy. You know that those all too few beautiful moments that

44

you've had in life have happened for only one reason -- because the top of your bottle had, in some way, been loosened and some ocean water got in and some ocean water got out. It mixed for awhile and your feeling of isolation and separateness abated. It was okay and you were okay -- in fact, it was bliss, and you want more."

"I do want more," I said, "and I don't want more. I'm afraid to want more and I still want more. It feels a little bit like flirting. It's scary, and most of the time all I want to know is if it can be done painlessly."

He completed my sentence. "...and without changing anything -- your address, your car, your hair, or whatever. I sympathize. I understand that we've learned that we have only one thing. We have a bottle. We have not learned anything else. We've learned a thousand things about that bottle -- make your bottle beautiful, make your bottle rich, make it talented, impressive, successful, make your bottle impregnable so that it will never break. We've had inklings that there is something else, but we've learned to discourage them. This spiritual inkling, this other deep stirring that you've had is that the impregnability of your bottle may actually be the problem."

Long car rides have never been among my favorite activities. I did, however, learn to appreciate them while listening to my friend. Although most of what I describe to you, the reader, circulates around what he had to say, there were also long periods of silence, as well as listening to music tapes and rarely, but sometimes, listening to the news on the radio. The circumstance of being a captive audience in this situation proved to be very supportive to really grokking his ideas. I don't think that I could possibly have endured on this particular occasion had I been able to go anywhere. I even encouraged him to continue, and he did.

"You've heard my ideas on this situation of separateness, the possibilities of service, and identification with something greater, and the obstacle of self-importance. I don't want you to misunderstand and think that I'm saying that it all comes down to your actions, your imbalances, your obstacles, and your possibilities. In actuality, the creation is a lot more impersonal than our experience of it. There are energies at work."

This seemed an unusually obscure statement as compared to the way my friend usually talked, so I asked him what he meant by energies.

"We have these bodies and these thoughts and these feelings. We appear very tangible to ourselves, but really, in a way, we're energized puppets. I don't mean puppets in a deprecatory way. I mean that when our time comes and we're lying there dead, we don't perform good and bad actions. When we're enlivened and operated by the forces and energies that exist, then we perform good and bad and whatever else a person can do. So in that way, there are really no good people and no bad people. People are operated, from moment to moment, by various forces. They are the agents of those energies. They are the puppets of those forces."

"That sounds like the idea that we're not responsible for our actions," I said, surprised that he would be putting forth such an idea. "Is that what you mean?"

"Not at all," he denied. "Take this example. If you wanted to be a good person you'd seek out a job with the American Red Cross and not with the American Nazi party, because what you did in your job would be decided, to a large degree, by who you worked for. So in a similar sense, if a person becomes the agent of a more giving force, that person is then thought of as a more giving person. It's really very simple. It's not so much that the person becomes a good person, but he acts the part of a good person in those moments when he is operated by a more magnanimous force."

We drove in silence for a while. We were heading due east and it was getting close to sunset. It was a completely clear day and the Sun was flooding in the rear window. I had to re-adjust the rear view mirror so as not to be blinded by the glare. I spent a few grunts complaining about the Sun until he interrupted me.

"The Sun is actually an extremely giving force. It doesn't ask for our credentials or what we've done today. It asks no questions. All you have to do to feel its warmth is come outdoors, and nowadays even that's becoming a problem. But aside from that, it shines equally everywhere. Nobody thinks of the Sun as benevolent. This big orange ball doesn't have generous qualities attributed to it. We all understand that the Sun obeys the laws of its existence, and the forces which operate it tell it what to do."

I told him that I could see that easily in relation to the Sun, but that it was hard for me to make the jump to seeing people in that way.

"Of course!" he said. "When we think of people, we lose our common sense. We attribute all the qualities that people manifest to the people themselves, when actually the forces which operate those people are what should get the credit. If a person's actions were to be directed by some higher and finer source of energy, the possibilities are considerable that his or her acts would become more and more benevolent. Of course, what's required for our actions to become greater and greater is that we become aligned with forces that are greater and greater."

"How does that happen?" I asked.

"For that to happen," he answered, "paradoxically, we have to become less and less, smaller and smaller, so as to be malleable by some of this bigness. If you can become an agent of that bigness, people will think of you as a giving person, as a good person, as a benevolent person. This can happen. It's rare, it does not happen as often as most people think, but it can happen."

I told him that I looked at being a puppet as the opposite of the way I wanted to be.

"Of course you do!" he responded. "Because you have no concept that there could be a puppeteer so benevolent and all seeing that it would be okay. If you could relax into that puppeteer's hands, you might even find that you were pleased to be a puppet.

"You want to feel the power that exists, but right now you feel you're sitting alone in your bucket seat. You're all alone. You're not being assisted by anything. You don't feel that there's something operating you at this moment. You feel that when you turn the steering wheel, it's you who's doing it. You don't feel the energy that's empowering you to do that turning. That's the way life is -- our attitude is, 'I have to do it, I have to do it.' Well that's a very distorted feeling.

"I'll tell you something that you might find interesting. Have you ever read about descriptions of various spiritual practices and that people from numerous traditions learned how to incorporate concentration on the breath into those practices?"

"I don't think so," I said hesitantly. "Is it important?"

"One of the reasons is because your breath is something for sure that you don't give yourself. You're always concentrating on things that you give yourself -- your possessions, your friends, your relationships, your property. A puppet has nothing that it gives itself. A puppet waits for the puppeteer, but we're real shaky about experimenting with that concept."

In the distance, to the northeast, the night sky was beginning to reveal the glow of millions of lights. We were approaching Las Vegas, the mecca of the western world's common aspirations, and I in this car contemplating the atmospheric conditions on Jupiter.

5

CARS WITHOUT GAS GAUGES

Men for whom an entire life was like one Sunday afternoon, an afternoon which was not altogether miserable, but rather hot and dull and uncomfortable....then suddenly it was over; it was already night.

Carlos Castaneda

In recent years, my friend had greatly absented himself from daily poker and relegated his playing to what's known in our circles as the "tournament trail." To explain: Most larger poker establishments, of which there are probably fifty around the country, hold an event once a year for publicity in an effort to increase attendance. These tournament events go on for several days and anyone can play as long as they put up a 'buy-in' (a term meaning an amount of money, anywhere from a hundred to a thousand dollars or more, which becomes the prize pool and is divided by the winners and runners-up of the tournament).

We travelled to numerous tournaments together, and although neither of us was often a big winner, we always did well enough to keep it going. In his earlier tournament days, my friend had played in Europe, mostly London, but our travels were limited to the western United States, mostly Las Vegas, Reno and Los Angeles. As the months passed, I became far more excited by the learning experiences and the discourses than I was about the poker scene.

49

It happened to be that my friend (as I will call him for now) was at one time a full-time professional poker player of the variety that I aspired to be. He explained that he never quite reached the top ranks of players because of two particular detrimental qualities that he either naturally possessed or developed along the way. The first was that he had an inherent dislike for making other people feel bad, a normal occurrence that one must endure when one is trying to beat another at something. The other, was that as rewarding as the winning part of poker was to him, there was always a certain other something, something that called out to him. So whenever he stooped down to pick up the golden key of fame and riches, an inner voice called out to him and distracted him from his personal accomplishment just long enough for someone who wasn't hearing that voice to swoop down and scoop up the treasure. Anyhow, that's how he explained it.

This particular trip to Las Vegas lasted about two weeks. We actually only spent four days out of all that time in the casinos. We were involved in so many, what he would call mini-adventures, that when I think of that particular trip, I don't really relate it to poker. Maybe also because neither of us won any money.

Las Vegas is in a valley with mountains on two sides. Some of those mountains, especially Mt. Charleston, are high enough that even though they're located in the Mojave Desert, one of the hottest places in the country, they keep their snow well into the spring.

After two days in Vegas, my friend suggested that we spend a little time hiking in the mountains. Some time ago he drove a couple of hours from here to the top of this 7,500 foot mountain and saw a valley 2,500 feet below on the other side. It was a half-mile drop and a great climb, so he got the idea that it would be a far-out place to hike. It looked like a very steep descent, but he figured that once we got down there, it would be a nice place to hike around.

We took off with small backpacks because we were going to stay out there for a few days. For half a day we climbed and slid down the half-mile hill and eventually got down to the bottom. It was beautiful, it was primeval. There were more signs of game there than he'd ever seen in Alaska, Asia, South America, even Africa. There was even a waterfall coming out of the rocks. I'm sure very few people have been there in recent years. There was no way to get there unless you drop down that steep hill, and no easy way in from the bottom either.

We walked around down there and it was just like paradise, like Narnia-land. We put our arms around a fir tree and with arms outstretched we still couldn't reach around that tree. That's a pretty big fir tree, like sixteen feet around. There was a brook, and bear tracks and deer tracks, and the sounds of nature were everywhere. We camped for a couple of nights by a stream and the following day, after a few hours of hiking, we got to where nature was starting to give way to man.

We were walking down this semi-arid valley with mountains on both sides. We walked for a few miles and some fences started to appear. We were still a long way from where we would have a chance to get picked up on the road, about twelve miles on down.

Eventually we got to the fences that we first saw from a few miles back. At that moment, we spotted a bull, a very large bull. We didn't know what to do. *The bull won't charge us. Just walk by and he won't charge*. It's not the kind of thing you want to test out. *Hey, you`re not going to charge us, are you bull?*

We walked along outside the fence and then climbed over the fence into the bull's area, carefully checking him out to see if he'd follow us. We went on a little further walking next to the fence just in case we needed to make a quick exit from his pasture.

As we were walking inside this fenced area, we saw more cow like animals in the distance, and the closer we got, the more obvious it became that they also were bulls. So now we were fenced in with these bulls, and there weren't too many options available.

The night before, I had been a little concerned about bears. There were a lot of noises around, and we were right by this stream. Bears probably even came down to drink. I saw some deer but never any bear. We never thought that bulls were going to be the wildlife that we would have to deal with on this trip.

Well, the situation that developed was that in order for us to get through this valley, we had to walk between these two particular bulls. They were a good distance apart, but we had to walk between them. We couldn't walk around them because the hills were steep on both sides and the bulls were set like bookends.

So as we were talking about what to do, I could see this adventure that we were in the middle of, but the way we were talking about it, you'd think we had to work out an ordinary problem. Really, here we were on an African safari adventure in Nevada.

Before us were two, large, potentially dangerous and unpredictable wild animals. They may have been docile, but we didn't know one way or the other. They could have been rhinos in the distance and it would have been the same. If you don't know how they're going to act, and you don't know the particular individual animals, then you're in with wild animals.

In the midst of contemplating our fate, my friend said, "Hey! We can play safari here! Of course what people ordinarily do is make the least of the situation. All they have to do is convince themselves that the bulls are nothing. 'They're nothing, there's no adventure here, this isn't unusual.' But here's a situation that we can make the most of, so let's play safari, let's not pretend they're nothing. Let's deal with this like it's really dangerous."

"I'm not going straight through there," I insisted, trying to muster the spirit of adventure that he was describing. We talked about it for a while and agreed that we had to go back a mile, keeping the bulls on one side of us, just in case we had to make a run for it. So instead of walking on through the valley past the bulls to the road where we planned to catch a ride back, we'd go straight up the first hill and then up another hill. It was really difficult because we were carrying packs and we had the "toe-jams" from the day we descended the steep hill.

I was really loving it because we were getting to play this safari adventure just five hours from Los Angeles. If we had made less of it, and somebody asked me in six months where we had gone on that hike, I probably wouldn't even remember. I know I'll remember it now, maybe even for the rest of my life.

When we were a few miles from the road and clear of bull-danger, my friend began to talk. "You probably think that you have to go to some exotic land or happen on some super adventurous circumstance for that memorableness to happen, but it's not really so. There is a way to live life dynamically even when events are ordinary. And it's not even a skill that you have to develop. It's more that we've become muffled. Other than our problems, which we magnify, we've made most other things into less, and the rest into nothing. We've found a way to explain everything away. We just eliminate the unpredictability.

"If the electricity went off in your house on a cold night, and you had to take out the sleeping bags and light candles, you'd remember that incident for years. 'Hey! Remember when all the neighbors came over and we huddled around the fireplace?' But you don`t remember all the other days; they're like a blur, they're muffled days. Wouldn't you think that a person would do anything possible to make sure that the lights could go out at any unpredictable time so that they'd be in really dynamic circumstances that would be memorable?

"But really it's the opposite. How curious, it's the opposite. Everything we do, all the systems we've developed are to prevent anything unpredictable from happening. Can you relate to what I'm talking about?"

He caught me by surprise with that question, because as he was talking, my mind was wandering to an incident that happened to me years ago when my car broke down.

I told him my story of breaking down in the middle of nowhere, and how I first felt, *Oh my God! What am I gonna do?* But it worked out, somebody stopped to help me out. I ended up spending several days at this couple's house till the car got fixed. To this day, I actually remember those people and that incident.

At the end of the story he began to laugh. "But tell me, do you remember any incidents from the following week, the week after your car broke down? Tell me what happened the week after that, or the week after that. You don't remember anything from those days, nothing at all from those all too predictable days.

"I'm not saying that the way to live is to never know what's going to happen, so let's build cars without gas gauges. Actually, the way we live is equally extreme. We do the opposite of that because we figure that we always need to know just where we are, without realizing that the result of eliminating unpredictability is that we become muffled and don't remember anything.

"At one time my life was like that, and it didn't feel good. Maybe sometimes it didn't feel too bad, but it sure didn't feel good. What I'm talking about here is not that the world outside of us is muffled, but that people are muffled. The world doesn't have to change. We're what has to change. People are their own worst enemies. They're creating systems so as not to feel anything really alive, so that they know what's going to happen tomorrow and what's going to happen next week. Don Juan told Carlos: 'An entire life was like one Sunday afternoon...not altogether miserable...then suddenly it was over.' And really that's what success is, when you create a life that's a not all too unpleasant Sunday afternoon."

It was a curious quote for that moment, because here it was Sunday afternoon. Fortunately, the experience I was having couldn't have been further from the very safe, semi-numbness to which he referred. In the distance I could see the highway, our destination. My feet were in terrible shape, and I was hungry and ready for a rest, but another part of me associated return to civilization with return to that semi-numbness. I asked him what a person had to do to keep it from going that way.

"Many people aspire to be someone else, " he answered. "They aspire to get what somebody else has. They have an imagination of what their life is going to be like when they're that other person. When they have that possession or that position or that relationship, they imagine that it's going to be different. But it's not that way. Because if you were to meet that idealized person, you'd see that his life also is dry. That person, in his way, is setting things up so that he too knows what's going to happen.

"Those are the skills that we learn. The skills of eliminating unpredictability. Some people are really good at it. They've been successful at learning how to set up life so that they always know what's going to happen. They're very scientific about excluding those unpredictable circumstances, those unpredictable people, and those unpredictable situations."

I definitely could relate. Wanting to becoming one of those people with that level of control was probably what fueled my poker aspirations. My dreams were beginning to seem more like nightmares. I asked him if he thought there was a way to avoid the chaos of unpredictability and still maintain a sense of freshness.

"Every once in a while," he began, "the creation will trip you. Sometime you'll climb down out of the woods thinking that the bears are behind you and the bulls will be in front of you. Sometime that will happen and then you'll have a story to tell. Otherwise, you really don't have a story to tell. Life is really beautiful when you have a story to tell. I know that people like to listen to me because I have a lot of stories to tell, and I don't have to go that far back in time. I can go far back, but I can tell you about today. Not because I'm a wild and crazy guy, but because I don't work so hard to make everything ordinary. Because life 'as it is' is really an adventure."

What I heard didn't seem to answer to my question, but I might have gotten something even more important.

As we re-entered town I told him that I was really hungry. He suggested a particular hotel, so we went there for lunch. One of his favorite pastimes was eating, so a fringe benefit of this poker life were the "all you can eat" buffets which were popular in many of the hotels and casinos that we frequented. He preferred this type of eating because, as he explained, "You can see and choose what you're going to eat before some stranger, who is always in a hurry, puts a plate of food in front of you, accompanied by the meaningless expression, 'Is everything all right.'" Buffet dining also allowed him to feel free to reach over and pick something off my plate to see if he would like to get some of his own. This actually startled me at first, but then became a sweet source of intimacy between us.

His modus operandi for eating at one of these places was to take small portions and make a lot of trips to the buffet line. I tried it as an experiment, though my modus operandi was generally to gorge.

After resting for the remainder of the day, we spent that night and the day after at the card tables.

The following day we went to the downtown business part of the city to see someone from whom my friend had to collect some money. We were trying to get into this building but couldn't find the way in. The front of the building was all black painted glass. The door was locked and we could tell that they were out of business, but he thought that the guy he wanted to see might be in there anyway.

Since the door was locked, we circled around the back and down an alley way. As we were walking, we wandered into a nearby store, thinking that maybe we got into the back of the right store, but it turned out to be the wrong store. The owner there told us that the out-of-business place was near by, but, "They won't let you in." He showed us the correct door; we knocked on it for a couple of minutes -- no answer!

As we started walking away, a man came over to us and said, "Hey! There's somebody going in the door that you were just trying to get into. Hurry up! Come this way and you can get in now." Neither of us had ever seen this guy before, but we followed anyway. We turned and jogged back down the alley and the door was open, so my friend walked in. He spent a while in there, took care of his business, and then came out.

As we were walking back to the car, we saw the stranger that helped us. He was about a block away carrying his lunch pail. My friend called out to him and started walking up the block toward him, and he started walking toward us. We all met in the middle of the block and introduced ourselves. The stranger's name was

Gustave. My friend told Gustave that he didn't know why he helped us out, but that he really appreciated it.

Gustave looked like he could use some money, so my friend gave him some. "This is incredible!" Gustave said. "I just spent my last dollar. I was hungry, and when you're hungry you should eat. So I spent my last few bucks on lunch. I said to myself this morning, "Today you should just try to do the right thing. You don't have much money, you might not have any way to get home, but try to do the right thing and see what happens."

You see he never asked us for anything. After he helped us to get into the store, he didn't even hang around.

So back on the street, we all shook hands and walked together for awhile -- it was special.

When we finally got back in the car to head uptown, my friend had something to say about what had taken place. "Money isn't a big thing with me," he began, "so it's not giving him the money that counted. In order to approach him, I had to call out and then go deliberately toward him like he meant something to me. He wasn't expecting me to come down the block. He didn't even know I was there.

"I know how it goes in the world. A lot of times you want to do something for somebody, but you can't. Well this guy went out of his way for me. 'Hey, c'mon c'mon! The door's open.' He was being a nice guy. I think that's far-out. So I went down the block to thank him. The money is nothing, but going down the block was making something special out of the incident."

"Why was going over to meet him so special?" I asked.

"It put me in a vulnerable position," he answered, "because whatever was going to happen was unpredictable. That's what's scary in life. We had this neat experience because I took that chance, and we got close to a person that would have otherwise been a stranger. We shook hands and walked down the street like we were on this planet together, and I have a sweet story to tell, instead of, I got in my car and I left -- you understand?"

I was beginning to get the idea, mostly because I wasn't sure that *I* would have called out to Gustave.

"What made it that now you have a story to tell?" I asked. "Was it that you didn't let it end with getting into the place?"

"In order to come away with a story to tell, I had to leave something behind, but not the five bucks. That's not what I had to leave there; that almost anybody can leave, that's paper. I had to take a chance with an unpredictable situation, with an unpredictable person, one that I didn't know. I walked down the street and called to him, and I survived. He liked it, you liked it, and I liked it. We all liked each other. So maybe next time, you'll go a little further and do a little more, and you won't be so scared that there's going to be danger in being a little vulnerable.

"Maybe there weren't any wild animals around, but the formula was still the same. See the specialness that's there; don't make it into nothing. It's always so easy to make life into nothing. Take little chances to be more alive, to be more childlike. Be the opposite of everything you learned, a little less afraid, a little crazy. Then slowly but surely, life will become less boring for you. Big people say, 'Do you want to play tennis?' Kids say, 'Do you want to play?' That's a very big difference."

That night my friend returned to the tables, but I spent the time in my room trying to absorb all that had transpired. Sometimes when I've felt like this, I gravitated to playing a little musical instrument which I usually carry with my stuff. It's a hollow little box about as big as a deck of cards with five wire bars attached to it. You can pluck it so that each bar sounds a different note. If it has a name, I'm not aware of it.

As I was lying on my back, plucking my no-name box, I started to think about all those little particles that were vibrating each time I hit a bar and made a sound. What do those particles think is going on? Their story of what's going on could be anywhere from some cosmic explanation, to a very personal story about why they're being put through all that shaking around.

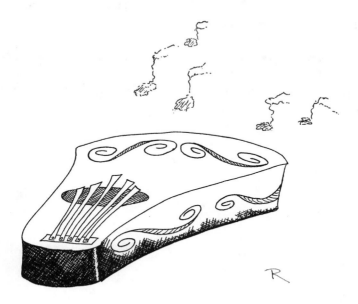

It occurred to me that as a very small particle, I am also in the same position, and there are numerous possibilities of how I could explain *my* situation. But whatever my explanation is, what is actually taking place is less personal than my explanation of it.

Sometimes I try to get really impersonal about my explanations, like to the point that there are pulsations going on and they're causing matter to move around. Those particles of matter think, "I went here, maybe I should go there -- I did this, maybe I should do that," or maybe even, "Why is this happening to me?"

Those particles could think whatever they want, but what's really happening is that pulsations are going on. I'm not saying that I do visualization or any kind of technique. I'm saying it's interesting to think in terms of an impersonal point of view for a change, because I usually think of my problems very personally.

I don't know where all these vibrations started. All I know is that they appear to end at me, and that's usually the only part that

I'm interested in. Maybe my life, that I read as a very personal story, is actually very impersonal at its source.

I thought that I'd share that bit of insight with you, the reader, not only for your enlightenment, but so that I could establish that my friend was not the only quality person about whom you are reading.

6

PALE PINK, FAKE FUCHSIA

Advertising signs that con you into thinking you're the one
That can do what's never been done
That can win what's never been won
Meanwhile life goes on all around you.
Bob Dylan

The next morning my friend informed me that at the game the night before, he had been invited by his friend Tony Hall to spend the day and probably the next night at a cabin that he had in fact helped build, high up on Mt. Charleston, and that I was welcome to come with him if I wished.

I should clarify that over the three years of our association, there were periods of weeks and on one occasion even months that I didn't see my friend. I rarely did, however, pass up a chance to spend time with him and this invitation didn't warrant an exception.

My friend explained to me that several years back he had helped Tony Hall build this place in the tall pine trees, and that he came up for a day or two whenever he was in the area.

When we got up there it was hard to believe that only an hour away from Las Vegas, the environment was so different.

"One of the ways I spend time here," my friend explained, "is being a semi-amateur astronomer. You couldn't put in enough 'semis' to describe what I am. If you're familiar with telescopes, there's a C8 Smith Cassagrain there, and maybe if it's clear tonight we'll get to play in the sky."

Well the sky started off very clear, but as it was getting to be eleven, twelve, maybe one o'clock, some clouds came over and we quit playing in the sky for the night and went to sleep.

The next morning when I woke up, there was a foot of snow on the ground outside the window. Tony Hall (as far as I could tell he was always called by both names) was also at the cabin and we all said the same thing: "Snow doesn't make any noise when it's falling." Because when we went to sleep it wasn't there, and we woke up and it was there. Everybody had the same thought. "God, it's beautiful, it's beautiful, but it didn't make any noise." It was quiet when the snow fell, and we were quiet for the rest of the morning.

I wasn't having my usual "what'll I do" thoughts. I was looking out the window like a little kid at this phenomenon of nature. There had been no snow there before, and then there was all this snow. It was a feeling of being part of a miraculous happening; I felt a certain spirit of wonder.

Toward noon we gathered in front of the fireplace and my friend started to talk about what had been happening. "I've been around children a lot, and something that you get to see with little children is they're always surprised -- life is always special, new and exciting. So we know it's within a human's capacity to feel that, but when we grow up we lose it. That's really too bad, and if we understand that it is too bad, then maybe we should do something about it."

"What can we do about it?" I asked.

"If we can look at a little kid," he responded, "and see those bright eyes, or if we can feel satisfied simply to look at the snow and appreciate its beauty, then we certainly have to find some way to wake that feeling of wonder within ourselves. Maybe then we won't have to demand that so much snow fall or that wild animals attack us in order for us to open our eyes."

I contributed a thought I had a while before -- that it wasn't fair and that it was too much to demand of little human lives that it take so much to evoke wonderment in us.

"It really *is* too much of a demand," he agreed. "It's not fair to the creation and it's not fair to ourselves. I'm talking about the quantity of hype that has become necessary for us to feel excited. It's really too bad.

"In order to be considered exciting, everything has to be extreme. How about the Buffalo Bills football team? Those guys worked and struggled and they got to where football players want to go, into the Superbowl. Did you see their faces? They lost the game and had a terrible time."

"That *is* ridiculous!" I contributed. "Every other football player in the world -- high school, college, pros, all of them want to get into the Superbowl and those guys got there and they had a lousy time. They lost the game so it just wasn't enough for them."

"That's exactly what I'm trying to say," he continued. "We've gotten corrupted. I heard somewhere that George Lucas, the movie director that made *Star Wars*, didn't used to like to make fast action movies. Now he sees that that's what you've got to do to hold people's attention. You've got to have an action every second. So now that's what he's into. Every second, you've got to have some action."

Tony Hall, who probably hadn't said ten words since we got there, started laughing and said, "Yeah, like the joke, I don't care how the food is, so long as there's plenty of it. The food is lousy but the portions are big."

I picked up on his joke by giving some examples of the buffets in town that proved that axiom, and we all had a good laugh comparing our preferences for where we liked to stuff our faces. It was a few minutes before my friend returned to the subject we had been talking about .

"That's the story," he went on. "That's what we've learned -- bright fuchsia colors, big movies, big portions. Remember when I came in the other night and you were watching the *Tonight Show* in your room at the hotel? There was some guy who was eighty-eight years old or ninety-six years old, whatever. The host said, 'How old are you?' The guest said, 'Ninety-six,' and everybody clapped. Nobody asked what those ninety-six years were like. Have you been bored for ninety-six years? No, nothing about the quality. That's a lot of years, and the quantity is enough to impress. 'We had somebody here who was ninety-two before, so you broke the record, you're ninety-six, incredible!'

"What were those ninety-six years like? Nobody cares, just put up those big numbers. That's what we've learned to respect. The 'Fortune 500,' the biggest of everything. The highest grossing whatever, no matter how gross it is."

"So what's the alternative in a society where all that's available is hype of one kind or another?" I asked.

"Forget about what the society deals," he said with increased volume. "Fuchsia is a hype. What I'm interested in is a very, very faint pink; it almost looks like white, but it's not white, it's really pink. It's not *very* pink, but it's *really* pink. You know the difference between fake fuchsia and really pink? One's real, it's a real color, it's really there. The other can get your attention real fast, but there's nothing really there. Our senses have become a little bit dull. We're a little more attuned to hype than to reality."

He looked away from Tony Hall and directly at me. "Those quantities of hype need not be required. Life, just as it is, is very, very special. I don't really care how much you're interested in what I have to say, as much as that you realize that you've lost something that you had -- that feeling of specialness. That's really the essential problem. Then maybe you can find some way to get re-involved in trying to find what you've lost. I think that would serve all of us and the creation as well."

Later that afternoon, he gave me another demonstration of his vast knowledge of the subtleties of human nature. I was getting a little restless. Spending such a protracted period of time being calm and quiet was unusual for me, and I guess I was getting ready to bounce to the other side.

Both he and Tony Hall were gazing out of the big picture window, when I spotted a guitar leaning against the wall behind an overstuffed chair. I picked it up to play a little. I muttered, "Hey! Look what's here," and picked up the guitar trying to appear like I'd never realized it was there. Then I started to pluck it a little and play one of my favorite guitar tunes. It was enjoyable for awhile. I sounded pretty good -- maybe not impressive, but at least not unimpressive.

My friend had been sitting facing the window on one of those swivel rocking chairs. He spun around and proclaimed as though he was making a speech, "Well one thing's for sure, if people are listening to your plucking, you're not going to try something that you've never tried before! You won't do that."

"What do you mean?" I said nervously.

"What you do when you pick it up," he said, "is you play some sequence that you've played before and know will sound good, right? If it's okay to play real quiet, you might not go for your very best. But if that instrument was by some chance electric, you would, without a question, 'go to the well.' Absolutely, you would go for your best."

Over time, I had gotten more and more used to his unpredictable behavior, so even though I was taken aback, I resisted going into shock. I had no idea what he was talking about, so I assumed that he didn't like either what I was playing, or that I was playing at all and disturbing the quiet.

I asked him if he'd prefer me to stop, and after smiling at my pitiful response, he said that he was actually impressed at my ability, not having known that I played at all, but that how well my guitar playing sounded had nothing to do with his comments.

I was still not on level ground so I asked him slightly defensively, "So what's the problem?"

"Let me tell you something that happened to me years ago and maybe you'll undersand where I'm coming from. Okay?"

"Okay," I said from behind my blindfold.

"One time years ago," he began, "a friend and I went into a music store. There was a man there demonstrating on an electric guitar. He may have been from a company that manufactures instruments because he was spending the day at this store demonstrating this amp and guitar.

"He was looking for people to play it, and since we were walking by, he asked me if I wanted to try it. Of course when he asked me, I was (for the reasons that I described earlier) playing around with some of the acoustic guitars that don't make so much noise. "He said, 'Hey! Try this one,' and he stuck this electric guitar in my hand. Well I can play a little bit, so when he stuck it in my hand I twanged a string and the whole store reverberated with that note.

"There I was with this guitar in playing position, and he said, 'Go ahead, try it.' So in my head, I went through all my possibilities in order to come up with the absolutely most flawless thing that I could play, because everybody in the store is going to hear it. The rest of the story isn't important. It might be entertaining, but it's not important.

"That's why I know how it goes when you're in somebody's house and you pick up some instrument. You try to make the best possible sound that you can. You're not going to start by playing a song you've never played before."

His "read" of my behavior was so precise, and his story so benign that I could only relax with the realization of how well this person knew the intricacies of human behavior, especially mine. I was captivated by the enthusiasm he could muster for such subtlety. It seemed to me that this "real pink, fake fuchsia" business was worth hearing more about.

The events of the previous days all seemed to have elements which related to that theme of subtle, versus extreme. I asked what it would look like if a person behaved differently.

He answered, "If by chance sometime you see someone pick up a musical instrument, while surrounded by strangers, and try to play a tune that they've never played before, you'll know that either that person is very drunk or something out of the ordinary has happened in their life to give them the capacity to perform this act of courage."

"Isn't that a little exaggerated?" I ventured.

"It may be that we're talking about a small thing, but as small as it is, it's a real thing. Real pale pink is much better than fake fuchsia. The way we've been taught and the way it is in our lives now, believe it or not, fake fuchsia has become preferable to real pink.

"If you don't think courage would be required, the next time you're in a situation with a musical instrument and a bunch of strangers, *you* try it! *You* try it without any booze. *You* pick up that instrument and play something that you're unsure of, something that you've never played before. You won't do it. Or even if you start with that intention, somewhere in the middle you'll get scared and change to something familiar, something more impressive.

"Anybody who's tried to live life like each moment is a new opportunity for adventure would know what I'm talking about. To the others, it's an idea, a theory. But anyone who has tried to live life without falling victim to denying that something subtly special is always happening, knows that it would be very, very hard to do."

It was almost dark when we headed down the mountain back to town. It would have been a harsh re-entry to ordinary life, had my friend and I not kept up a conversation about the ideas that we had previously been talking about. He started after we said good-bye to Tony Hall and had barely gotten past the driveway.

"Do you know the Bob Dylan song that goes (he droned):

Advertising signs that con you
Into thinking you're the one
That can do what's never been done
That can win what's never been won
Meanwhile life goes on all around you.

"The song's called *It's All right, Ma, I'm Only Bleeding.* Have you ever really listened to the words?"

I actually was a Dylan fan some years back, but only since meeting my friend had I first begun to appreciate how much I'd missed the first time around. "If those are the words, I guess I didn't," I confessed.

"If you close your eyes," he said, "and imagine some vivid color, you'd have this incredible color in your imagination. Then, if I asked you which color do you like better, the pale pink wall in front of you, or the deep blue, purple or fuchsia of your imagination, which would you prefer? What are you going to say? You gotta say, 'Pale pink is hardly any color at all.'"

What he said reminded me of the little wrinkled organic apples at the health food stores, the ones that cost three times as much as the regular ones. I mean how can a person buy those things, $3.69 a pound for a little wrinkled apple and it's hardly even red? Especially since you can go across the street to Safeway and get this picture perfect thing -- it's like a living steroid.

In my enthusiasm for the subject, I got sidetracked a little, talking about the exorbitant prices at health food stores. My friend finally had to interrupt.

"I was telling you about some little event, like being able to go into a house where you don't know anybody and where you don't know what the rules are or how much of an impression you have to make to be accepted. If you pick up this instrument and start playing something that you'd play if you were by yourself in your room -- *that* would be adventure! It's not an imaginary fuchsia adventure, it's a real pale pink adventure.

"Learning how to live life moment to moment like it's an adventure regardless of the circumstance doesn't sound like such a big thing to you. It should sound like a miracle, because it's a little mini departure from the way things normally go. People don't recognize that in ordinary life there is no departing because everything is so completely channeled and directed that there can be absolutely no departing."

"It's hard for me to believe," I interrupted, "that everything is that consistent. It all seems pretty random to me."

"So you think," he answered, "that from time to time there is departing? You think that something happens that's outside of the really deeply grooved channel? Well I can tell you from my experience, *there is no departing*. There's this groove, and everything that happens is in that groove.

"I call that groove the 'mechanical flow of life,' and it really is that. It's the way life flows, mechanically. It's like railroad tracks. The train is on the track. The train travels only on the tracks. There is no departing."

I was beginning to feel frustrated. "So how do these subtle adventures fit in?" I asked.

"It's like the color of a pink wall. Just a little bit off white, nothing dramatic. Just a little bit outside of the railroad tracks. Not exactly down the groove of the tracks. Not fuchsia, just a little bit off white. It's not an imagined extreme adventure. It's a real departing."

I was having trouble getting in synch with his explanation. I still couldn't see why he was going on so much about my picking up that guitar. Why was that such a big deal, and why is such a slight departure from the railroad tracks a big deal? I told him what I was thinking.

He explained, "You know what happens when a train departs slightly from its tracks? It's all over. You know what I mean when I say, 'It's all over?' There is one law of the railroad -- zero tolerance. It's not like driving a car, where one wheel goes off the road a little and it's still okay. On the railroad, one wheel slips off and it's all over.

"The railroad tracks make one requirement and the mechanical flow of life has one requirement -- you must stay exactly in it. Obey the laws exactly. You can imagine all you like; imagination is within the laws of the mechanical stream of life. You can even imagine you're not part of the mechanical stream. Any imagination is allowed. The only law is, you must stay on the tracks.

"It's against this law to live each moment of life like it's an adventure. Having a sense of wonder about the small events we live through, taking chances to be vulnerable, and resisting the urge to eliminate unpredictability are also against that law.

"If one wheel can get off the track, you've broken the law and then anything is possible. Once any departing whatsoever happens, then even freedom is possible."

We were approaching town and I was getting a little fidgety knowing that shortly a myriad of possibilities of how I would be spending my time would become available.

In the few moments of silence that followed his last comments, I reached restlessly for the two day old newspaper lying rolled up between us on the front seat. Below the main headlines, in only slightly smaller type, was an article that caught my attention. I read the first line and laughed out loud.

My friend asked me what was so funny and I told him. "Listen to this! The advertising for the state lottery: *Thirty million dollars is going to be won. Go out and get your tickets because thirty million dollars is going to be won by one person.*"

I went on. "If ten people won three million dollars each, I bet they all would be deliriously happy. I certainly would be. But to get our attention, it always has to be more. If they write, 'One million dollars will be won,' it won't even attract enough attention for the newspaper to carry the story. That's sure an example of what you were talking about."

My friend nodded his head in agreement and then added an example of his own. "It's the same in the movies. I saw an old one a few weeks ago, and they were doing this robbery for five thousand dollars. 'Big deal! I already stole ten million in the movies last week.' Don't you feel like that?

"More people have to get killed, more things have to explode, bigger and higher. So if you see a documentary where they show the first explosion of an atomic bomb, you think, 'Darth Vader would have no trouble tripling that.'"

"I think I get what you've been trying to tell me," I said. "It's the difference between the imagination and actuality. To live adventurously, I only have to be able to take this train and move it infinitesimally off the track. You know, it's going to be real hard to get me interested in something that subtle. I guess I'm like the lottery ads."

He told me he was glad that I was finally catching on, because he was getting tired of talking about the subject. He wasn't as tired as he claimed, though, because he still had a few thoughts to add.

"The seed of an adventurous life is when one wheel gets off the track and then the whole train is off the track. It's broken out, it's an outlaw. It may not have careened down the hill, but it's an outlaw train. It's a rebel train. The seed of freedom is within its reach.

"But there's a very unfortunate agreement between people-- that we're only entitled to a moment here and a moment there. Maybe your story is that it takes special circumstances or that you don't deserve too much of that specialness. Someone else might have some other story, but the common agreement is that it's not readily available. You can only get it once in a while.

"In actuality, there's not a limit. Limit is a reasonable word. Life can feel very exciting, dynamic, wonderful, dangerous, all those good things, like mysterious, like loving. It can be like that. I know that you know that, because it's happened to you for a moment here and there."

We sat quietly for a while -- as I was slumping down in my seat for comfort, I remembered a show I had seen on T.V. about the eastern block countries. It was about their meager food supply. The part that struck me, at the time, was that they were now seeing pictures on their own T.V.'s of stocked supermarkets in other countries. Then they would go to their own supermarket, and it was beets or radishes? After a while they said, "No go!" If it was beets or radishes all over the world, it would have been okay, but now they have T.V.

I straightened up quickly. I was now understanding the full thrust of his message. I became excited and agitated. I blurted out, "That's a major rip-off!" I told him what I had been thinking, and he was delighted with my story. He urged me to go on but that seemed to be all I had to say.

My thoughts left a question unanswered, and I asked it of him. "How did we ever get into such a sorry state?"

"Sorry or not, that's our situation." he answered. "I'm not saying that we've agreed to go out and have a mediocre time. Nobody says that. People say, 'Let's go out and have a good time.' But what are they actually willing to do when they go out? Will you do what you see people in the movies do to have a good time? Will you talk to a stranger? Will you live your life like an adventure? Very, very difficult, very difficult.

"Listen, your part in this rip-off system is that you've been told that you can't live your life as an adventure but you can hope for things like wealth and power and fame and acknowledgement. Like I said, or like I said that Dylan said: *You can do what's never been done, you can win what's never been won, meanwhile life goes on all around you.* I'm telling you that you don't live even a miniscule portion of what you deserve. What you're being told elsewhere is completely false."

I told him that I grew up on cynicism and I never seemed to be able to shake it. Maybe I never wanted to.

"It's a gift to aspire to more wonderment and adventure," he said. "We're in a rough spot here. Ordinary life will really take it out of you. It's like a rasp. It files down hope. It makes people cynical, which is in no way a quality of a child.

"I've travelled to some remote places and have met people that Westerners don't often get to meet. I've seen very simple cultures, where cleverness and sarcasm don't exist. They haven't discovered cynicism -- yet. That takes complexity to develop."

"Well they're one up on me!" I said, with a tinge of blame and self-pity. "When I was growing up, I don't think I ever really met anyone that *wasn't* cynical."

"We have to have patience and compassion with each other," he said, "because we're in this together. We've grown up in these circumstances and have all been maimed. There's really nobody to blame. It's not like you can blame your parents or your teachers or the politicians, because everybody's a victim.

"We're all these battered babies who have undergone some harsh stuff. So if you can say that you still have an active hope or wish within you to feel more wonder, that's a marvelous gift. It's a wish that you should be very thankful for. Because in order to have that wish, you have to accept the existence of what you're wishing for, because you won't wish for something that you don't think is in some way possible."

I told him that what he was saying made me think of poor people. They lose the ability to wish, because achieving their aspirations appears to be impossible for them.

He nodded in agreement and said, "If you still have that wish for wonderment, then that makes you a tremendous recipient of grace. The first step is to appreciate how much you already have. Remember, there's a lot to life that you don't yet know about, even though the way life has been presented to you has caused you to think that this is not the case. You think that the possibilities that you've been presented with are all there is. You're taught to apply yourself to what's been presented and to put your hopes in that practical arena.

"So if you have in some way escaped with both the ability to cope in the world, as it appears that you have, and the ability to wish for some of the experiences that I've been telling you about, then you are truly fortunate. Because a lot of people who have the wish for something else, have not been able to maintain the ability to cope. They're locked up somewhere.

"If you've escaped with both of those, you're a very fortunate and graced person. Don't you think that it's about time you started appreciating just how lucky you are?"

7

THE BABY & THE LAMP

In those eyes that had never seen the day, in that half-shaped brain was a sensation of light! Light -- that it never had seen. Light -- that perhaps it never will see. Light -- that existed somewhere! And already it had its reward: the Ideal was real to it.

Dreams, **Olive Schreiner**

Several days later we left Las Vegas -- I by car, to play poker in Southern California, and my friend by plane to Oregon, to spend time with some old friends. We had arranged to meet in two weeks; as events turned out, I wasn't to see him for almost a month.

It was both an interesting time for me and a difficult time. These two have often gone together in the patterns of my life. This had been the longest separation from my friend up to that point in time, and it affected me greatly. I found myself often imagining what he might think or say, or how he would react to this or that situation.

I never conceived of myself as the type of person who would think of another as superior in the skill of being a human being. But along with the knowledge and understanding that my friend reflected, was a way of being that was undeniably grander than any I had known.

75

I did, in fact, have a phone number in Oregon where I could contact him if I saw fit. But as it turned out, I only used it to establish and confirm our eventual meeting place in San Jose, about sixty miles south of San Francisco. I guess that I had so many conversations with him in my thoughts, that when the possibility arose to actually talk to him on the phone -- I was all talked out.

When the day arrived, I picked him up at the San Jose Airport, and within three minutes, maybe even two, he was again explaining the mysteries of the Universe to me. I found it hard to listen to him at first, mostly because I was involved with wondering if he remembered who I was. I asked what he'd been doing for all that time, mostly out of nervousness, but partly out of curiosity.

"I guess you know," he answered, "that I spent most of this last month on a farm, a farm with all kinds of animals. Actually I spent most of my time feeding them and cleaning out their stalls -- basically hanging out with them. Watching animals is certainly an education. It was for me anyway. I had some very interesting thoughts about this world of life around us. I'll tell you some of them if you're up to listening, but maybe later would be better?"

Later probably would have been better, but I said that of course I did want to listen and now would be fine.

He proceeded, "Most of us subscribe to the point of view that people are inherently different from other living creatures. We think that there is a continuum that starts with roaches or maggots and works its way up, more complicated and more complicated as it ascends, and then somewhere, it goes to dogs and horses and monkeys and then humans.

"But you know, it's really hard to accept that there is a continuum that includes us, because our lot as people is really so uniquely strange. It's really beyond strange, and to me, there's only one reason for this strangeness. All living creatures have things to do and to take care of. We have all that too, but in addition to that, we have this unique ability to perceive the situation that's going on. We can even perceive the situation that contains the situation that's going on. We can theorize about it and try to figure it out. So we can't just go along in life and simply take care of business like the animals can. That's not our lot, because we have this other thing that we do, called thinking about things.

"Now maybe at our present stage of development, our thinking is mostly taken up with how to improve our ordinary circumstances, but that doesn't mean that we don't have some additional potential for thinking and feeling about life."

Even though I had been a little fuzzy, by the time he mentioned that "we couldn't just go along as the animals do," I caught up and was actually interested. It seemed to me that what he said had contradicted an idea that I held in regard for as long as I could remember. It was Saint Francis' idea and Jesus' idea before him, that we could be as simple as the animals. I asked him what he meant by this "additional potential for thinking and feeling about life."

"Stop for a minute (not the car) and really feel the situation," he answered. "There's not another living creature on this earth that has the option of contemplating the ideas that you and I have been dealing with. Think of other creatures getting together to discuss the evolution of consciousness or some similar subject. There's no other creature that even comes close to that.

"The way it actually looks, is there's this continuity, you know, the life chain, and then there's this big space -- then there's us, with our very strange situation. Hey! You know what I think the question really is? Is it curable or is it incurable?"

We were interrupted by the necessity of stopping at the exit booth to the airport parking lot. I gave the attendant the ticket along with two dollars that my friend had put in my hand as we pulled up to the booth. The attendant asked me, "Will this be okay?" as she handed me a fifty cent piece as change. I looked at it for a moment because they're not so common anymore, told the lady that it was fine, handed it to my friend, and drove out.

What followed was an unprovoked, as far as I could tell, and un-usually extended flurry of laughter from this man sitting next to me holding a half dollar in his hand. I asked what was so funny.

"Remember to ask me later," he said.

When he calmed down, he continued talking about our lot as human beings. Not having any idea what had taken place to cause the hysterics, I was all the more relieved when he resumed talking.

"Are we stuck with this weirdness," he continued, "or is our situation only weird because we don't know what to do with what we are? That's really the question.

"No therapy session or making peace with husbands or wives or bosses is going to work this one out -- more money won't even help. Because here we are, these beings that operate standardly according to nature's laws, same as the other creatures do, but having the capacity to ask questions like *Where's it all going?* and *Does it matter what I do?*

"I think that we have to start by recognizing the strangeness of our situation. After that, maybe we can assess whether we're part of a permanent catastrophe. No, let's not call it that. Let's call it a permanent disability or maybe a permanent ability. So far it has been a burden, but maybe there's some hidden capacity that's been given to us that we haven't yet discovered, much less figured out how to use."

He suggested that we switch drivers because he was familiar with the turns that we had to make while going through the downtown area. I pulled over, and as we passed each other walking around the back of the car, I asked him what he was laughing about back there at the airport. I guess he either didn't hear me or didn't want to answer, because when we resumed driving, he continued with what he was talking about.

"Think how it all starts for us. Before a baby comes into the world it's unborn, it's unnamed, it's unseparated. It barely senses its own individual existence. It's tactilely part of something else before it's born and before that as well. So this pre-baby was part of something, because obviously, the less separated you are, the more a part of something you are."

When I got back in the car after our driver switch, I unconsciously picked up some old piece of paper and was nervously tearing little pieces off of it. Our month apart had obviously taken its toll.

He chuckled and called it to my attention. "As you tear off a piece of paper, the more you tear, the more separate it appears to become. Before you tear it off, it's part of the rest. If you want to cut a little circle out of a piece of paper, before you actually cut it out, it's separated in your view only, but it isn't really separated at all.

"Initially a baby is part of something, and then it becomes born as a separate individual. It's no longer physically connected to anything. It's not even given what an ordinary electric lamp is given, a cord to a power source, so it can look back and check, 'Ahhhh, all right.' It's not given that -- it's completely floating."

I dispensed with the fidgeties and was now following him so closely that I actually winced, or maybe a better description is I cringed, and the words spontaneously came out of my mouth, "That is very, very freaky!"

He agreed and went on. "It could only be expected that in a situation like that some quick action is necessary on the part of this little newly separated being. Something to restore assurance of its connection to what it had in the old days, because everything has changed.

"We humans are entities without any physical connection to anything. People don't even walk on the earth anymore; we walk on floors. There's a description in one of those 'Don Juan' books that you've read of his friend Don Genero swimming on the earth, the earth being his lover. That's very remote to us, very remote. We walk on carpets; our feet are not connected to the earth. We live under ceilings and between walls, so we're also removed from the sky. Our hands are in the air, but unless there's wind, the air feels like there's nothing there until we hit something that we recognize. So really, we're dangling, and we're not even dangling *from* anything."

We were driving in heavy traffic through downtown San Jose, and he started to gesture semi-wildly in order to enhance his description of dangling. "We're like that guy in the movie *2001, A Space Odyssey*, who floated out into space while all his appendages were moving. He was flailing out there. That's our condition.

We have no tangible connection to anything that we can recognize."

Flailing his arms and legs as he drove actually didn't enhance his description at all for me, unless his purpose was to make me feel like I was that helpless baby. I finally started to grab for the steering wheel and he calmed down. I felt like I was in a Laurel and Hardy movie. We both had a good laugh. For the first time since I picked him up, I really felt like we were together again.

"Can you feel the impact of our situation?" he continued. "A simple lamp at least has the advantage of a cord which plugs into a socket, and inside that socket there are wires which lead to bigger wires. If that lamp could tangibly trace where its life was coming from, it could go back all the way to huge generators that it could depend on. That's phenomenal!"

He plucked the cigarette lighter out of its holster, and holding it up in my face he said, "This ridiculous inanimate object has so much advantage over us. Think of that. We have no such tangible opportunity. For us to be able to do what this thing could do is almost inconceivable. Where would you even start?"

I shrugged my shoulders. I wasn't sure I knew what he meant, and even if I did, I certainly wouldn't know where to start.

"But inconceivable as it might seem," he said, "we must start somewhere, because unless we rediscover that connection which is no longer visible, we will continue to dangle and flail. What keeps us alive is an invisible mystery to us, and we know no tangible connection to it."

I thought that I detected a flaw in his explanation. I asked if our heartbeat, which we don't wind and for which there's no cord or battery, and our respiration, which gets pushed in and pulled out without any visible bladder, were not physical evidence of our connection.

He paused, I think as a sign of respect for my question. "You're right!" he said emphatically. "That *would* be evidence, if we were cognizant of their presence, but as it is, we aren't. That leaves us in the dark, and since we can go for hours without realizing that we do indeed have a heartbeat or breath, we have no tangible connection to what keeps us going.

"We don't know where our thoughts and feelings come from. We proceed as though everything is self-generated: 'I think, I feel, I think, I feel.' Like we have some kind of motor in us, one which generates thoughts and feelings. Certainly no one has ever, during an operation, discovered a motor in us which generates our breath or causes our heart to beat. Unlike us, these lamps can't move very far because they have cords, but at least they know where their life energy is coming from, and we don't."

For some reason I related what he was saying to the realizations that I had that night in my room playing my plucking instrument. I told him the story (pretty much as I told it to you, the reader). After my story, I added that it seemed mind-blowing to me that even though there was this huge missing piece in life, I could still spend most of my time asking questions like, "I wonder why I have a tickle in my throat?" or "She doesn't like me, I wonder why she doesn't like me?" or "I was the best player, I wonder why I couldn't win in that poker game?" While beneath it, beneath it, beneath it, there are these questions: "What in the world is going on? Where is the fuckin cord? Why did He leave out the cord?"

He said simply, "If a person understood the importance of asking those missing questions, those most basic questions, he would recognize that he's going to have to answer them before he can get answers to any of his others."

I asked him if he'd ever seen a little pamphlet called *The Word That Was Lost*. I didn't remember who wrote it. Somebody I barely knew gave it to me for my birthday a few years before. It explained that all the efforts that people make to enhance their lives, no matter how sincere and no matter how energetic, are useless, because there's something missing at the base of it all. And if that something at the base of it isn't experienced, then everything that's added on, for whatever sincere reason, is not going to help.

He told me he'd never heard of it, but that it sounded exactly like what he was talking about. "We have to surmise the presence of a life force," he said, "because we've lost the actual sense of that energy alive in us. Having lost touch with that experience, we find ourselves in the tremendously vulnerable position of trying to artificially create the security that's naturally given to us.

"Something's been lost, and this something that's been lost is unsubstitutable. But since we don't know this, we spend our lives trying to find substitutes for that something that's been lost, that connection that's been lost. We try to create this security with people, with objects, with hopes of travelling to new adventurous and exotic places, with variety, with stability, and with entertainment of every conceivable type.

"Not because we mean to go further away from truth, but because we're dangling, we're not touching down anywhere. We have woven this tremendous fabric in an effort to try to protect ourselves from harm. We've become so protected, that we have hidden ourselves from our creator and our maintainer."

When my friend was talking about something he considered really important for me to absorb, he would tend to repeat himself an inordinate number of times, sometimes with merely a change in inflection or tone or alteration of a word or two. It took me a while to get used to it. I eventually realized that it was extremely deliberate on his part. And when I began to appreciate the importance of his instruction, I likewise began to value the repetition.

I have left some of the repetition intact in the text that you're reading. If it was appropriate for me to listen to it, it probably is for you too. As I said earlier, the method of payment that I assumed for the incredible gift that I received was -- to pass it on as best I can.

"Something has been so lost to us," he contended, "that everything that we've added, all the attempts that we've made to enrich our lives are actually starting from a point which is not the first point. Like building a house starting from the second story without having a foundation.

"But really, even more basic than that, we're starting without something that was lost that's so intangible and so unknown to us, that we don't even know what it is, or that it is. If indeed this is the case, it would be vital to have a glimpse of what's really taking place, even if in the beginning it is just a theoretical or intellectual glimpse."

I felt that this past month must have been good for me, because the quality and depth of my input and understanding had definitely changed. Each time he described his point of view, some example or understanding jumped up in me. In the past this had not so often been the case.

I told him that this idea of a house without a foundation reminded me of a family get-together that I went to while he was away. It was a birthday party. The kids were making a lot of noise and having a miserable time. They were throwing stuff around, and my brother-in-law blurted out, "I know what we need. We need more candles and some different color candles too. Let's try that."

It sounded ridiculous to me, but all the grown-ups including me scurried around setting up candles. For a few minutes, the kids were even looking at them and shouting, "Hey! Look at all those new candles." Then they started up their crazing around again.

After I finished telling my story, I looked over and noticed that my friend seemed to be immersed in thought. I asked him what he was thinking.

"They have to recognize what the problem really is; they have lost the direct experience of being connected to a permanence which gave them life and maintains it at every moment, and no alteration of the variables in their lives is going to substitute for that 'Word' that was lost."

We arrived at our destination. He pulled into the parking lot and stopped the car. Instead of moving to get out, he turned to face me and said: "But how can you more clearly recognize this problem? When do you ever take enough time to think about life in a different way? Everything for you is so fast paced. Mostly you're thinking about coping with your problems, plans, and relationships. How often do you really try to settle in on yourself, and try to figure out where it's all coming from, where it's all going to, and what it is that you're connected to?"

Instead of falling victim to my "defending myself by blaming my circumstances syndrome," I thought of a question that had occupied me earlier in the day. "How about babies?" I asked. "If they're in their natural state, is it hard for them as well?"

"Babies seek touch from their mothers," he answered. "It's vital because it's their lifeline for a time. Still, they suspect the impermanence of that touch; they cry and are anxious from the very beginning. Babies come from an unmanifest state where everything is connected. They're hatched out as individual entities that have individual and separated needs, and those needs increase. It's a very insecure position, and one that should be looked on with tremendous compassion.

"To be a human being is a difficult position to be in. The anxiety is there, the shakiness is there, and it doesn't go away; it increases, and increases, and increases till we have to start learning ways to keep it under control. No normal, healthy person wants to walk around feeling tremendously anxious. Unfortunately, the situation of experiencing separation carries with it tremendous potential anxiety."

I thought that I was understanding something about this question of babies. I told him that I had a newly formed theory.

"Yes! Yes! Tell it to me. I'd like to hear it," he said with sincere enthusiasm.

"Maybe when babies aren't crying, it isn't because things are good. They can be distracted from crying, but maybe things are never good. Sure, we can divert them from recognizing that they're no longer physically connected to what they, at one time, were connected to. They are, what you've been calling, separated entities, and that's painful, so they cry.

"So when we say, 'Oh don't cry, everything's all right,' maybe they know it's a lie, because everything isn't all right. Sure, we can make them stop crying by distracting their attention from their disconnectedness, but really, we only cover up the situation till the next time it's uncovered." I never found out what he thought about my theory because he brought it right back home -- as usual.

"Here's an interesting question," he said. "How come *we* aren't always crying, and what have we done to stop crying? I'm not saying this in any accusatory way. A person doesn't want to go through life crying, so we start learning ways to divert ourselves from the problem, from the pain, from the separateness that we experience.

"We learn (and in these times we've become experts) the many ways of diverting ourselves. *How's it going? -- Oh, great!* (That means you've successfully linked together all your methods of diverting yourself, very few spaces in between.) *It's not going too bad.* (That means you're having some spaces in between these ways of diverting yourself, and when in those spaces, even though you blame your condition on anything and everything, you feel the pain of that same separation that you felt as a baby.)

"It's an interesting point of view to think that a baby or a grown-up cries when it feels the emptiness that occurs when all these diversions are abated and there's a moment when none of them are effective. Right then and there we feel the turmoil of disconnection."

He reached for the door handle and almost instantly was out of the car, leaving the echo of his last few words in the car with me. If I said that what I had just heard made sense to me, it would be a ridiculous understatement. In actuality, it seemed as though all the muddled thoughts that I ever had about man's basic problem had just been explained, uncovered, and simplified. It was awesome, and I felt at home.

8

TURMOIL, COVERED & UNCOVERED

He who knows in truth this Spirit
and knows nature with its changing conditions, wherever this man
may be he is no more whirled around by fate.

The Bhagavad Gita

We had come to San Jose for a yearly tournament held there for medium to good players which was also attended by the usual bunch of locals trying to get lucky and win one. I had never played in San Jose before, nor had I actually ever even been there. This was of little consequence, because once you got inside these casinos, your location on the planet quickly ceased to matter.

It was about eleven o'clock in the morning and the tournament was due to start at one in the afternoon. People were signing up, a procedure which involves waiting in line, paying your buy-in money, and picking a little piece of paper out of a bowl with two numbers on it -- one number indicating the table at which you will be sitting, and the other, the seat number you've drawn at that table. I was to be in the #6 seat at table #14. There were twenty-two tables in all. My friend was in the #1 seat at table #7. The way the tables were arranged, I faced him directly across the room. I hoped that it wouldn't affect my concentration.

Everybody was milling around waiting to take their seats when my friend came up behind me. He was smiling broadly, about what, I didn't know, but his smile did remind me of his laughing fit in the airport parking lot.

"What was all that laughing about at the airport?" I asked.

He laughed out loud, though nothing like the airport performance, and went on to tell me why he had been laughing. "I went to pick up a present for my daughter at the airport in Portland before I got on the plane. It cost $15.50. I've had this fifty cent piece stuck in the little watch pocket of my jeans for about a year. It's even been through the laundry a number of times -- it's gotten to be kind of a good luck piece. When the clerk asked for $15.50, I spent a moment digging out this fifty cent piece and started to give it to her. As I did, I looked at it and realized that I hadn't seen it in maybe a year, and I wondered whether or not I really wanted to give that half-dollar away. Since I didn't come up with any profound philosophy on the subject, I gave it away.

"Remember when you picked me up and we were driving out of the airport lot? The attendant looked at you for a long moment, held up a fifty cent piece and said, 'Would this be okay?'"

I liked his story and broke out in a big smile.

"How come this story makes you so happy?" he asked rhetorically. "Why is a story like that so pleasing? What does it mean anyway? Does it mean anything? I gave away fifty cents, I got fifty cents back. It's like watching little kids and the really simple things that they can get excited about. It's a little story with a sweet little twist in the ending. If our days were filled with little stories like that one, our experience of life would probably be very different than it is.

"Think of how little was involved in my having this delightful little experience and having this story to tell. Think of the risk I took, the sacrifice I made. That coin wasn't really even a keepsake for me. I was just too lazy to get it out of my coin pocket. That's why I ended up having it for all that time. It was stuck in there. Probably the last laundry was what loosened it. The laundry created a tiny little space for delight to come through. If it weren't for the laundry, *de-light* might still be stuck in there!"

I liked what he did with this story and I wanted to get in on the fun. "If it can be loosened so easily, maybe dat light isn't dat far away," I joked.

"Maybe," he said, ignoring my fooling around, "there are only a few little obstacles between us and the light. Obstacles, that if removed, would give us a chance to experience life in this simple delightful way. If that were the case, then energy would be really well spent to find out what those obstacles are, and remove them."

The tournament coordinator was up at the microphone announcing that everyone should take their seats. I went to my seat with a feeling of unaccustomed lightness. Maybe there *are* only a few obstacles between us and the light.

This was an elimination tournament. That means that all players receive the same amount of chips to start off with. As players lose their chips and drop out of the game, the tables are consolidated, and the final person at the final table, the one who is left with all the chips, is the winner. The person who drops out before him gets second place, and so on. Ten places receive prize money, though tenth place is usually about equivalent to getting back your buy-in.

Pride is involved in the fact that I'm dwelling inordinately on the details of this particular tournament. Both my friend and I made it down to the final table before each of us was in turn eliminated. We each picked up a sizeable chunk of cash and went to the buffet to eat and celebrate our co-victories. After the expected poker talk, which went on for some time, and our multiple trips to the buffet line, my friend resumed explaining to me about this "turmoil of disconnection."

"This diverting, this covering, is what you do to keep the turmoil of feeling your lack of connection from overtaking you. You have to scramble your feet very quickly because turmoil is gooey -- even the word turmoil, like leeches crawling around in black slime. So much of life is spent scrambling to try to convince ourselves and each other that okayness is right around the corner. We can actually have discussions like: 'How are you doing with your new house?' 'How are you doing with getting a raise at your job?' 'How are you doing with your new girl or boyfriend?' or even, 'How did you do at the poker tournament?' We think that if the answer to that question is, 'I did well at the tournament,' then it equals, 'I'm doing well.'

"Now you may have done well at the tournament, you may be doing well with your new house -- but you're not doing well, because the turmoil of disconnection is always threatening to surface. It's either raw, meaning uncovered, where you're close to tears, or it's covered, which means you're successful at setting up life so as not to have to look at it. And that's understandable; a person isn't really screwed up because he's trying to cover his turmoil. What's a person to do?"

After seven straight hours of card playing, we both had enough of the inside of this building, so when my friend told me that he had arranged something interesting for us to do, I was ready.

We had reservations at one of those suite hotels where you get a couple of bedrooms and a living room. For a small price, you get to feel like you're in a house instead of on the road -- definitely a tangible benefit of sharing. On the way over to the place, he explained what he had planned.

"I have a friend Paul who lives here in San Jose. He just got back from travelling in Africa -- lions and tigers Africa. I spoke to him on the phone last week after I was sure that I was coming down here. He told me that he had taken some videos while he was there and had been editing them to show to friends. He knew that I'd like to watch them, so he asked me if some of his other friends could come over to wherever I was staying, so he could show them to all of us together. He said I could invite anyone that I wished, as well. He would have done it at his place, but he was having some trouble with his neighbors complaining about too many cars parked there. So that's what's happening. I also asked a couple of guys that I knew from the tournament."

That evening Paul showed up with his wife and their video. The four poker players were already there, along with two ladies that Paul's wife had invited. That made eight of us sitting in our small living room in the All Suites Hotel. A little later, two more people came in that Paul had invited. They didn't know whose place they were coming into, so they were in this curious situation of having been invited by someone other than the person whose place it was. We live in a pretty informal time, but there are still social rules and regulations -- standard procedures.

So these two people walked through the doorway into the little entrance hall. They were standing under an arch that lead into the living room. At that point they didn't give a shit about the video; the only thing they wanted to know was whose place it was.

They were standing in the doorway and the only two people they knew were sitting on the couch, but they knew it wasn't their place. They knew it was somebody's suite, but six other people were there, and they didn't know which one was the host. Maybe they wanted to know in case one of them had to go to the bathroom. They wouldn't want to ask the wrong somebody.

It wasn't like they were panting heavily. We didn't have to give them a paper bag to hyper-ventilate into. But they couldn't help but let on how anxious they were, and it was *very* anxious.

Finally they said to Paul, the only person they knew, "Hi, how are you doing? Whose place is this anyway?" They said that. Some people might have preferred to try to figure it out, but these guys asked. We made some jokes like, "Oh, we thought it was yours," which made them even more anxious, but then we all laughed and they laughed too.

I really liked watching the videos and I think everyone else did too. Paul gave a great running narrative, and his wife knew a lot about the animals. Later that night, after everyone left, my friend put down his glasses, turned to me, and started talking.

"I hope that you can appreciate the uncovered turmoil that those two people experienced as they walked into the room. They came through the birth canal of the doorway, in through the different parts of the anatomy that was the arch, born into this new situation -- and their turmoil was definitely uncovered.

"What happens when you're a newborn baby? What happens when you're a fifty-year-old baby and you're born into a new situation? You try to cover the turmoil that you feel -- that same turmoil that arose when you first lost the awareness of being connected to your life source. It doesn't take much for that turmoil to be uncovered, so we've had to develop some very definite skills to cover it back up, to coat it over.

"Think of how little it took for those two people to have their turmoil uncovered. Think of how little it takes for *your* usually covered turmoil to be uncovered. How did you go about covering your turmoil tonight?"

I guess I was a little tired from the events of the day and feeling not at all sharp. His question caught me completely off guard. For a few seconds I struggled unsuccessfully to come up with a reasonable reply. He obviously knew I wasn't all there, but for some reason of his own, he went on anyway. I think that sometimes he used me as a sounding board for verbalizing and developing his ideas. As long as I was not actively snoring, I guess I could realistically serve that particular function.

He proceeded to answer the question he put to me. "You covered your turmoil tonight by protecting yourself whenever that turmoil was in danger of being uncovered. Since you live in a constant state of anxiety, worrying that your disconnectedness is going to be revealed and that you will have to re-experience that pain, you find it necessary to protect yourself from whatever you fear will uncover it. When you understand that, you'll be able to watch for specific examples of just how that happens."

I was tired but still curious about what it is that I could watch for. I asked him when he thought I would be ready for something like that.

"Maybe sometime," he answered, "but for now just try to understand the idea of uncovered and covered turmoil, okay?"

I said okay and he went on.

"I call those methods of protection that you surround yourself with, your 'protective devices.' You've set up these protective devices because you feel in danger an enormous amount of the time. So much so, that in each situation, you have a new and different story for yourself about what you have to do, this time, to protect yourself.

"Unfortunately, none of your stories are accurate, and all the danger you imagine, is just that -- imagined. The two people in the doorway would certainly tell *their* story differently. They would describe an awkward situation, one in which they should have been told instantly whose hotel room they were in. They probably thought we were insensitive to their difficult position.

"Believe it or not, regardless of the specifics of the circumstances, however varied they may be, all your frantic protecting is focused at only one thing -- to avoid, at any moment, coming face to face with the turmoil of feeling your disconnection from the energy that keeps you alive. That energy that you were, at one time, merged with, but since birth have become more and more unaware of.

"This enormous collection of protective devices that encircle us, become encircling. If, by chance, there were a force that could be called 'The Grace of God,' even *it* would be obstructed by these encircling clouds.

"When we create the pollution that shrouds our cities, the Sun, even though it had nothing to do with causing that pollution, begins to lose its ability to get through to us. Should the Sun increase its power every time we create pollution? We don't expect that. Well the power of the clouds is nothing in relation to that of the Sun. In fact, the Sun is so powerful that we still get light, we still get heat. The plants grow distorted, but they do grow. Still, as the clouds increase, the sun becomes more and more obscured."

He noticed that my eyes were starting to close involuntarily and I was beginning to nod-out. An overwhelming exhaustion was overcoming me. This day started a year ago, it seemed, with picking him up at the airport and my success at the poker tables. I had my limit and that's where I was. I went into my room, and in less than two minutes I was sleeping with my clothes on.

I awoke early the next morning. Feeling sure that my friend was still asleep, I went into the windowless living room and turned on the lights. He was sitting cross-legged on the couch with a cloth covering his head. We had never shared the same living space before, so I was unaware of his private routines. I quickly turned out the lights and retreated to my room. My best guess was that he was doing some kind of meditation, but I couldn't be sure.

After about an hour, I came out again, more discretely. This time the lights were on. I told my friend that I was sorry and hoped I hadn't disturbed him.

He laughed and said, "If at some time in the future you practice meditation, you'll discover that no amount of noise that comes from outside yourself can compare with the distraction of the noise that goes on in your head from talking to yourself constantly.

"Let's go on talking about what we were talking about last night before you fell asleep on me."

I said that I'd like that and sat down across from him. He backtracked enough so that I could remember the point at which I had zoned out.

(If you, the reader, feel that you also need to backtrack, you can go back and review his earlier remarks.)

"You go through life," he began, "feeling a constant sense of danger, the threat of an unknown void. You don't know about this basic turmoil of yours, so you don't recognize what's happpening, but you feel a certain discomfort, an awkwardness, and you try to do something to alleviate your difficulty. Of course there is no such situation, and the constant need you feel to take care of something makes you old before your time.

"We learn protective devices for almost every potential situation and we apply them moment after moment. If a situation occurs for which we don't have a way of protecting ourselves from one of these imagined dangers, we talk to ourselves and make everything come out the way we want -- at least to come out that way in our thoughts. Talking to ourselves is the catch-all protective device. It protects us from the imagined dangers that the other protective devices miss."

I was beginning to understand the basic concept. I thought it would help if I could relate his idea to something tangible.

"What would be an example of an imagined danger?" I asked.

"*Silence* is an example of an imagined danger," he answered. "Actually silence is beautiful. Silence is where you can hear 'what is.' Silence is where the sounds of creation can be heard."

"Why are we so afraid of silence?" I asked.

"My kids used to think that silence was the enemy," he said laughing quietly. "I would tell them to have quiet-time. 'We're going to have quiet-time now,' and the kids would look at each other like, 'Why would a bunch of kids get together to have quiet-time?'

"They would say to each other, 'He's coming! I think he's going to give us quiet-time now.'

"What a weird thing to think. I'm not making up a story. That's what they used to do. They'd hide behind trees or something, and when I would find them and suggest Q.T., they'd say, 'Aww I knew you'd say that.' How strange for a kid to be afraid of that, and all *we* are is big kids, right?"

"So why do you think we're afraid of quiet, or silence?" I asked.

"We feel that quietness is empty, like a void, like an absence of stimuli and it's bad, it's scary. Maybe if we could get to experiment a little with silence, we might discover something new. Have you ever tried some kind of meditation or other?"

I told him that I was one of the thousands that had tried T.M. (Transcendental Meditation) for a while and then dropped it.

"Well, then you've probably experienced a second or two of silence, and even that's beautiful. I won't go to three, because I know you've never gotten there," he joked. "But you can't be okay with the silence past two seconds. Most people can't even tolerate one second of silence. They have used their protective devices, especially talking to themselves, so much, that sitting still for one second of quiet can't even be expected of them."

"It sounds like you're saying that we're all drug addicts hooked on talking to ourselves," I said with minor alarm.

"Exactly!" he said. "People are addicted, habituated to something that really works. Because not only does the noise in their head protect them from the fear of what they'll find in the silence. Not only that, but also the details of that noise can explain things in an acceptable way, so as to make them blameless for whatever's taking place."

"That's a powerful tranquillizer," I muttered, mostly to myself.

He went on, I don't think he even heard me. "You have something that can create noise inside your head that's always with you, so you're never alone with your uncovered turmoil, and what's more, the details of that noise calms you. It's satisfying. It explains things the way you want them explained. You're always in the right, even if you say to yourself, 'I was really wrong there,' you can still be right about that! Always in the end, by talking to yourself, you come out right, *always!*

"If not, you just keep on going till you do come out right. That's a powerful thing to have sitting up there on top of your neck, and you've certainly used it, I should say, misused it, in an extreme way."

"Are you saying that there's a reason to uncover that turmoil other than to just get it all out in the open, you know, let it all hang out?" I asked, not as a challenge, but with hope that there really was another reason.

He answered enthusiastically, "What if there was some fabulous place where you could go if you didn't have the extra weight that comes with the constant effort of trying to cover up. Maybe we have a little bit too much bulk, with all those extra layers of protection. Maybe without those extra layers we might be able to experience something that we couldn't otherwise, something remarkable, something really worth living for. If that were the case, there would be some reason to deal with this turmoil and scrambling. Otherwise, why even acknowledge that it's there?"

9

YOU'RE NO GLIDER

I believed...that time was at least as real and solid as myself, ... I said 'one o'clock' as though I could see it, and 'Monday' as though I could find it on a map...

The Last Unicorn, **Peter S. Beagle**

By this point, you, the reader, have had a chance to evaluate the wisdom contained here-in, so as to decide for yourself whether it's worth sticking with, or maybe find some better way to spend your time. It would be best if you made that decision on the basis of your valuation for my friend's understandings, rather than on some hope that something attractive, exciting, or extreme happens in the story. I can save you the wait. In terms of happenings, this is a pale pink story, not a fake fuchsia story. Or more simply stated, nothing happens in this story that would make this book a suitable movie for T.V.

You and I, the reader and the writer, may have very different perspectives on the matter of these written words. To me, they are precious, because they represent the most valuable commodity that I have ever found in this world. To you, they are at worst, a form of entertainment and at best, a clue to the location of the secret of freedom.

To the extent that you are magnetized to the second possibility, you are already blessed. As to the lure of that which entertains, I hope that you can persevere with these writings long enough to discover the precious wisdom and insight that my friend conveyed to me about this seemingly innocent addiction to entertainment.

The San Jose tournament is made up of five separate events. Each day a different type of poker game is played, and each day, people who want to play in that event gather in the late morning to sign up.

The first event, which had already taken place, was hold-em. Today's event was called lo-ball, a game that neither my friend nor I played, so we had what you might call the day off. Tomorrow we would both be playing again in seven card stud.

We spent our day off separately, I, walking around downtown in search of some items of clothing that I had been wanting, and he, at a local health club, getting some exercise and working out. I dropped him off at the gym and arranged to pick him up before dinner. As it turned out, my interest in clothes was nonexistent that day, so after a couple of hours of aimlessly walking past stores, I went to the health club myself for a little exercise.

Our paths crossed in the sauna, where I headed directly upon entering the gym, and he, after a strenuous workout. We were alone, and my friend didn't miss the opportunity.

He asked me to describe my picture of what was going on with both of us at that moment. I didn't know on what level he was asking. I fumbled around trying to describe the idea of sitting and sweating as a leisure activity, while people in other parts of the world sweated naturally because they worked so hard. He ignored my bumbling social commentary and started talking about his own view of what was going on.

"There's something benevolent and beautiful operating us, even at this moment," he began. "Something putting life force in my voice to speak these words, and in your ears to be able to listen to them. In order to experience this benevolent and beautiful force, some of these clouds of yours have got to go. It would be convenient if you could keep all these protective devices, be safe every moment, and still be open to the experience of the creator, but it doesn't happen to work that way.

"With people frantically protecting themselves from imagined dangers, and talking to themselves constantly to remain convinced of the existence of those dangers, it's no wonder that there's a restlessness to peoples' actions. I don't think you have to pay a lot of attention to life to know that there's a certain frenzy out there. So many activities seem to have 'rush' attached onto them. There's no way that you could reasonably construe that all these things should have to be rushed, but everything seems to have a little bit of 'rush' hooked up to it. With all this rushing and restlessness, we're really very hungry for rest -- we are. It would be very fortunate if we could acknowledge that this is our state and not have to pretend so much."

His statements were timely. I had done basically nothing but roam around town, but still I felt the need to unwind, the need to rest. I told him that I had gotten used to feeling restless, like that's the way life is.

"Actually," he jumped in, "ninety percent of your time is spent feeling restless, or judging that things have to be a little different for you to feel just like you want to feel. I'm not saying that you're not well-adjusted. I'm not saying that you can't cope or that you're a basket case. I'm saying that we're all well-adjusted, we're all confident and we all, to different degrees, know how to do the 'stuff' that we're called on to do in life. But we're all really weary, and we're all really tired."

His words seemed heavy, I seemed heavy. The awareness of being weary that his words engendered seemed to multiply my state. Still, curiously enough, I was agitated. "That's a weird combination," I said, "to be both tired and restless."

"It's not as weird as you think," he responded. "Even when we're tired, we're on to the next event almost as immediately as the current one arrives. If you've ever watched yourself, you know that's the way it goes. You're constantly moving along to protect yourself from the next danger. You're never quite okay. You always need something more, and you hope that *something more* is going to be supplied to you in the next moment."

Even as he was talking, what he was describing was happening. In my thoughts, I had started out the sauna door on my way to what I was going to do next, what I was going to think about next, where I was going to be next. It was like I really was running from some kind of danger, but of course there was no danger.

He knew me well enough to know that I knew exactly what he was talking about. He poured it on.

"There's a certain armed feeling," he said, "one that you might even have right now. Like you may have to run at any moment in order to protect yourself. Like you can't relax and agree to be here, because if you do, this danger will catch up to you. So your hopes are always in the next moment, you think that whatever is next holds the secret to your okayness."

He looked over to make sure I was absorbing what he was saying. The sauna was a good place for listening and I think that he knew that. After all, where could I go? I was drenched in sweat and naked.

"How could we not be tired," he said, "with all this frantic renovating and maintenance of our protective devices and our launching pads. Like in cartoons when Woody Woodpecker runs to the edge of the cliff, and keeps on running. His feet go around like a helicopter blade and he doesn't fall, till he looks down.

"That's the nature of our lives. What keeps it all going is our frantic movement, our monkey cage agitation. We're spinning our legs the same way that Woody Woodpecker, or the Road Runner, spins his legs. He's just like a helicopter, but you know the way it is with a helicopter, the minute it slows down, it goes down. A helicopter has no relaxing mode. A glider has a relaxing mode. But you're no glider.

"If you listen to the buzz of the rotors, you can hear them. The din of the blades is going on inside your head. They're trying to keep it all going. Somewhere inside you, you recognize that if you relax, there will be nothing to keep these protective devices together, because *you're* keeping them together. You built them, you're maintaining them, you're keeping them together.

"Maybe now, sitting in the sauna, you get the idea that you need to relax. But of course that's like telling this helicopter, 'Listen, take it easy, calm down, stop those blades once in a while.' Your concept of exactly what will take place is accurate. If you stop, all your protective devices will stop, because nobody else will keep them going, so *you* have to keep them going."

My mind wandered to a time when I owned a small restaurant. It was the hardest work and the longest hours of anything I ever did. I knew if I didn't show up, there would be nothing to keep it going. My friends would say, "Listen, relax, take a vacation." And I would tell them, "If I relax and take a vacation, it'll be gone. The customers aren't going to keep my restaurant going."

When I returned from my thoughts, I told him that he was obviously right about all of it, but that I felt incapable of altering the situation. I was a little annoyed at how well he knew me, and I showed that annoyance by asking, in a curt tone, if he had a constructive suggestion.

"I'm not telling you this in a casual way or making a joke," he said with a sincere tone. "I recognize that we're talking about what you've set up as a life, and I'm not suggesting that you do anything like stop spinning your rotors. I'm presenting this really essential problem, that we're doing stuff all the time. I don't mean doing stuff like hammering nails. I mean like thinking about the situation we're going to be in later, and what we're going to say, and what we're going to be, and what we're going to do, and how we're going to act.

"This nonstop frenzy has developed through trying to protect ourselves from experiencing the turmoil of our disconnection. But no action that you perform that involves any variety of this rotor spinning is going to change anything whatsoever.

"If change is going to happen, you're going to have to recognize that there is life coming into you, and that the life which is coming in has a source of power as tangible as the electric turbine generator is to the lamp. Then, when the rotor blades slow down and even stop, and something crashes -- something else will survive the crash. Something that doesn't have to be sustained by your monkey cage agitation.

"As you walked around downtown today, you weren't calm. You may not have been mad at anybody, you may not have been recognizably agitated, but still you were at war, you were unsettled. You were juggling variables and making decisions and protecting yourself from imagined dangers. But since you're surrounded in life with other people in the same circumstance, you imagine that that's the way it's supposed to be -- that's most unfortunate, most unfortunate."

He reached over and poked me in the side to get some extra attention from me for what he was about to say. It was an unusual gesture for him to make towards me, so it really worked. I wiped the sweat out of my eyes and straightened up as he went on.

"The most fortunate thing that could happen to an agitated person is for them to cross paths with a person who has some capacity to be calm -- a person who is no longer involved in the frantic and frenzied manufacture of protective devices. Someone who doesn't need to keep that turmoil from overtaking them, because they've rediscovered the connection to the energy that keeps them alive. Meeting a person like that doesn't happen often, but sometimes it happens."

He poked me again, a little harder this time and repeated with a grin, "But sometimes it happens."

I decided against working out, which I really didn't want to do anyway. After the showers, we left the gym and headed to the casino. We were going to have some dinner and see who was winning the low-ball tournament. On the way over, I asked if he could tell me more about being calm, because it would probably be the closest I could get to it.

He told me he was glad that I had lightened up. He proceeded to complete his thoughts about agitation and calm as though my question were a sincere request, which I guess it really was.

"Living properly really requires being calm, because when you're calm you can absorb what's coming in, you can receive. When you're not calm, you have one big catcher's mitt around you, and you're dodging: 'Catch it! Quick, throw it back! Throw it back! Catch another one, throw it back.' That's what you're doing, you're juggling everything that's coming in. You're juggling and trying to put out the right thing. You're an actor on stage trying to deliver the right lines, trying to make the right impressions, trying to defend yourself, trying to look good, trying to stay out of trouble. That's exhausting and frustrating work."

"It sounds crazy!" I said. "Why do we exhaust ourselves like that?"

"We do these things because we think that they will bring us peace," he answered. "We juggle because we think that peace will come when we're successful in covering the turmoil, but peace will never come that way. Peace will come only when we rediscover our natural effortless capacity to experience the energy that keeps us alive. The energy that was there before we were born and will continue on unchanged after we're gone."

As I've said before, I frequently asked him questions during his discourses to clarify my understanding of what he was saying. I have only included some of my questions, because the others would not help to clarify his explanations. They would merely give you a better idea of where I was coming from, and I can't really see the benefit of that. I do, however, consider it relevant for you to know that I did ask him my usual question at this point:

"Is there anything that a person can do about this condition that you're describing?" And instead of his standard brush off of this type of question, he alluded, for the first time, to an actual program for change.

"There actually is a science," he said seriously, "for learning about the scrambling that we do to cover our turmoil. In that science one looks at scrambling with precision, humor, and perspective. It's difficult to do, but it's possible to do."

The endeavor to which he referred seemed like it would be very arduous. I guess if I had any other alternative I wouldn't even have listened, but our relationship had moved me closer to being burnt-out on my own bullshit and everybody else's too.

"Wouldn't it be great," I fantasized aloud, "if people knew these things about themselves and about each other. Because then we wouldn't have to keep pretending that everything's okay. We could cut through all that posturing. I'm really tired of it, it always seems to go the same way. You meet somebody, they tell you how everything's okay with them, you tell them how everything's okay with you -- then you leave. Basically, it's a non-happening. Then you wait for the next time and the next, hoping and hoping, but nothing ever happens."

We drove in silence for a while. After a few minutes he broke the silence.

"You and I have a tremendous potential advantage," he said. "You don't have to waste time convincing me that you're okay. We can get right down to talking about this strange situation that we, as human beings, find ourselves in."

10

REMEMBERING & FORGETTING

It is like a finger tapping against the skin of the chest,
like a finger on a drum, telling the ear to listen
and hear talk of things from a far-off place.

A Story Like The Wind, **Laurens van der Post**

After eating dinner together, we each went our separate ways in the casino. My friend seemed to have acquaintances wherever he went, and this place was no exception. At different times, over the next hour or two, I spotted him conversing with at least five different people.

I went over to try my skill at one of the non-tournament poker games that was going on. I sat in on a game for about an hour and a half. I didn't have much financial success but I did have fun playing, due mainly to the fact that most of the players recognized me from the final table of the tournament the day before.

I spotted my friend sitting alone at a table in the bar that was attached to the casino. I had never seen him drink, so it did strike me as somewhat unusual. I walked over and stood in the doorway until he noticed me and waved for me to sit down. He was drinking a bottle of beer, so I had one too.

The recorded music was a little loud in the bar, so I didn't expect that he would try to talk to me, and he didn't. I drifted in and out of listening to the oldies that were making their most

105

recent efforts to invade my eardrums. They were all songs that I'd heard a few too many times before. My friend however seemed to be engrossed in the music, or something, because each time I glanced over at him, I noticed that his eyes were closed.

After a while, we left to go back to our hotel. We had barely been in the car for a minute, when my friend started humming one of those all too familiar songs. A few minutes later, we turned on to the freeway, he stopped humming, turned to me, and said, "Is there a dance to remember? Something hidden in some covered up place inside us? Is there really something to remember that's been forgotten? Is there really a 'Word that was Lost'?

"Trying to remember that *something* is one option a person has in this life, and trying to forget that *something*, by covering the turmoil caused by its absence, is another. It pretty much comes down to that. You know when you ask me sometimes what I think of this or that activity, or this or that book or idea? Well the answer is, it really comes down to -- some try to remember, and some try to forget.

What he was talking about reminded me of something my Dad used to say. I couldn't recall his exact words, but I told my friend what I did recall. It went something like: *It doesn't matter so much what gets put in your hand, as it matters how you intend to use it. If you have a baseball bat, you could start a game, you could start a team, you could start a little league, or you could do a lot of damage. It's the same baseball bat.*

"It's the same for trying to remember or to forget," he said. "You can go to a movie to remember, and you can go to a movie to forget. The movie isn't the key. You can play a musical instrument to remember, and you can play one to forget. You can read a book to remember, or you can take a walk to remember, or you can do your job to remember, or you can listen to me to remember. And you can do all those things to forget. The tool is really not as important as the tool user. And like I said, some try to remember, and some try to forget."

For some reason what we were talking about made me recall the launching pad and rocketship analogy that he had introduced

to me. One thing I knew for sure about myself was that the forgetting part, which I associated with redecorating the launching pad, was far more tangible to me than the remembering part, or to wherever it was that the rocketship could fly.

I was listening attentively for instructions or some further references to the "method" to which he had eluded; I had a feeling that they would be forthcoming.

"It's such a tricky situation," he explained, "because it always seems like there's hope. I mean the world of forgetting is really hopeless, but still, people have hope that the next variety of forgetting is going to be the cure. How is it that a person can actually think that if they do tomorrow what they did today, that something else is going to happen except what happened today? All the evidence is that it won't, but still there's hope. There's a certain beauty to hopelessness, especially since there *is* no hope, and of course I mean there's no hope in forgetting, all there is, is repetition. But once you have even the slightest inkling of what you've forgotten and what there is to remember, you're already separated from so much that's ordinary."

"I think I have that sense," I said, "but I certainly don't feel separated from so much that's ordinary -- and why would that separate me anyway?"

"Because now you have a standard," he said as though it were obvious, "because you have a frame of reference. Without that, a person is stuck with imagining that the world of forgetting is all there is. That's a very deep hole to be in, because there are millions of colors in that world of forgetting. There's so much variety in that world that you couldn't think of all of it. You would just keep thinking and thinking and thinking, and after a year you'd still be thinking about the world of forgetting. The entertainment, the adventures, the sadness, the fantasies, and everything else that's been created to help people forget that they're missing the connection to the energy that maintains their lives. That world of forgetting even has its highs and lows, so you can actually think you're going up and down and that something is really happening. But it's really only one thing that's happening -- a big snore."

If I did, as he said, have a standard, I knew that it was rarely applied. I wanted to shout, "So what should I do." But I never had any success with that question. So instead I said demurely, "What can be done to increase that frame of reference?"

He laughed and repeated my question while mimicking my voice. He knew I was trying to con an answer out of him, but he gave me one anyway.

"What's called for is really very simple -- entering the world of remembering and beginning to see what that world is all about, and making enough of a study of the world of forgetting so that you can't be tricked by it -- so that you can't be fooled. That would be amazing -- for you to become a person that couldn't be fooled by the world of forgetting.

"Maybe you can start off by finding out where your love affair with this world of forgetting started. Where did the romance begin? How did it build? How is it going on right now? Do you want to perpetuate this relationship with the world of forgetting? Or do you want to rediscover the connection that has always been and will always be there?"

He synchronized his last word with our arrival at the hotel. We didn't speak any more that evening. He had given me so much to think and feel about, that now, I suspected, it was my turn.

11

THERE'S A BIG DEFICIENCY OUT THERE

*Perhaps this dread of transience explains our greed for the few
gobbets of raw experience in modern life,
why violence is libidinous, why lust devours us,
why soldiers choose not to forget their days of horror.*

The Snow Leopard, **Peter Matthiessen**

The contents of these writings have probably, by now, either encysted or expelled you. Those of you who have been expelled are now outside of the realm of my immediate concern. Those of you who have persevered are entitled to, among other things including congratulations, an accounting as to my consistency in my relationship with my friend. One might assume from reading to this point, that the road was without stones, and that I never doubted the value of my friend's utterances, nor did I ever question that I was receiving some inestimable gain from my contact with him. Later on, I will present one of his theories which will explain why this would have been impossible, but for now, let me tell you the following.

I did, for a short while, question whether or not I was wasting my time, and wonder if I were to stop all this philosophizing around, that I might become the world's greatest poker player. Fortunately, I had the good sense to divulge my doubts to him before this mood of mine had gone too far. One night, I called my friend on the phone and was whimpering and complaining about what I might be missing by getting so involved with him. I can see now how much patience and wisdom was manifested by his response.

"Really, if you could feel in you that something could take place without *your* being the one who made it happen, that would be a most wonderful feeling. Then you would recognize a hope of a different kind. All your life, you've been taught that finding the right kind of activity would solve everything. What has been taking place with us can point you toward seeing that *real* relaxing could yield results. When you listen to me, there's nothing required of you, yet there's still something happening. Of course, the 'something' that's happening is not in the world of activities, it's in the world of relaxing."

"Maybe I'm just not ready for all of this," I pleaded. "That's possible isn't it?"

"You won't have to deal with questions like that if you try to think of those occasions when you're with me as a really simple and reasonable way to spend some time. It's a relatively small commitment for a relatively big possibility. Of course it might come to nothing also. But you go to the movies or out to eat or you sit home, and you don't get anything out of those things, and you're okay with that. So there are a lot of things that you do without great expectations.

"If spending time with me is the best thing that you have on your list of things to do, then do that. That way, you're always where you want to be. That way, you can be without demands and expectations. And then, something may transpire in you that comes more from the inside out, than from the outside in. Of course this might take a little time, and you might have to calm down a little."

I told him that what usually happened when I relaxed was that I drifted toward numbness and lost most of my motivation. We obviously were talking about two different kinds of relaxing, so I asked him to clarify his variety.

"I don't mean for you to calm down in order to make your dissatisfaction disappear. Because dissatisfaction with the way your life was going is probably what brought you to get to know

111

me in the first place. It's critical to feel dissatisfied. Being dissatisfied can give you a really wonderful attitude.

"Of course once that dissatisfaction brings you into a situation where something can be done to alter your course, then you have to calm down. You might have to hype yourself up to get to the dentist or the doctor, but once you get there, your hype only gets in the way. Let yourself be taken care of -- that's why you're listening to me, isn't it? I'm not talking about how you should be out there in your everyday life; I'm saying the times when you're with me."

"It's not like that doesn't sound good to me," I whined, "but you're talking about stuff I'm just not good at. What you're asking me to do is really hard for me."

"The only reason I feel I have the right to ask you to do anything is because I'm also saying, if you have a better way of spending your time, then you should take that better way. So if talking to me on the phone right now is where you want to be, then try to be here. See if you can relax -- see if there's something else happening."

The mood I was in made it difficult for me to absorb the subtleties of what he was saying, and hearing it over the telephone didn't help much either. I asked him if he could be more specific.

"Have you ever been in a situation where something attracted you and enveloped you? You couldn't really say that you were giving it your attention. It won your attention and carried you away. Not that I'm such an eloquent story teller. The way I talk is often inconsistent. Sometimes it's dry, sometimes more entertaining, sometimes fast paced, sometimes more informational, sometimes more esoteric. The idea is not for you to find your favorite style so you can like the way I talk. The idea is for you to trip over the experience of simply being here."

After reading my description of what was, for me, a critical phone call, I find myself wondering if you, the reader, might not apply my friend's wisdom to your position, in relation to you and me and this book.

112

Before saying goodbye on the phone, my friend invited me to a lecture (or meeting, I think he called it) that was to be held the next night. After he gave me the address, he left me with the instructions: "Come only if you have no better possibilities."

The next night, after considering the guidelines he had suggested, I drove to the address he had given me. It was a meeting in a large gym-type room, sponsored by a local spiritual group. I spotted my friend down front, but since there seemed to be no empty seats around him, I found one in the middle somewhere.

The first speaker began by mentioning that she had never spoken to a large bunch of people before. It was interesting to watch and listen to someone who was really awkward at talking to a big group. That's a scary thing to do, and this lady was obviously nervous.

The first twenty or thirty seconds after she sat down in the speaker's chair she didn't say a word. Her mind was probably spinning out with thoughts going so fast that no words could come out. I know how it goes, she's sitting there spinning and everyone's staring at her. It's a little awkward for us, because we know it's awkward for her. But we have the mandate to look at her and wait for her, so we don't have to feel on the spot, like something is expected of us.

The meeting lasted for about an hour and a half, and there was another speaker after the nervous lady. By the time he started to speak, there were probably three hundred people there, and a bunch of those people were kids and some of those kids were babies.

This guy was speaking from a slightly raised platform. The kids were making so much noise that I couldn't hear, and I was only about ten rows back. Since I couldn't hear, of course I had tons of opinions about how everything wasn't going the way it should be going. I started thinking: *What's this guy doing? Why doesn't he have a microphone? I can't hear what he's saying. He should have a microphone.*

As he was talking, I was soaring into my opinions of his shortcomings and his inconsiderateness. But while I was sitting there

113

with my opinions, he started to explain his point of view on this matter. He said that a lot of people had suggested that he get a microphone, because at one time there were only twenty or thirty people at these meetings and there wasn't so much noise then, but now there were a few hundred and it was really different.

So as he was explaining his point of view I was sitting there still not hearing him too well. But now I was really interested in what he was talking about. I was so interested that I got up, moved to the front, and sat on the floor (along with a bunch of people that were already there), so I could hear him clearly.

Now I was hearing every word and he brought up the idea that he thought talking without a microphone was really where it's at, because then it was really up to us to hear what he was saying. Since I was sitting up front now, I was a living example of what he was talking about.

It really hit me that my opinion about this microphone business made so much sense to me, until I experienced the value of the opposite point of view. I wanted *him* to do better. I wanted *him* to make it easier for me to be entertained. That's what I was demanding, but actually what I really needed was to give *my* best. When I got up and moved down front, everything changed.

I eventually left the meeting, between the question and answer period and the socializing period, but my friend stayed for a while to talk to the nervous lady. We met outside and he suggested that we walk. As we did, I asked him casually what he thought about that lady who spoke.

"In a situation like that one, she had certain expectations of herself and no doubt the people listening had certain expectations of her. One of those expectations is that when somebody sits in place 'A', generally known as 'in the audience,' and somebody else sits in place 'B', usually thought of as 'on the stage,' the stage person has a responsibility to entertain the audience person. Don't you think that's an unspoken agreement?"

I nodded at his question.

"I find that interesting," he continued, "because most every-body at that meeting wanted to get something special out of it.

People don't come to meetings and gatherings like that if they don't want something special. There are movies, the tube, people have friends, places to go, making money things to do. There are even a lot of classes around that a person can take. There are ways to be occupied in this town and most other places as well. So if a person goes to a meeting like that one, they must have an aspiration for something special, something different."

I asked if he really thought that just because a person came to a meeting like that one, it was reasonable to assume that they had spiritual aspirations.

"Well," he answered, "my guess is that most of the people at that meeting were looking for something other than entertainment. I even assume that some of them have very deep aspirations, ones that have not yet been realized. Then on the other hand, people have had years and years on the 'dayshift,' where they've developed so many concepts and picked up so many habits."

I asked him what kind of concepts and habits he was talking about.

He stopped walking, looked over at me like I was a little stupid, and said, "One of those habits or concepts is -- when you sit on chair 'A', you are entitled to be entertained. You have expectations as to what extent the lady who is sitting up there should be giving *her* best, and how much you are supposed to be giving yours. You're pretty confident that she's supposed to be putting out more than you are, right? That's so, isn't it? You feel okay waiting for her to come up with her better stuff, you feel okay to wait.

"It's not your assumption that *you* may have to pay better attention or hear more deeply into what she's saying, or feel more for her life. In other words, your point of view is that it's not on *you*, it's on *her*."

When he said that, I realized that what I had experienced in the meeting over the microphone business was an example of exactly what he had been talking about. I told him what had happened and what I understood from it and he seemed to agree. He had more to say on the subject however.

115

"Here we have a situation where some number of folks have deep aspirations. They go through life, and from time to time they see a possibility or an opportunity to further the realization of those aspirations. Eventually, they find something that seems to be connected to their hopes, so they start to move toward that something. It could be a book, it could be a person, it could be an idea. Then at some point later -- later that day, later that week, later that month -- they recognize that that something, that possibility, is no longer in their life. It disappeared. They were driving toward it, they blinked their eyes, and it was gone. All they know is what they once saw as a possibility is no longer in front of them."

I certainly followed what he was saying; it was simple enough. But it was too big a jump for me to see the connection between expecting someone to entertain me and totally losing my way. I asked if he could explain the connection.

"I've been describing a frequent little happening," he answered. One that might be a clue to why this disappearing of possibilities occurs -- a happening where you consider yourself to be in the 'audience.' Something one learns very efficiently in this culture from movies and T.V., you know, entertainment. This place called the 'audience' is supposed to be an okay place to be.

"But here's another point of view. When I was listening to that lady, her name is Patricia, I tried to have my experience depend on how much *I* could give, not on how much could be given to me. That way, there wouldn't be a substantive difference between listening to someone like that nervous lady, who was a little halting in her speech and unsure of what she was saying, and listening to the other guy, who was something of a scintillating speaker. The difference wouldn't be a big deal, because what does it really take to give your best? What does it take to really put in what you have to put in? You could give your best with whoever was speaking."

Curiously, not at that time, nor actually ever, did we discuss the content of the speeches at the meeting. For some reason it never even seemed important for me to ask him why he suggested that we go there.

Before we parted, he told me that he was going to be involved in some kind of volunteer work that weekend. He said that if it were within the guidelines that we had established for my spending time with him, that not only was I welcome to come along, but that I was invited to participate.

On Saturday morning I picked him up in my car and we drove to the place where this participating was to happen. On the way there, he gave me a short introduction to what was about to transpire.

"Okay, so let's talk about the experience of giving your best. I'm sure we agree that it's supposed to be a richer one than the experience of taking -- good theory! So why are all our efforts pointed toward trying to receive more? More pleasure, relaxation, spare time, credit, cash. Because for us, this idea of 'the richness of giving our best,' is only a theory. We are of course willing to give our best if we're rewarded accordingly. But giving our best, aside from receiving potential rewards, is not an area with which we have yet tried to experiment.

"I want to try to prove to you, because it's proof that you need, that giving your best is where it's at. At one time, I was also a machine for self-gratification. Giving my best was always linked to the hope of a payoff. I'm not like that anymore because somebody took the time to try to convince me that giving my best was worth experimenting with. Today I'm going to take that time with you."

We had arrived at a high school athletic field which today was being used as the practice site for the Special Olympics for mentally and physically handicapped children.

We spent the day there, and I can say without reservation that it was one of the most memorable days of my life. I don't know if my friend would agree, but I would advise anyone who has never participated in an activity of this sort, to push through whatever resistance they might have -- and do it.

If at some time in the future I write a book for the purpose of recounting my personal experiences, the details of this day will definitely warrant a chapter. As it is, I'll skip those details and will give you what I consider to be of even greater value -- a compilation of what my friend explained to me during the day and after we departed from the stadium.

"This is incredible!" he said shortly after we arrived. "At the Special Olympics everybody can participate, everybody can give. You can sit in the stands or you can walk out on the field. The customary distinctions of observer and participant are not so clearly drawn. One year, I even played music with some friends for these Special Olympics. Basically, there are a bunch of kids out there trying to do their thing and they're terrible at it. It hardly can be compared to what you see on T.V., the best in the world, the best in the world -- but these kids are out there having a good time. And you can get out there and root for the them and give them hugs and all that kind of good stuff.

"But go to the regular Olympics and try to get out on the field -- you'll end up in jail. Try to even approach the track, and the security people will check you out. That's pretty interesting. Here are two situations. One is extremely entertaining because of the competence of the athletes, but we're not permitted to give our best. All we can do is sit there and be overwhelmed by the skills of the participants. In this other situation, we can do as much as we want to do. We can run around the track along with the kids, or whatever. So in my way of looking at things, you have a much better shot to give your best while listening to some nervous lady awkwardly trying to talk about her experience."

The connection that he made between this event and the lecture of a few nights before became clear to me. The conclusion that one had to draw by using his point of view was that by not giving our best, we're constantly hindering ourselves and not even knowing it. I asked him if this was indeed the case.

He answered enthusiastically, "It's an interesting dichotomy that we're part of, an interesting situation that we're in. My hypothesis is that we may be seeking the fulfillment our dreams in a way which will pre-guarantee failure. We're seeking to get close-up seats so we can be entertained by the stars performing in the Olympics, when our dreams could be better fulfilled by running around a track with a bunch of handicapped kids who aren't breaking any records, but who are giving us the opportunity to put out as much love as we can put out. That's pretty interesting.

"I'm not from Mars, I know what boredom is. I know what it feels like to want to be entertained. I've walked out of Swedish films where every fifteen minutes somebody scratches his nose and that's the drama of the movie. Sometimes I've even walked out with a feeling of self-righteous indignation because *it* was boring, not that *I* wasn't prepared to give so much. I wanted to be a couch potato."

I told him that I agreed with everything that he was saying, but that people didn't organize our society in that way.

He answered me with extreme definiteness -- almost adamantly, "Like I've been saying, giving your best is where it's at. I've got a lot to say on this subject, and I'm going to keep on saying it until it becomes obvious to you that you gotta forget what's right or wrong with what other people are doing, and begin seeing what life is like when *you* concentrate on giving *your* best.

"We're made in the same form and we're taught in the same schools, with the same parents, within a fairly small variance. We're taught to cover up. We're taught to protect. We're taught how to keep, not how to give away. We're taught how to get the best, not how to give our best.

"Some of us feel secure enough to take some chances here and there, that's true. But still, that represents such a small percentage of our time that I don't think a person would want to sew those moments together and claim that their life was complete. I don't think a person would want to do that because there wouldn't be enough of those 'giving your best' and 'being yourself' moments."

I certainly had no illusions about my life being complete, but I still couldn't see how I could reasonably be expected to tackle a system that was set up to defeat me. I expressed my reticence, and he began to talk about my personal situation.

"I'm talking about the world being a very deficient place because of this lack. So who can I talk to about this problem other than you, who have everything? You have the time to hang out with me, so you have everything. Think of the leisure you have, and then think of the rest of the world and how it is.

"I know you came to that meeting the other night to get a little entertainment, get a little information, get a little enlightenment, get to sit on your ass for a while. You're even listening to me now to get something -- but think of all you already have. You already have so much and you want to get more. That's weird. So I'm not saying all this to tell you how to get more. I'm talking to you to show you that you have so much that you can afford to give your best. You can go out in the world and start being yourself -- you can be loving, not so that you yourself can have a better experience, but because the world needs that honesty and loving. Those qualities are sorely needed. There's a big deficiency out there."

12

ARE THEY LESS FORTUNATE THAN WE ?

...It was a Bushman point of honor...that the one who went to fetch food and help for stricken companions only ate and drank ...when all could eat and drink together again.

A Far-Off Place, **Laurens van der Post**

As I explained earlier, I have arranged the material in this book so as to keep my friend's explanations on similar subjects near each other. The effect of this has been and will continue to be that the events described will not necessarily be chronological. I'm mentioning this because the next two happenings that I intend to describe took place much later, and not near in time to each other. I bring them up now because they relate to the subject that my friend called 'giving your best.'

One of my sweetest memories of these three years was a most unexpected trip on which my friend invited me to go along. It was to Mexico, and our travelling group consisted of my friend, his two children, ages ten and seventeen years, and me. Although I will not go into the details of my interactions with his children in these writings, I do want to tell you, the reader, that it was indeed an education to be around children who had grown up with the extraordinary influence that my friend provided.

121

One day, we all went to this little island called Isle De Mujeres off the Mexican coast. We had to take a ferry to get there. We were coming back late at night, and my friend, the two kids and I were all sitting on the top deck. It was dark and mostly stars and balmy weather.

Sometime after the boat got going, this man came over and asked if he could play something on his guitar for us. So he started to do a little bit of what I might call "his act." You have to expect that in Mexico because a lot of the people are really poor. You know, they have all those zeros on the end of their money. Any opportunity they get to have contact with a tourist is obviously an opportunity to get some of our zeroless money.

He was singing a song and my friend started playing along with a harmonica that he often carried, and of course I had my no-name strum box. Everything was fine and the kids listened. Then after the Mexican played his song, he said in Spanish that he'd like to ask for a little tip.

My friend told him that he thought that playing music was beautiful, and asking for money was okay too, but that they didn't go together so well. He said that he would like to keep the money over there for now and the music over here, and maybe later we could do the opposite. I don't know how much the guy understood, but he started to play again, maybe because he was a little drunk or there was nobody else around to solicit.

The song that he started to play was *Lodi* by Credence Clearwater, except that he sang it in Spanish. It took me a while to recognize what he was playing, but once I did and since I knew the words, we sang together.

After that, the kids sang *Puff the Magic Dragon* for him, and then he sang some rock and roll songs like *Good Golly Miss Molly*. I could pronounce the English words better than he could and that fascinated him. After a while he got up and knocked over a couple of beer bottles, and walked off.

The only other people on the top deck were two affluent looking Mexican men from Mexico City or Acapulco or somewhere like that. They were standing about twenty feet away from us and one of them was holding one of those cameras that go beep, beep, and can take flash pictures at any time. So the one with the camera came over, looked at my friend's nine year old daughter, and said that he'd been watching her and he just had to take her picture. She was wearing this big sombrero that she had gotten over on the island, so he took some pictures of her with the hat, and then he left.

When he came over, I was pretty sure that he wasn't really interested in my friend's daughter, the sombrero, or the picture. He had been standing twenty feet away from this scene, and something about it was tremendously magnetic. He wanted to involve himself in some way, but all he had was a camera, so he came over and took a picture.

He was magnetized to something, but what could have drawn him over? It was pretty dark, there were no lights. He was there with another guy and didn't appear to be looking around for something to be interested in. He was watching this scene of someone who he looked down on, a slightly drunk Mexican peasant, and some other people that he obviously had opinions about also -- American tourists. Here they were together, and there was joy happening, or there was something happening and he didn't know what to call it, because it wasn't the kind of thing that one normally sees. So he came over with this absurd pretence, "I just had to have a picture of you," like he's going around looking to take pictures of little gringo girls.

After a while the kids fell asleep on deck, and my friend had some things to say about what had happened.

"When the musician was looking for a tip, everything was ordinary -- *I'll entertain you if you pay me.* But when that changed to -- *let's both give our best and see what happens,* then something so magnetic took place that a person who was in no way involved felt that he had to get in on it. You see, whether or not he knew it, he also was looking for a way to give his best.

"What an interesting orchestra we'd make if each one of us gave our best and kept the beat as we heard it. We might not be entertaining, but we sure would be something unique. People wouldn't pay money to come and listen to us, but maybe they'd want to come and play with us."

I asked him if he thought that people could really be like the ones he described.

He spoke in a melancholy tone, "We've lost the value of the simplicity of giving our best. At one time, say in the middle ages, there were people called entertainers -- entertainers like court jesters. A very ordinary somebody whose job it was to play some background music at the whim of the host, and then was sent away with a little money or food.

"Obviously things have changed tremendously. Now that we've lost the understanding for the need to give *our* best, the people who are entertainers, basically politicians, professional athletes, and show business people, have become larger than life. They're the best known people on the planet. We've made them that, because we're willing to pay with our money and respect to watch them give *their* best.

"We've lost ground from the times when entertainment was a casual happening. Now a mammoth amount of our life is focused around events that are arranged for our pleasure. How can we maintain a value for giving our best in a culture where entertainment is really the most important thing? As the importance of these diversions rise, the significance of each person giving his best is going to decrease. The more fascinating these words that I'm saying are, the more passive you can be while listening to them."

I could really feel the accuracy of his statements. I told him that it was amazing how much my expectation of what I was hearing right then was that it should be entertaining to me. At different moments, I thought his presentation, or the way that he was talking, was rambling a bit. I let him know that it sounded to me like he was jumping from idea to idea, and wasn't getting to the point quickly enough. There were actually times when I felt that he was demanding too much of me -- that he should be more clear because he was explaining something to me, so he should put on the whole show.

It wasn't an easy thing for me to divulge to him, but it seemed important, so I took the chance. I was rewarded not only by his response, but by a feeling that I was really participating in something unique and remarkable and adventurous.

He acknowledged my confession with a good laugh and then went on to say a few more things about the subject. "You become focused on me giving more, so that you can give less. What happens is that your expectation of me becomes so great, that you want me to do whatever it takes to entertain you. You no longer want to know what I'm talking about, or what I'm about at all. You no longer want to know what *anything* is *really* like. Since you've gotten in the habit of avoiding giving your best, all that becomes important to you is that the scene you're watching and the people in that scene are putting on a show for you.

"You understand? Your expectation is there, even if you think it isn't. That's most unfortunate, because you're demanding that I be something other than myself for you. With people demanding that others be the source of their entertainment, it puts a tremendous pressure on each of us to be entertaining. So we put aside being ourselves, acting as we naturally would act, in exchange for the acceptance and regard that we hope will come from being entertaining. That's the way life goes."

The next day, while we were at the beach and the kids were playing in the surf, my friend told me a story about someone he met at a party. Even though I was neither present at the party, nor have I ever met the guy involved, this story has stuck in my head, and I think of it from time to time.

"Years ago," he began, "I met a man named Bobby at a major poker tournament. I think it was the championships up at the 'Horseshoe' in Vegas. There was a reception for the VIP's and the press, and I was invited by a friend who was a sports reporter. They often have parties on the day before the big tournaments, probably to get some press coverage.

"Bobby was really small, maybe even under five feet tall, but he had a really athletic look to him. I got to talking to him, and eventually got to know him. He was a jockey, a fairly well-known jockey.

"He quit school when he was really young, before high school, I think. Basically his life was horses, and eventually he became very successful as a jockey. He started to make a lot of money and get invited to places and associate with people that he would never otherwise have had the chance to associate with. He could converse about ordinary things, but he didn't really know about things that more educated people talk about.

"So he got an idea. He was going to learn about something, anything. He decided to learn about impressionist art, a subject that held no particular interest for him, but someone happened to have given him a few books about it. So he read the books and even managed to find a few more.

"His idea was that whenever he was at a party or some gathering where there were people who appeared intellectual or wealthy, he would at least know something, and whatever was being talked about, he would try to turn the subject to impressionist art. He became very skillful at that. In fact that's how I met him, because he started to talk to me about art, and I couldn't figure out what impressionist art had to do with our conversation."

I liked his story and wondered if it were really true. It seemed hard to believe that a person would go to all that trouble. I couldn't picture anyone I knew doing something as crazy as that. I asked if he thought that this guy was the exception or the rule.

"What he was doing is not as unusual as you might think. He was just doing his thing, trying to entertain me in the way that he thought he was supposed to. Entertain me, not by giving his best and being himself, but by being what he thought I wanted him to be. This act that he adopted was completely covering up who he really was, because in his estimation, he wasn't going to be okay if people found out who he really was.

"Not understanding that the way to give your best is to be yourself leads and has lead to extremely diabolical circumstances. We live in a world where faking it is more acceptable behavior than being real. You meet someone, you scope out what they expect of you as quickly as you can, and then you try to be that thing. What happens to who you really are? Who you are is long, long lost."

I told him that I felt sorry for anyone who was so insecure that they had to make up stuff like that, but it was hard for me to see that there could be major implications to that kind of behavior. I put it in the category of innocent bullshitting -- my friend didn't.

"You told me," he explained, "that at one time you read books about cosmic consciousness, states of being, powers, and inner peace, so I know that you must have ideas about those subjects. Maybe you even feel that those experiences are still worth pursuing.

"Whether you do or not, the facts are the same -- whatever kind of peace you're seeking is hidden by your ordinary state of being. The way you are now, you can't be 'as you are' in any circumstance whatsoever. You are always under the influence of your self-image -- how you come across, are you being entertaining, are you being accepted? Anyone who has taken the opportunity to watch themselves, even casually, knows that this is the case. I'm presenting the hypothesis that if there indeed is an expanded reality, an inner tranquility, they are hidden beneath veils -- starting with the veil that you've lost both your sense of value for being who you are, and your sense of value for giving your best."

Several months after our return from Mexico, I convinced my friend to accompany me to L.A. It was not one of his favorite places to play poker, but he agreed to go on a condition. I am not at liberty to inform you of that condition, but I can tell you about something that took place there that would definitely be of greater value to you.

Some of the best poker games in the country are in the Los Angeles area. There are two large casinos there, each having virtually hundreds of tables dedicated solely to poker games of every variety and every limit. The term *limit* refers to the amount of money that can be bet in that particular game. Those amounts run from a dollar or two, to a thousand dollars or more. There are actually poker games in these two particular casinos where each player at the table has ten or twenty thousand dollars worth of chips in front of him.

One of the shortcomings of playing at these places is that you have to go into the bowels of Los Angeles (if ever this expression fit, it fits very graphically in relation to L.A.). On this particular occasion, the magnet that pulls poker players from around the country to play there, pulled my friend and me as well.

The afternoon after we had arrived in L.A., we stopped downtown to make a phone call and put some gas in the car. My friend was standing on the other side of the car cleaning the windows. (He had a thing for clean car windows. He once said to me, "You would never look through glasses or eyeballs that were that dirty, so why look through a piece of dirty glass that is one foot in front of your face.") While we were standing there, a guy who looked like a semi-bum (I hadn't yet made the transition to calling them homeless people) came over and started to tell my friend a story about how his car was out of gas a few blocks away and that he needed some money.

My friend listened attentively, laughed a little, and started to talk to this man -- at length.

"You know," he began, "I'd be glad to help you out, but first let me tell you about something that happened to me. I've lived near San Diego on and off for about twelve years, so I can recognize some of the faces around town. I don't walk downtown as much as I used to, but I'm down there every once in a while.

"So this one day, I parked my car, and as I was walking out of the lot, someone wearing a baseball cap and work shoes came up to me. He looked like kind of a middle of the road person, not like he was a derelict or anything, and he said to me, 'Do you know where Mission Boulevard is?' I told him I did, but before I could start giving him directions, he said, 'My car broke down a few blocks away and I'm from out of town,' and he told me his story. 'I need a few dollars for gas, here's my driver's license. I can mail the money back to you blah, blah, blah...' like that. He had a real good presentation. Well, I gave him some money for gas and then he left.

"I usually recognize people that I've seen before -- so two or three years go by, and maybe six months ago while I'm walking around downtown, this guy comes up to me and the instant I see him I know who he is. Of course he proceeds to tell me the same story."

Now I'm still pumping gas and watching and listening in disbelief to my friend telling this long story to a bum. And most of my disbelief came from the fact that this bum was actually listening.

My friend paused at the end of the story and then went on.

"That's pretty rough for honest people like you who are really having car trouble."

After saying that, my friend pulled out a couple of bucks and gave it to him. When we got in the car and drove away, I asked him why he told the guy that story and why, if he knew it was a con-game, did he give him money.

"I told him the story because I wanted him to know that we were both in this together, he on one side of the question, and I on the other. Then I looked at him, and I asked myself the only really important question for someone in that situation who wants to give his best."

He stopped talking and looked over at me, so that I would fill in the blank. I was pretty good at *Jeopardy*, but I couldn't guess this one. After a few moments, I told him that I didn't know what the question was.

We played poker that evening and my concentration was less than usual. Whenever I saw someone in the casino that looked a little down and out, my friend's comments resurfaced in my thoughts. Later that evening, I cornered him and asked what that "only really important question" was.

"Before I tell you," he began, "... at a game I was playing in the other day, the guys around the table were talking about the subject of giving money to people on the street who are panhandling. It's one of the challenges that a person who lives in a big city has to deal with. If you don't live where many poor people live, you can usually bob and weave and dodge those kinds of situations pretty well. You know, you see them coming, you cross the street and walk up the other side. But for some people it's a never answered challenge. Unless you develop rules for yourself like -- you'll give to anyone if they're lying on the ground, if they're over a certain age, if they're a certain sex, if they look a certain way.

"So a lot of us have guidelines for when we'll donate of our resources, but for the ones of us who don't -- it's always a spinout. We're always hoping that the situation won't come up again. After the spinning out is over, we're so glad it's over that we don't sit down and put together some guidelines for the next time.

"It's an interesting question, because how many things in life are like that? We've figured out most things fairly well, or if we haven't, we've arranged to be where they're not. We don't want to mess with questions that just kinda fly up at us.

"But here's one that I think most people would admit is disquieting. Even if you come up with rules, they only work if you convince yourself that you're justified. Like, 'They could get a job,' or, 'They're probably drunk,' some kind of story like that. However it goes, you have to either be disquieted or have made up arbitrary guidelines."

He glanced over at me and asked simply, "How do *you* handle it?"

I usually appreciated when he asked for my input, but for some reason I wished he had left me out of it. I didn't like this whole subject. Maybe it hit a weak spot. I was definitely one of those people that preferred to cross the street and hope the whole thing would go away. I guess I wanted to conceal something really yucky about myself, because I made up some comments that sounded relevant, but actually had nothing to do with the way I really felt.

"Yeah," I said, "I'd want to do the right thing, but how can you tell? I mean, even if that guy wasn't a con-man, who says that giving him money is really going to help? Maybe he has to learn to take responsibility for his actions."

My friend, of course, knew that I was bullshitting, but must have considered it more important to stay with the subject than to confront me about whatever it was that I was hiding.

"The most interesting thing about this subject," he said, "is how difficult it is to recognize that all that really matters is that this person is less fortunate than you, and forget the reasons why or the ways how. How much simpler our choice of a course of action would be if *we* were looking to give *our* best. Then we wouldn't have to spend all our time and energy assessing where the other person was coming from. If this guy does what he's doing, he has to be less fortunate than we are. What he's doing is not an uplifting thing to do. It doesn't feel good to panhandle or to con people. It's not the kind of thing where you wake up, rub your hands together, and think, 'Ahhh, another day, let me atem!' It dosen't matter whether he's successful or unsuccessful, that person has a rough life.

"So to keep it simple, all we have to do is give our best. And since anybody who's panhandling is obviously less fortunate than we, to give our best would almost always be to help him out."

I understood his premise, but it seemed to me that there were other issues. Like maybe this guy is ruining it for all the other people whose cars really do break down.

He responded quickly, "I understand that, I understand that there are other questions, but the interesting question to me is -- is there anything more important than for me to give my best? Is there anything that I really have to know in that situation other than that most important question: *Is this person less fortunate than I?*"

His words reminded me of a movie I had seen years before. These priests were taking care of people with leprosy. The lepers were really scarred and distorted and if it had been a video, I would have put it on fast forward. I knew that my reaction to this subject was connected to some squeamishness that I felt. This was actually the first time that I had ever even allowed myself to think about the less fortunate. Since it wasn't his style to pull me into it, I rallied the necessary courage to tell him where I was coming from.

His comments, although not directed at my personal aversion, were easy for me to interpret.

"Let's use kids as an example. Kids are really little machines for giving their best, even though it may seem that they act like little taking machines. They're little machines for being themselves, in that there's nothing held back. They're giving you their complete selves. Whatever they are, they're giving it to you. They don't rehearse or prepare or manipulate.

"A human being, in its most natural state, is a giving-its-best machine. That isn't how it usually goes because we're not in our natural state. But the more we approach our natural state, the more we become giving-our-best machines.

"When a little baby delights you, to thank the baby or to say, 'I want more,' would be ridiculous. The baby is doing its thing naturally -- it's giving. It's not holding back, and that's the part that you're missing. It appears and feels to you like you want more -- but in giving your best, you realize that *that* is what you've wanted, because giving is the natural state."

I really appreciated his comments. They made me feel that whatever the reasons were that caused me to be uncharitable -- they weren't important. Because if I could relax into that state of naturalness, then I would be as giving as I was supposed to be.

For some reason, I flashed on the feeling of 'going home.' I didn't know how it was related, but I asked him why people like to get back home to their family, or if not to their family, to wherever they feel at home.

He knew what I meant and how it fit in.

"Why? Because giving is more readily accessible when you're home. If you went to a Denny's in a strange city, the opportunities to be a giving person would demand so much more of you. Say somebody's sitting next to you at the counter and you ask him, 'How're you doing?' Maybe that person responds by complaining about something or other -- maybe the weather, maybe the food, you know how it goes. Well even though you know that complaining is not what's best for him, think of how impossibly hard it would be, for you to give him your best by telling him what you understand about the damaging effects of complaining.

"So people wait to get back to the place they call home. They want to be where it's safe to give their best and be themselves. It really feels good to be in that natural state when nothing is held back -- but there's more to life than fucking. Believe it or not, when it comes down to it, that's all there is -- this society is based on fucking. This is a fucking society. The movies, the magazines, the newspapers -- everything is based on getting laid, and it's only because those are the only moments when people are not holding anything back.

"Obviously, life is made for other things as well. What we want is to feel like we're not holding back. People think they want more. Of course they want more, because they're still holding back."

13

IT TAKES A CLEVER PERSON 30 YEARS

My story is not a pleasant one; it is neither sweet nor harmonius, as invented stories are; it has the taste of nonsense and chaos, of madness and dreams - like the lives of all men who stop deceiving themselves.

Demian, **Hermann Hesse**

His cumulative input was impacting my life decidedly. In less than a year, I began to notice a distinct change occurring in my outlook. Before meeting my friend, I had been a reasonably self-confident and somewhat cynical person. Recently, I noticed the edges of my character soften a little. I seemed to be becoming less judgmental and more tolerant of the shortcomings of others. But oddest of all, I noticed that I was less excited about my "possibilities." This was disturbing to me because I usually got the energy to do things by getting hyped-up about whatever it was, and I was having trouble getting hyped-up.

It occurred to me that this lack of my old enthusiasm was due to my friend's input and the shortcomings it frequently directed me to notice in myself. I sometimes found this depressing and occasionally even questioned the value of this often humbling process.

I intend to use the following chapter to tell you about a very defined phase of our association. As they say in the movies, or somewhere, "It doesn't paint a pretty picture." What I want to ultimately describe, however, is the gentle, thoughtful, and infinitely wise council of a person who always seemed to know exactly what to say to help me notice for myself just what my next step should be. Of course my last statement is made in retrospect. I did, from time to time, manifest resistance to listening to what my friend had to say, and only now do I really appreciate what I heard.

In the late fall of the second year of our friendship, we took a rather long tour together. We attended several poker tournaments, one each in Reno, Las Vegas, Los Angeles, and Lake Tahoe. This trip remains in my memory for two reasons: first, because it was the most financially successful period of my life, and second, because a small and almost insignificant event (that I clearly remember to this day) powerfully signalled to me that I had actually begun to change my ways of being and thinking.

I was riding a "high" when we arrived in Lake Tahoe, which was to be the last tournament that we would be playing in for awhile. This "high" was due to two first place finishes and two second place finishes out of the ten events in which I had participated at the previous three tournaments.

On my first visit to the poker room, I discovered that I was a celebrity at the hotel that was hosting the tournament, and as we all know, people like to associate with celebrities. On the second day of our stay in Tahoe I was strolling around acknowledging my fans, when the driver of the hotel limousine asked me if I wanted to take a ride a little later that day. Their limousine was a new white stretch Lincoln that looked about forty feet long and was impressive, to say the least. I had never, and have never since, ridden in a limo, so I said okay and asked how come he chose me and where were we going. He told me that he was going to pick up one of the owners of the hotel at the airport, and that this owner, who was also his boss, suggested that he bring along "the guy who has been winning all the tournaments."

The boss was coming in on a private jet and would call when he was getting close. So if I wanted to go, I should stick around the hotel, and he would let me know when the call came in.

I told him that I'd be playing cards in the poker room, and that's where he could find me when he was ready to go.

A couple of hours later, the chauffeur came up behind me and told me we had to go right away because he was running late. I cashed in my chips and met him out front.

He ushered me into the back seat because the boss told him to give me "the full treatment." We didn't talk during the trip. I was sitting in the back playing with all the toys -- bar, T.V., etc. The few times that I did look out of the window, I noticed that he was cutting in and out of traffic and obviously rushing.

About ten or fifteen minutes into the ride, the limo made an abrupt swerve, skidded, and hit the back of another car -- not too hard, but not too soft either. He glanced back at me with a glazed and troubled stare, asked if I was okay, and then got out to talk to the driver of the other car. After a few minutes of what I guessed were the usual procedures, we resumed our trip to the airport, and the chauffeur resumed his previous mode of driving.

When we arrived at the airport his boss was waiting at the door of the small terminal building. He obviously noticed the damage to his limo because when we stopped, he walked directly over and started to run his hand over the dent. The chauffeur got out, to tell his story I guessed, and I got out to see the damage, and because I didn't know what else to do. As I stood there, about seven feet away, I overheard the following:

Boss (annoyed but controlled): I told you that I'd be landing in twenty minutes and to try not to keep me waiting around the airport, but I also told you that I knew there would be a lot of traffic so no need to rush. Isn't that exactly what I said?

Chauffeur (looking down at the ground): Uh huh.

Boss (continuing more calmly): I can't say that I'm not pissed off about the car, but we can always get it fixed. What I do hope is that you learned a lesson from this.

Chauffeur (thinks for a few seconds and says): I sure did. Never take Lake Tahoe Blvd. during rush hour.

I stood there in disbelief. To say that I saw my life flash before me in an instant, would be an understatement. In actuality, every excuse I ever made and every distortion that I ever created, so as not to see myself "as I am," rushed before me. The rest of the story would only dilute, what was for me, a most powerful moment.

That night over dinner, I told the entire story to my friend and added what I had learned and experienced. He listened extremely attentively and then responded. "A person is entitled to want a better experience of life and to spend a number of years in quest of improved conditions. A clever person needs about thirty years to discover the value of what ordinary life can deliver. A very clever person doesn't even need thirty years, but for some people, no amount of time ever seems to be enough."

I interrupted him and asked what catagory he thought I was in. After the question came out, I wanted to stuff it back in my mouth.

He smiled and went on without answering. "After a while, a person may start to recognize that his attempts to improve his lot are not really improving his lot. As I said, a clever person takes about thirty years, but most of us aren't very clever. We've watched too much T.V. We've heard too many opinions. We're pretty slow, so it takes us a little more time. But eventually, it should become clear to you that getting what you think you should be getting is not going to give you what you really want.

"Some people get despairing and depressed and even get to 'the edge,' but maybe *you* can recognize that there's something else without having to get so close to that edge. When I say 'something else,' I don't mean trading in blue and getting green, or east coast for west, or eating vegetarian food instead of meat."

I was still wondering which category I fit into -- clever or very clever (I couldn't see myself as neither), but I was clever enough to know not to ask again. Instead, I asked if he could say more about this "something else."

"There's something else that's needed, and that's the something else I'm talking about. That something else requires a really different perspective, philosophy, way of doing things, and even more than any of that, to have someone around who knows what's really going on."

I asked him if the reason that people knew so little about 'what's really going on' was because not everybody was ready for it.

"Everyone should have an opportunity to taste the ordinary things and see what they're all about. If a person doesn't take the necessary chances to do that, and prematurely aborts his attempts to go after what's attractive to him, sooner or later those attractions will return and get that person's attention again. You can't get around that by pretending.

"The question then becomes, how many repetitions does it take? Of course the best case would be the fewest repetitions. Do you know that Bob Dylan song that goes:

> *An' here I sit so patiently*
> *Waiting to find out what price*
> *You have to pay to get out of*
> *Going through all these things twice.*

"Then, of course, there's four times and six times and fifty times. You're the one who eventually decides how many times you're going to have to go through all these things. Something constructive that a person can do is to experience each happening in a way that will decrease the likelihood that he will need to experience it over and over again. This requires, among other things, that we experience events 'as they are.'"

"Which was what didn't happen on the way to the airport," I added.

"That's right!" he applauded. "The chauffeur had a lesson. *Do not drive like a maniac -- recklessness causes problems.* But his explanation of that lesson was very different. In fact, his explanation of that lesson necessitated that it must all happen again. Required, absolutely required, that it will happen again. What I'm talking about is not a skill that we learn in school. What we learn there is how to make excuses, and excuses are probably our single greatest enemy. Because if you make excuses, it means that even though you've been taught something by circumstance, you refuse to look directly at that lesson. Instead of looking at that lesson, you develop another explanation for what's taking place, one that can only result in more repetition.

"Circumstances come to each of us to teach us about life. A person has to learn how to see those circumstances 'as they are,' and not as we prefer them to be. That is no small endeavor, and it is also not something that people normally know how to do. We've learned a lot more about making excuses than about taking responsibility."

High in the Sierra Nevada mountains, Lake Tahoe straddles the border between California and Nevada. The Nevada part of the lake, though equally picturesque, is dedicated to casino gambling, and the California side contains some of the best snow skiing in the U.S. along with water sports and camping. It is truly one of the most scenic places in the country, and unbelievably enough, many of the card players that I know have never witnessed its beauty.

On the way up to Tahoe, we made the agreement that we would spend our days outside and our nights at the tables. The first snow had not yet fallen, but the air was cool and conducive to brisk walking. The morning after my limo ride, we arranged to get an early start, drive into the Sierras and hike around a bit.

Walking in the forest on a crystal clear morning was intoxicating enough, but having a companion such as the one that walked along with me, created an unreality about the whole scene. We were silent for a long time. It was not until we crossed a small stream and sat down on some rocks that I thought of something that I wanted to ask him.

I understood the idea of unconsciously repeating our mistakes, and the importance of limiting those repetitions, but sometimes I just felt the oppressiveness of seeing fault after fault after fault. I asked him if it was really necessary that such a huge amount of attention be placed on all these weaknesses. I think I had probably asked him the same question before in another way. I guess I needed reassurance every once in a while.

He answered patiently, as though we had never talked about the subject before. "The reason that I talk to you so often about your shortcomings is to help you to see more clearly that they are keeping you from something. In this way, maybe I can also help you to recognize the possibility that something wonderful can still happen. That's not a small thing, that's a very deep, extraordinary thing, because I'm not referring to a 'something wonderful' that you already know about.

"It's a stretch for you to accept such an optimistic possibility, because neither you, nor even the most optimistic person that you know, is very optimistic. Your aspirations and expectations are very, very modest. In a certain way, you're burnt-out, because you've given up on real hopes, and the only hopes that you have left are the imaginary ones. You're burnt-out because you've read all the words and heard all the stories. You've heard about the possibilities -- you especially, at this time and in this place. But since it still hasn't happened for you, you're not really hoping for the best any more, you're hoping for the 'best.'

"Since you're limited by aspirations that are so modest, I've been trying to evoke your hidden aspirations. The aspirations that you've given up on, or the ones that you're embarrassed to let on that you have. You've confined your hopes to things like travel and relationships and various victories. But these conversations that I've been having with you are about something else, cause I'm not talking about success and conquest or any of the things that are ordinarily hoped for in life. I'm talking about something different, and in this area that I'm talking about, your hope should run rampant."

He got up and so did I. We resumed walking, this time in the direction of a steep hill that was about a mile away. I felt really energetic and wanted to tackle climbing it. He was wearing tennis shoes as opposed to my hiking boots but he said he'd give it a try anyway.

Often when he adopted that cheerleader enthusiasm, like that "hope running rampant" stuff, I reacted with a skepticism that was regurgitated from my youth. We got to the base of the hill and I saw no reason to conceal my feelings. Fortunately for me, he took the opportunity to straighten me out.

"There's no reason to ever be cynical about this stuff, because the ideas that I'm putting forth are very natural ones. We didn't plan this creation. The whole scheme was created long before it reached us. There's a way that it is, and there's a way that we, and all the other happenings, fit in. Anything we do to distort that 'way,' is going to take effort -- our effort. It's going to be like paddling upstream. There will never be a moment when you can put the paddle down, because when the paddle goes down, you relax into the way it really is. But you're afraid to relax into the way it really is, because you've created something else, something false that you depend on. So you have to keep paddling to keep it going -- and paddling is a nonstop effort on your part.

"Unless you change your perspective and begin to see life *as it is* -- unless you relax and begin to live life *as it is* -- whatever you do will take constant effort. The only time you can experience the simplicity of being yourself and giving your best, is when the need to make that effort isn't there."

His enthusiasm was beginning to win me over. I could see that cynicism might be okay to have about things people do. But maybe cynicism in this other world doesn't apply. I said quietly, "Maybe I'm too small to be cynical about something so big."

He acknowledged my realization with a nod and said, "My picture of the world is that it's all possible. It's not that only a lamp can do it, but it's possible for a human being to experience its source. It's also possible for other questions that people ask to be answered as well, but not until after that thing that's been lost has been found.

"You see, I haven't been trying to inform you about a subject. I'm giving you these words so that maybe you'll find hope somewhere in you. Very few people are in a situation where they can sincerely hope that 'this is really it,' that this is the beginning, and that they're going to travel back up that extension cord to discover where it all comes from. It's too daring to have a hope like that. But still, I'm going to keep giving you these words and maybe you'll become willing to take another chance at feeling that the sky is the limit for a human being. I hope that you understand what I'm talking about."

He didn't wait for me to answer but took off straight up the hill at a pace that I doubted he could maintain. I trailed along about a hundred feet behind figuring that he'd slow down and then we'd climb together. He didn't, and we didn't.

When I got to the top of the hill, he was sitting on a log looking over the other side. The view was magnificent. The casinos were visible in the distance, though in that panorama they represented an extremely insignificant portion of the whole. He stood up and asked me if I thought it was time.

I thought he meant 'time to leave,' so I started telling him about what it was like to see so much nature surrounding the silly little casinos which usually represented something so important to me.

He laughed and said he wasn't talking about leaving the hilltop, but was asking me if I was ready to 'get serious.'

I told him that my interactions with him had become the only really meaningful part of my life, and that if there was another step to be taken, I felt that I was ready to take it.

He proceeded with an explanation that seemed to have a different flavor from others that he had given me. He alluded once again to the fact that there might be some course of action that I could take. One that might start me on the road to change. He even mentioned the word 'method,' a word that I had never actually heard him use before, and one which was successful at getting my attention.

"The way we are, we act as needed," he said. "Of course, everybody has a few areas where they do a little extra -- like somebody might have a thing for the faucet in the bathroom, and they polish it all the time. Everyone has little things that they're like that about, maybe checking the air in the tires every day. But most of us notice our tires when they become like pancakes. Then we put air in them. That's the way we are with most things, we act as needed. All the discussions in the world, all those words won't convince a person that action is necessary. You decide for yourself when action is necessary. In other words, if you're getting away with what you're doing, the way that you're doing it, you're going to keep on doing what you've been doing. It's only if *you* think and feel that you're not getting away with what you're doing that you'll consider the need for new action."

"How does a person get to that point?" I asked.

"If you don't feel a demand within yourself to change the way it is for you, then you won't try to change the way it is. You must feel that demand. You must feel that you're not making it. You must feel like you're faking it. You must feel that *it's no longer acceptable*.

"It's the same with people who are addicted to anything, because being addicted to living on the surface of things (where nobody gives their best and everyone is performing for everyone else) is the same as being addicted to a chemical substance. That's right, being addicted to settling for a mediocre experience of life is the same as being addicted to any substance or person or job, or whatever people become addicted to. It's all the same. You must come to the point where you say to yourself, *This is no longer acceptable*."

I told him that as much as I would like to have a positive attitude about what he was saying, it all sounded pretty devastating to me. I noticed that he was smiling while he was talking, but I found *that* level of lightness totally out of my grasp. I said something stupid like, "It's easy for you to say."

"I know that it might sound really depressing to you," he said in a sympathetic tone, "but what it really is, is exciting, because that's where this whole process of change gets its motivation. The idea of trying something really different, going for something really new, starts from knowing that what you've been doing up to this point is not making it. Yes, people may be buying your act, but you know in yourself that you're faking it.

143

"This is a confronting and uncomfortable thing to talk about, but it's impossible to skip this particular step. So I'm taking a lot of time and effort to help you to draw, for yourself, this picture of being broken. Because no one can tell you that your life is not happening. You have to realize that for yourself. Anyone who has a feeling for his heart wants more than the ordinary possessions and relationships of life, and sees his complete and absolute inability to transcend that ordinariness."

We were silent for a while. I remembered something that had happened to me a few days before. I had this really neat idea to send my sister's kid a present from Tahoe. When I got to the store I realized that the quality toys cost a lot more than I was willing to spend. There went my sainthood out the window. Later, I felt that my cheapness was really disgraceful, and that I didn't want to be like that. I told him the story.

"But you're not only like that in this one area," he added. "It's this area and that area and all the areas that I've mentioned. So at some point a person says to himself, 'This is not okay with me anymore. I don't care that other people may think that I'm doing fine. I don't want to be like this anymore.'

"If a person is dissatisfied deep in their feelings -- not so much that they're the grunting around type dissatisfied, but they're tired, and tired is really a good word. Tired of the next hope, tired of adding more things in order to make the situation okay for the next chunk of time. If a person is tired, then there's a possibility that maybe they can learn to change their perspective and begin to learn to relax and see things as they are. But it's really necessary to have that feeling of tiredness."

I was beginning to get agitated over his repetition of this idea of dissatisfaction. I said, "So say I'm tired. Do you think I'm really tired? I think I'm really tired. So if I am, what do I do then?"

He ignored my agitated state and went on calmly. "After a while a person who's tired can begin to recognize that there's something in themselves that needs repair. Now a reasonable person will start by considering a simple repair. You wouldn't rebuild your car engine first thing. If there's a little noise in your car, you wait until it's really clear that there's something really wrong. Then you might try adding a little oil, and if that doesn't help, changing the oil, maybe putting in new spark plugs."

I told him that I dealt with my health in the same way. A few years before I had gone through a period of poor health. So I started my cure with changing my diet. It seemed like a viable place to begin. Later I stopped smoking and drinking; those seemed like reasonable steps also. I was hoping there was some possibility that I could get healed without disrupting my life, and that's where I wanted to start.

"A person certainly would want to try changing their living situation first," he said, "rather than turn the whole thing inside out to see what the guts look like when they're on the outside. It's only if that person is tired and it's unavoidable, that they would involve themselves in that kind of extreme procedure.

"Those that still hope that the new job will make everything okay, that the new relationship will do it, that the move to the new place will do it, find it very difficult to make proper use of methods that were developed to remove obstacles and see things 'as they are.' It won't happen if a person still has hopes that peace and satisfaction will come with the proper resolution of his problems, plans, and relationships."

"I don't know for sure how tired I am, but it all looks really hopeless to me," I said with a hint of a whine.

"Sometimes," he explained, "hopelessness is a positive thing, and sometimes hopelessness is not a positive thing. It depends what you feel hopeless about. If you feel hopeless about the rewards of the ordinary world, then that's a positive thing. If you feel hopeless about making contact with the energy that is within you, that created you, and is maintaining your life, then that's not a positive thing. It would be wonderful if you could see those two types of hopelessness as separate and different."

The patience and kindness he exuded had a pacifying effect on me. I stopped resisting and got into the flow of his words. The idea of two types of hopelessness made a lot of sense to me.

It reminded me of a short story, "The Father Confessor," that he had suggested I read. It was about two priests in medieval times. They knew of each other's existence because they were both well-known ascetic monks who had spent years hearing confessions.

One day, one of the monks was feeling the falseness of his pretence of holiness, and that he couldn't go on hearing confessions. So in his despair, he went to visit the other monk, who, at about the same time, was feeling the same way, and similarly, went to see him. They met close to the second monk's hermitage. When the second monk, who was older, saw the younger monk, he didn't let on that he had also been experiencing doubt.

They end up living together and discovering renewed faith and love. When the older monk reaches the end of his life, he tells the younger monk about despair: "God sends us despair not to kill us; He sends it to us to awaken new life in us."

I told him about the story, which, it turned out, was one of his favorites, and he proceeded to meld it into his explanation.

"Failure may be the best thing that can happen to us, because success builds the illusion that we can win. But you know, everyone is a failure. and everyone feels it to some degree. There are no successes. It just depends how long it takes to learn that you don't want to go through another set of repetitions. So this monk said that despair comes to give us new life, not to kill us.

"There is no peace brought about through the quest for ordinary things. Peace is somewhere, but it's not brought about through manipulating the ordinary things of this earth. When we try to get our peace there, we end up despairing. A despairing which has the potential to bring us to new life. Peace will only really come to us, when the obstacles are removed from between the illusory way we live our lives and the way the creation actually is. When we can see and be with the creation *as it is,* in both its cosmic vastness and in our moment to moment behavior, the capacity to truly relax, be ourselves and give our best will return to us naturally."

14

GOING DIRECT

Those who see us, even though we cannot see ourselves,
opened the door for us, answering our puerile calculations, our
unsteady desires and our awkward efforts with a generous welcome.

Mount Analogue, **Rene Daumal**

Later that week we left Tahoe and headed back toward San
Francisco. It was a sunny day and a beautiful drive, up past Reno
and then down through Truckee and the Sierras. There's an
alternate route that took us through the old "gold rush" country,
Nevada City and Grass Valley. We traveled on smaller roads
whenever possible. My friend was a big proponent of not getting
ahead of ourselves; the freeways are proponents of the opposite.

Somewhere, as we drove that country road, my friend suggested that I turn north toward a small town a few miles off our
route. When I asked what was there, he told me about a pre-
school that some old friends had helped set up. He wanted to see
if it was still in operation after all these years. He wasn't
volunteering any more details, so we drove there in a silence that
was only broken by his directions.

I'm going to skip the description of the school and the people he used to know, and tell you about an experience that I had in this place, which was now a pretty ordinary (as far as I could tell) nursery school.

When the teachers heard that my friend knew the folks that started their school, they invited us in and welcomed us to look around as long and as much as we wished, as well as to stay for a surprise cookie time.

I wandered off into a room with a fish aquarium in it and three kids looking for something to do. When they spotted me, they asked me to read them a story -- instead I offered to play a game with them. My intention was for the kids to have a nice time. Maybe they'd learn something, maybe just have fun -- not because I'm such a good guy, but anyone in that position would want that.

When I was a kid, I liked to perform little magic tricks. I guess it went along with playing cards. So I made up this game for these three kids using some magic and a little green rubber ball.

I told them that whoever guesses where the ball is will get some cookies. Now my idea is that they're *all* going to get the cookies, because I have the ball and I can do whatever I want. How are they going to know what I'm doing? They're little kids. In relation to them, I'm all-powerful. I can change the trick any time I want. They won't know, but they'll be okay anyway because my intention is that they all get the cookies. They all want cookies, so all we have to do is play this game and they'll get what they want. That's all they have to do.

Of course *they* see this game as a problem. They see it as a competition. But I'm holding the little green rubber ball and I don't see it as a problem at all. All they have to do is relax and they'll all get the cookies.

So what do they do? They start to fight with each other. They get aggressive, they worry, they start to grab. Is this going to help them get the cookies? No, it's going to postpone the whole thing.

Now feel the situation. I'm sitting there knowing that I'm in control of how this game is going to turn out. I know that sooner or later we're all going to be in the kitchen eating cookies, but these kids are going through all kinds of changes because they don't think that. They think it's up to them. They think there's a problem and they've got to perform in a certain way. They're having thoughts like, "How can I win this game?" "I hope I do it right," and "What if the other kid does it first?" They're all very frantic and concerned that they won't get what they want.

So what happened was these kids got over-anxious, ignored the game that I set up for them, and tried to run into the kitchen to grab the cookies. What could I say to them? "Come back, come back, come back." It's really simple. They'll have to recognize my position in this situation because I made up that game.

I wish them well. I'm not going to say, "Ha, ha, no cookies." That's not my idea. My idea is for something nice to happen. Who's causing the problem? I'm not causing the problem.

Well, this whole scene actually took only about five minutes, so it wasn't like I disrupted the whole nursery school or anything like that. But I sure had a story to tell my friend when we joined each other over cookies and milk. We sat off to the side at a mini-table for two, and after I told him the story he added some observations of his own.

"What would you think if you were the child in your game?" he began. "Not way back when you were a kid, but right here, right now. Worried that you won't win the game -- afraid that you won't get what you want -- struggling, only because you don't know that there's something that's watching over you, something on your side, something that wants us all to get the cookies.

"I'm talking about something benevolent and powerful, because it's manifesting all this life around us, and then it's keeping all of that life going. That's a lot of technique and a lot of skill, and it's all focused at caring for us. A complex operation is going on in this creation, to say the least. There's an intelligence out there, and it's not like man's intelligence.

"Man thinks God is ten feet tall. Man thinks God is like a very powerful man -- like a very super-powerful, very super-intelligent man. That power is something else entirely, and its idea is that we all get into the kitchen and eat some cookies."

His explanation was interrupted by one of the teachers informing us that nap time was approaching and that it would be best if we left. I said my goodbyes to my little friends (they all got the cookies) and we left the school, got back in the car, and headed on down the road. As we drove off, he added some final thoughts on the subject.

"Our feverish monkey-cage agitation demands that we rush into the kitchen, make a dash for the place where the cookies are stored, and fail to recognize that there is a benevolence that's on our side. We're constantly getting called back -- go back, go back, go back. And that's really too bad, because that's not the idea the creator has for us. Those cookies are there for us. All we have to do is recognize that we have a friend running the entire game -- one who has the ability and the wisdom and the love to play with us, and that it's for us to learn to be played with."

The weather warmed considerably as we headed southwest toward Sacramento. In a relatively short time, we descended in elevation from about seven thousand feet near Truckee, to just a few hundred feet in Sacramento. As we entered town, my friend suggested we hit the local Safeway to get some snacks for the rest of the ride. As we all know, in the U.S.A. a supermarket is never hard to find. Within five minutes of his suggestion, we were wheeling the aisles of Safeway, and I was about to get my next lesson.

"Our basic philosophy of acquisition has to be re-examined," he explained. "We want something that's over there on the table, but we're over here by the door. Our usual way of getting this thing that's over there is like the way we're doing this shopping here at Safeway. We go over there and get it. We wouldn't phone the president of Safeway and say, `Listen, I need half a dozen oranges,' and then he'd tell us where to get them. We wouldn't do that. We go to the orange bin as we're doing now. We pick exactly the ones we want and after we're done, we go to the checkout, pay for them, and then walk out of the store.

"We wouldn't petition whoever or whatever is in charge of this entity in order to get what it supplies. We go directly for it. I've learned that and you've learned that, and up to this point you couldn't have learned anything else."

"I can't see anything wrong with that," I interjected. "And even if there were, what would be the alternative?"

He picked up a can of pineapple chunks off the shelf and after checking to see that it didn't contain sugar, he answered, "Maybe no alternative is needed. That method often functions successfully with the ordinary procedures of the world. But everything does not operate by the same laws. The objects in this store are influenced by the law of gravity, and this can of pineapple responds to that law. But a certain distance above the earth's surface, which is not that far relatively, that law is not influencing in the same way, and this can would behave differently.

"What you see is not all there is. Yes, we want an orange and we want the rewards of being a conscious human being, but that doesn't mean that the process of acquiring oranges and our acquisition of that consciousness will obey the same laws. *I can tell you that they do not.*

"If you think that you're going to sign up for some program and perform some set of actions in order to get this consciousness from over there, where it is, to over here, where you are, like you would get oranges -- you will not succeed."

"Then how does a person get to be a conscious human being?" I asked.

"This goal of internal connection," he explained, "is not in the Safeway world of the things that people do. It was not created by man, it is not maintained by man, and if it is, it will not be destroyed by man.

"This process obeys a different set of laws, and one cannot go directly for it. It doesn't matter what books you've read. It doesn't matter what ideas you have or who you know. You must find some way to attract the force that has both you and your quest in its view."

I was beginning to understand what he was talking about. I asked, "So how can we learn to attract that force?"

"This self-importance of ours is so destructive!" he exclaimed. "It leads us to believe that *we* can work this out. It is not the case, you will never work this out. If ever you are the beneficiary or the recipient of any gifts from that orange bin, it will only be because you were noticed. And you don't get noticed by trying to traverse the space between here and there. You only get noticed by removing the obstacles between here and there."

I heard myself complaining as I said, "It always seems to come back to the same thing."

"Yes it does," he agreed, "because we're all somewhat similar to each other. We learn that if *you* are here and *it* is there, then if you go there, you will be where *it* is, and you will be in the best position to get *it*.

"The only time that people resort to prayer is when they are completely incapable of going over to the orange bin, completely incapable. Like when they're on their death bed, when control is gone and the flood waters are rising. If there's ever any chance to go directly over to the bin, that's what we do. That's what we've learned, and that's what we do. But every once in a while we find ourselves in a situation where that doesn't work."

What he was saying seemed extremely important to me. I was following every word (which wasn't so easy in the baked goods and candy aisle). I asked him what kind of situation he was talking about.

He stopped rolling and leaned against a shelf like we were going to be there for awhile. "Like maybe you really care about someone and you want her to care about you. Telling her, 'I really care about you,' usually doesn't make it happen. Saying, 'I really, really care about you,' still doesn't make it happen. So you try going to where she is, and it seems like now that you're at her 'bin' maybe it will all come together. But not only is it not coming together, it's probably getting worse.

"There's a saying, 'Only love can break your heart,' or maybe it's not break your heart, but break it open. There's something to that. You feel like you really care for another person and you try to make it happen, but you find out that you can't make it happen."

He looked at me as though he *got* me -- and he did. He had just described a painful event out of my past as accurately as it could have been described. I wondered for a moment if he knew the specifics of what had happened to me, or maybe I just wasn't as unique as I had imagined.

He gave me a few minutes to recover and then he resumed his explanation. "Maybe if you're a poor black person living in the ghetto, you can still become a famous millionaire like Michael Jordan. Maybe that's even possible if you're short. Maybe you can get a gun and rob a bank. It's conceivable that you might even get away with it. That's what happens sometimes on T.V., or in novels, or in the movies. But you can't make someone love you. For some people that's the first lesson. For some people that's the first time that going direct doesn't work. Because with everything else, there's a possibility."

"So are you saying," I asked, "that love is love, and romantic love is a reflection of this other spiritual experience, this finding the lost connection that we've been talking about for this past year?"

"Exactly!" he pronounced. "The idea of self-improvement is so heretical. There's something really coarse about the idea of improving our lot, improving our conditions. I mean coarse in terms of not fine, not subtle. I don't comply with the human agreement that this phenomenal life is given to us, and then it becomes our job to improve the lot of that life. What *is* meant for us is another job, another purpose, and another experience -- and it doesn't have to do with getting anything that's over there in the orange bin."

"What *is* meant for us then?" I asked.

He looked at me like I should have known the answer to that question by now. He answered anyway, "It has to do with finding out what we're connected to and how we're connected. The miraculous thing is, when we begin to realize this connection, the things from over there start to make their way over here. The oranges just seem to find their way over."

154

It's impossible for me, as the messenger who's delivering these words, to assess how you, the recipient, are receiving them. If your reactions are anything like mine were, your mind is now blown.

Where does this guy come up with this stuff? We're walking around the supermarket, and as he pops a few oranges in the cart, he proceeds to explain some mystery of the human predicament that I have never heard described anywhere before, and he does it using the metaphor of oranges.

I mean, is this really happening, or what? Well, if *you* don't think this stuff is extraordinary, you might want to read this last part about the oranges again. Maybe you didn't get it. Maybe you were spacing out; read it again!

At any rate, I'm going to go on and describe what happened when we left the store and headed back to the car.

It had begun to rain. We had to make a dash for the car, and in the process we both got pretty wet. As we were sitting toweling off in his van, I got up the courage to ask him something that I had been curious about for a long time.

"Since we're talking about the oranges finding their way over, can I ask you a personal question?"

He smiled and said, "If we're all basically the same, then there are no personal questions -- so go ahead, ask!"

"For as long as I've known you," I began, "I've never known how you deal with the money thing. I know you don't play poker that often, and when you do, you usually quit before you win very much. If you hadn't been talking about 'going direct' in the store, this question probably wouldn't have surfaced again, but since it has..."

I mumbled on nervously for a couple of seconds not knowing how to end my inquiry. I looked over and he seemed to be delighting in my squirming. Finally he put me out of my misery.

"Okay, calm down -- you asked, you did it. You see, that's what happens when a person keeps something from coming out of them for too long. When it finally does come out, it's almost traumatic.

"Over the years a few other people have asked me how I do it financially. For a while I said that I invented those round paper things that you put on the toilet seat in public bathrooms so you can sit on the paper instead of the seat, and every time people use those things, I get the royalties.

"I didn't have an answer for the question that people could easily understand. I really didn't want to talk about it, so I would say that. I told that story for a while, and the people that had an interest in my well-being would use extra ones -- you know, double up!

"Then one time I was talking to someone, and he asked me if I had a job, and what I did for money. That time I said, 'I'm in a position where I never have to worry about money again for the rest of my life.' So that became my answer, and that really is the case.

"Of course, what that person didn't understand was that the key word was 'worry.' That I didn't have to *worry* about money, not that I had it, but that I didn't have to worry about it. People imagine that the key is to have it, but really the key is to not worry about it. Having it doesn't preclude the worrying part. You know, rich people are not free from the worries about money. People who have learned not to worry, don't worry.

"Some people look at me as though I've got this easy life and travel all over the place, and they wonder how I do it. I don't work, so how do I manage to go to all these different places? Well, it has nothing to do with anything that I do. It's not because I'm clever, and it's not because I know the steps along the way. In fact, it's not for any reason.

"When a person is 'facing in the right direction,' the oranges just seem to find their way over! Not all the oranges, no, not all the oranges -- just the ones that I need to drive the road that I drive, and serve the purpose that I serve."

A few moments into his response, I gained my composure and was able to listen. My question, which was definitely on the surface of things, received an answer which was definitely not. I deeply appreciated his ability to take things higher. I told him so, and asked if he could say more about this idea.

"I like to think that you can really take to heart that striving for more in this endeavor of ours is futile. For the consumer and the oranges, it may be a realistic striving, but it's not a realistic striving when it comes to a human being and true peace, harmony, and tranquility. There is no peace that comes from anything other than discovering the true connection, the one that has always existed, between a person and the energy that keeps him alive. There is none; they're synonymous.

"When a person feels the connection to what maintains her life, to what created that life, and to what is eventually going to take that life, then that person has the proper perspective of things. That person is no longer a separated appendage. That person is no longer dangling in space, desperately needing to be reassured and made to feel secure. There is no other peace.

"Anything that I would ever tell you or ask you to do, or suggest, or teach, or talk about, would always be, whether it sounded like it or not, to lead you in that direction. Because there is no other direction. There is no acquisition of peace. There is only the removal of obstacles in order to feel the connection that is already existing. I know for a fact that this can take place, but it certainly can't take place if you're always frantically on your way to the orange bin.

"Despair also comes from the sum total of our efforts to go direct. To go direct for some special experience in life and not find it, not find it, not find it. And that despair comes not to kill us, not to tell us that it's time to give up, 'Fuck it, it's not worth it.' It comes to say, maybe you're facing in the wrong direction. Maybe you're going about this in the wrong way.

"For some people, that despair, that disappointment leads to the possibility of a new life. It leads to the possibility of discovering the source of what's here, and to start learning to look toward that source. So instead of trying to go direct, we can put our efforts into realizing our natural connection to that source and then see, in turn, what experiences that source sees fit to give to us."

15

DO YOU THINK FEAR TACTICS WORK?

...she had her first deep experience of real humility as she saw how little she had of it. ... after all the systematic slayings of small prides one by one, ... she had touched only the outer edges of that jungle where I, Me and Mine flourished in a thousand forms.

The Nun's Story, **Kathryn Hulme**

The idea that a clever person should be ready to look for a deeper level of life by the age of thirty gave me trouble. Being six years past thirty and considering myself one of the clever ones, it would seem that I should be prepared to act vigorously on some of the insights that my friend was bestowing upon me. Yes, I was definitely a changed person, but it seemed that the changes were due mainly to my exposure to him, and not to any effort on my part. In actuality, I felt unmotivated except for an occasional burst, and those bursts were generally due to wanting my friend to think well of me.

It was not so much that our relationship was getting stale or repetitious, but more that I felt I had to get up off my ass and add something to it. Unfortunately, whether due to laziness or inertia, I was unable to muster any kind of sustained effort. I didn't seem to have what it takes to even ask my friend what precisely that effort should be.

When we were traveling, there was a certain excitement that came from simply moving around. The increased activity concealed my lack of motivation. Whenever I returned to my home base, apartment, ordinariness, that lack would resurface.

On one occasion that I recall painfully, my friend took off on the tournament trail without me, explaining that the change of pace would do us both good. It may have ultimately done me good, but it sure was painful. I was left to my own devices, and it was scary to see how many of my stupid old habits and activities pulled at me when my friend wasn't around. His leaving without me was on his part purposeful -- and what's more, it worked.

When he got back to town, I phoned to see when we could get together. He suggested we meet at his daughter's school that afternoon because he was going to pick her up. That would give us some time to talk before she got out.

We met there in the early afternoon and I immediately assaulted him with a barrage of questions about my lack of incentive. He listened attentively and then responded with this story.

"This is a Montessori School," he began. "It's sweet, progressive, and pretty low key. She's at an age now, when a lot of the parents expect their kids to be taught something conventional. For the first few years she was in classes with very little focus on academics -- like I said, sweet stuff, mostly Kermit the Frog and circle time on Sesame Street.

"Then this year she moved on to the next color door. The door she was in last year was grey door. That's how they name their classes at this school -- not third grade, fourth grade -- but purple door, green door. Now she's in brown door and it's more brown there. The teacher in brown door has brown ideas about academics, and he wants some subjects to be taught, partly because parents are starting to expect things to happen other than singing *The Circle Song*.

"I don't necessarily agree, cause I think that *The Circle Song* can take you a long way. But Phil, he's the teacher, he doesn't think that. He thinks the kids need geography and like that, partly because of the parents' expectations.

"Phil is starting to let them know that they're in preparation. Preparation for junior high, high school, college, professions, old age, death -- you know, preparation. In school you're always being prepared for something. Really it's the slaughter, but they don't know that, so they can't tell you that.

"This preparation is always supported with well-known fear tactics -- like you won't be prepared, you won't be ready, and you won't be able to keep up with the other kids, so you won't do well and you'll be embarrassed.

"I'm not saying Phil's heavy-handed about this stuff. Certainly he's not at all like some of the teachers in public schools, but he still has ideas about preparation. Along with the preparation story also goes 'you better learn it because I'm going to give a test.'

"So the other day I was talking to her about this."
I said: *Why does he do that, give tests all the time?*
She said, like most kids that age would say: *I don't know.*
So I said: *Did you ever ask?*
And she said: *No.*
And I said: *Well why don't you find out? go and ask.*

"To a kid, that's an intimidating suggestion. I'm sure if somebody would have said that to me when I was that age, it would have been plenty scary. I remember that it felt like the teacher could do just about anything. There was no limitation to the amount of pain a teacher could cause you. That was my concept of a teacher.

"When my daughter said that she didn't want to ask, we talked about it. That's an important thing with me -- talk about it, find out what's the worst thing that could happen, take a chance, see. Not only with kids, with big people, with myself, see what happens. So we talked about it and she said okay she'd ask, because she's had some wonderful experiences with getting out there and taking chances.

161

"Like a few weeks ago she went to a track meet. She's small, but she runs really fast. It was a track meet with kids from all over the city, and none of her friends were going. It was mostly boys, and it was really scary for her. But she got a lot of encouragement, went anyway, and had a great experience.

"I'm not saying that she won or she lost. But aside from how well she did or didn't do, she had a great experience. She broke down at the end with tears of relief because she lived through it.

"I was there watching, and obviously it was beautiful for me too. I'm not talking about how many points she scored, but that she got out there, took a chance, and survived. That's what it's all about, really. Life is terribly traumatic if you think you're not going to survive.

"So she did ask the teacher why he gave them so many tests. He explained to her that tests are the way he gets the kids to remember the information, because they know they're going to be tested.

"I asked her: *Well, do you think it works?*

"She thought about it for a while, and she answered: *Yeah, I think it does work.*

"And I think she's right. I think it does work."

My friend then asked me, mostly I think, to make sure I was following him, "Do *you* think fear tactics work?"

I could relate so personally to the story about his daughter that I probably could have told it about my own life. In actuality, fear was the only thing that had ever motivated me to do anything. I guess what I had learned from life was that fear tactics worked, but worked to do what? I responded to his question from my understanding of this problem.

"It depends what you mean by work," I said.

He smiled at me, realizing that I had understood the subtleties of this subject, then continued. "Exactly! We both know that fear tactics are incredibly effective. They do work for achieving the ordinary things in life. So much so, that one could assume that fear tactics work, *period!*

"But I've been involved in this endeavor of removing the obstacles to being a relaxed and giving person for long enough to know that there is something else that has to be kindled in a person in order for them to pursue this endeavor. Something that has nothing to do with the motivational factors of ordinary life, nothing whatsoever.

"That's pretty incredible, because I've also seen people's attempts to run through their accustomed motivating factors, trying to see which one is going to work. One at a time, one at a time, one at a time, each one in turn gets shot down, until they realize that there's going to have to be some different kind of motivation here.

"Pride doesn't work, competition doesn't work, fear doesn't work, reward for the future doesn't work, getting attention and approval doesn't work, fame and fortune doesn't work. None of the things that we've known to have been successful for us in ordinary life, none of them work."

It becomes necessary now to let you, the reader, know that my friend did read the rough manuscript of this book. He made several suggestions, far fewer than I would have thought. I, of course, incorporated any suggestions that he made, and added or deleted according to his wishes. The following paragraph is one that he directly instructed me to include. It actually represents a direct communication from my friend to you, the reader. I might have thought the thoughts that it expresses, but probably wouldn't have taken the responsibility to tell you.

"This situation of proper motivation is a problem right from the beginning. So I'm seeing to it that this problem is presented to you now, in the early stages of your introduction to these ideas. You're reading right now for a certain reason, but the reason that you're reading is not going to work for you. If something that you read sounds like a suggestion of something to try, you may try it, but your reason for trying it is not going to work for you. You're paying attention now, but the reason you're

paying attention is not going to be the kind of reason that is going to face you in the right direction. You're going to have to discover something really new for motivation, and you're going to have to discover it within yourself, because that's the way it happens. It's not going to be the reasons that made you do the things that you've done before."

My reaction to this extensive explanation about motivation which was directed to me, is probably similar to your reaction to the above paragraph which was directed to you. "So what can I do to get properly motivated?" Well fortunately for me, by this time I can answer some of my own questions, so I'll answer yours as well.

A major recurring principle in my friend's ideas is that everything good is already built into us, and that all we have to do is learn to relax, in order to let the capacity in question come forth. I further have begun to understand that even the capacity to relax is built into us, and that it is simply our job to remove the obstacles to that natural ability.

16

DEAD-END U-TURNS

*Even the most vigorous and gifted among the others all failed and
were defeated in the end because their task or their ambitious dream
seized hold of them, made them into persons so possessed that they
lost the capacity for liberating themselves from present things, and
attaining perspective.*

The Glass Bead Game, **Hermann Hesse**

I was beginning to understand that even if rediscovering my lost
connection were an ordinary practical problem, which it isn't, my
attempts to go directly for a solution wouldn't help me. After all, I
didn't have any idea what to go directly for. It's even possible that
what I imagined to be the missing pieces to this puzzle may very
well not have been what was missing at all.

What was becoming more and more obvious to me, was that
my life was focused on changing circumstances, and that my
friend was trying to point me in the direction of learning to leave
circumstances as they are, and change my point of view. The
practicality of this latter way of living became clearer to me with
the help of an explanation he gave me in response to a story that I
told him.

Where exactly we were on that occasion is unclear in my memory. Sometimes I found that sitting and talking in his van created an environment that was so complete that the outside world disappeared. As I recall, we stopped to stretch our legs at a highway rest area. He began (what appeared to be) reminiscing about a hike we had taken together.

"It's really amazing how our view of a situation can be distorted when we can only see it from ground level. Remember when we took the hike down that steep hill and went through a deep canyon? I think it was the day before we spotted the bulls. The terrain went up and down, hills and valleys, and when we were in the valleys we were basically lost. We didn't know where we were going. We walked through those winding valleys but didn't know where they lead. We didn't know what was around the corners. Remember when you started talking about how lost we were?"

I nodded, the memory was very clear.

He continued, "When you're in a valley, you can't tell where it winds, if you can get through, or if it's a dead-end. You don't know if there's water ahead, or shear rock, or whatever. Then you climb up a hill. You look around and you see it all.

"Nothing changed. The land didn't shift. You get up on the top of this hill and you say, 'Oh, I see!' You see the way it winds, you see the obstacles that may be in your path, and you try to remember what you're seeing. Then you come back down to the valley and start walking, and after a while you forget again.

"I've hiked a lot, and it always goes like that. When you get up high, you know what's going on. When you're down low, you try to remember what you saw when you were up high, and you hope for the best. People want to feel like they know what's going on, even when they're down in the valley, but you can't. You've got to get up to where there's perspective. You don't have to change the world, you don't have to change the circumstances, you don't have to change anything. You've just got to get up there where you can see how it is."

His hiking example reminded me of an example of my own. It was a vivid memory, and I had no trouble recounting my story to him.

It happened in my early twenties. I was travelling around the country with some friends in a converted schoolbus-motorhome. It seemed to me to be the best way to go. You know, no hotels and motels, carry our house on our back, home-cooked food.

We were driving around somewhere in Florida. One of my friends was visiting a relative in one of those planned retirement communities. We drove off the main road through an entrance gate and then through all these one-way snakelike roads. There were hundreds of houses, most of them on winding lanes, and most of those winding lanes were dead-ends.

So we were there visiting for a while and eventually we were ready to leave. Of course when you leave, you've got to find the same road out. Well we think we're driving out the same way that we came in, but a half-hour later we're still driving around in circles.

Well if you've ever driven a really long vehicle, you know you'll do anything to avoid hitting a dead-end. A dead-end is the worst, especially with this bus, because it didn't have power steering. In order to make a u-turn, I had to get someone to come up front and help turn the steering wheel. On this particular night, we made a lot of dead-end u-turns, and this went on for longer than you want this kind of thing to go on.

Sometime in the middle of this odyssey, we stopped and somebody said, "You know, if we were in a helicopter only thirty feet above these streets, none of this would be happening."

When I finished the story, we both laughed for a while. I, remembering that ridiculous incident, and he, at my pantomime of turning the steering wheel. After a few moments he asked me what I understood from what had happened that night.

"When we were on ground level," I said, "we needed a course in directions. We would have had to memorize the map and figure out what to do, or we'd have to live there for a couple of years, and even then, if we weren't that good at directions, we'd still get

lost at night. But if we were up above, we'd see the whole thing. We'd say, left, right, left, right, no problem."

"You're right!" he said enthusiastically. "The answer to the problem is perspective. Perspective and the humor that can come from perspective. Humor, because you feel that lightness from being just a little bit above the situation and you can see it as it is.

"The only other possibility is that you study the specifics. You'd have to be a psychologist, and dedicate yourself to the study of driving directional science. You'd have to learn all the details that psychologists know. If you ask a psychologist he'll tell you, 'Yes, this type of person will do this and this and that because their parents did this and this and that.'

"And you know what? They're often right. But if you change the variables a little bit, they won't know the answers, because there is no perspective there -- all there is is information."

It seemed a very radical extension from the story I told him. Directions on the road is one thing, but to correlate that so directly with life seemed unrealistic. I asked him if he was actually saying that if you have perspective in life, you don't need information.

He exclaimed excitedly, "That's exactly what I mean! You don't need a street map of each community if you're above it. Because it's right there and what to do is obvious. But if your answer for how to get out of the maze of streets is a map, then you'll need a map of each community you're in. For every place you go, for every situation you're in, you'll need a separate map.

"That's one of the reasons that people are so tense. Because whenever they go into an unfamiliar situation, like a new job, everything is happening there for the first time. So a person wants to know, 'What's the map of this place? What are the rules? Who is it okay to talk to? What are they like? What do they like? Where do you get this? Where do you get that?' They don't want to make any radical moves before they find out what's acceptable behavior."

"I can see the value of perspective," I said, "but what's wrong with learning about each situation as it comes up?"

"That's a reasonable question," he answered. "If you learn each circumstance in order to be knowledgeable, I call that 'control.' Control feigns being relaxed, but it's not. Cleverness feigns being a human being, but it's not. When a person knows how to be in control, and has detailed maps of four hundred different situations, the thrust of that person's life becomes avoiding that four hundred and first situation. If life delivers him into that four hundred and first circumstance, then he's not relaxed anymore. He didn't have perspective, he had control and cleverness. A person is born with the capacity to have perspective. It's not a special attribute that you have to add on to yourself. If you stop punching and calm down a little, then perspective starts to come into you."

I told him that it seemed way out of my reach to give up my dependence on information, and even more than that, my need to be in control.

He saw it otherwise. "I see a very specific alternative to the way people ordinarily live their lives. Even though it's not really possible for them to stop doing what they're doing, they could add something a little different. I actually have more confidence in peoples' ability to do that than they have in themselves, and that goes for people I don't even know.

"I'm looking at this person driving around in circles in a motorhome in this subdivision maze and he's saying, 'I'll never get out of here, I'll never get out.' But I'm thinking, 'A left and a right, a left and a right, and you'll be out. It's no big deal. It's only a subdivision with a lot of curvy roads.'

"When you think, 'I'm trapped, I'm trapped,' I know what you're feeling. It's what you were feeling when you were driving that bus. But what if someone you knew was able to see and could teach you how to look down and see that maze in the proper perspective? Then maybe you wouldn't always feel like you need a personal consultation with the Creator of the Universe for help. All you'd need is to know the someone who happens to see."

17

HOW YOU SEEK IS WHAT YOU'LL FIND

...when I see or hear anything majestic which allows no doubt that it
proceeds from the actualization of Our Maker Creator. Each time, my
tears flow of themselves. I weep, that is to say, it weeps in me, not
from grief, no, but as if from tenderness.

Meetings With Remarkable Men, **G.I. Gurdjieff**

I knew at that moment, in the harsh florescent light of the freeway
rest area, that sitting next to me in that van was such a
"somebody." He had gotten through to me by using my own
innocent story, because for as long as I could remember, feeling
trapped was what I indeed felt. For the first time in my life, I saw
that escape was possible, that freedom was possible.

For two years, I had known this man who possessed an
infinitely superior perspective of life to my own, along with an
infinitely superior ability to live according to that perspective. It
had taken all this time and exposure for me to develop the hope
that (as my friend would say) "the sky's the limit for human
beings."

I wept warm tears. It was not the weeping of self-pity, nor of
any other negativity. It was a new weeping for a new possibility.

He took the opportunity of my openness and vulnerability to
talk to me in a way that seemed different, softer, and full of heart.
Probably he was the same. It was I who could hear differently.

"We're two people, you and I, who have gotten together over some ideas. Two people who have a heart with an opening. Two people with some recognition that life has become either turmoil or covered turmoil. And we've gotten to know each other for the purpose of making that life into something worthwhile.

"Right now you feel something sweet. I want you to look more and more for that feeling, that little opening, that heart that's buried so much of the time. Try to steer your way around to that opening, and see if there's some way to feel it again and again -- maybe even to increase the likelihood of finding those little openings. Because if that can happen, it'll be a precious thing. That's where it all starts. It all starts with a simple, pure, sweet intention.

"If you can find that little opening in your heart and in your life, that little warm spot in your thoughts and in your feelings -- then maybe you can use what's given to you, not by me, but given to you however it's given to you, to further open that spot. Then whatever happens will be beautiful.

"I've never told you that I want to describe my method, or that I teach this or that course. I've always wanted to get you to a point where you could focus in on that warm spot in you. I want you to learn to drive around inside your being. Steer around, walk around inside yourself. Feel a little, 'That's it, that's not it, that's it, that's not it,' a little sarcasm, a little doubt, a little hope -- all of it, and feel it.

"Then every once in a while you'll trip over a little sweetness. Maybe it's like the space between the inhale and the exhale, where there's just nothing happening. That one calm space that's warm and sweet and makes your eyes feel a little watery -- warm watery.

"You know that's where you want to be, but you don't have any idea how to get there, and you wish you knew what made it happen. Sometimes you listen to a song that's done it for you before. But you've listened too many times, and now it doesn't do it for you anymore.

"You don't need a new song. You need to know the secret of how that old song did it for you. That's the way I want it to go for you, because as far as I'm concerned, that's the only place to be. There is no other place to be."

The emotions I was feeling opened doors in my memory that had been closed for a long time. Amidst the flood, was a flash of something that had happened to me years before when I lived in Seattle. I knew that it was connected to what he had been saying, and thanks to my state, I was able to tell the story without rehearsing it.

It happened as a friend and I were driving down the street. I was pulling up to the curb when my friend said, "Hey! Look out! There's a book over there." It was lying in the gutter. We got out and looked at this book. It rained a lot where we were, but fortunately it wasn't the rainy season, so the book was in okay shape.

It was a scuffled up little book published in South Africa in 1898 or 1902 or something like that. It was written by a lady named Olive Shriner, and it described an incredible series of dreams that she had -- a wonderful book. In the prologue on the first page were the words:

The path to glory is paved with thorns,
but on the path to truth, at each step,
you place your foot down on your own heart.

I asked him if that was what he was talking about.

He answered in what seemed to be almost a whisper. "Yes that's what I'm talking about. If you can't find your own heart, you can practice any method or any system of any kind, with any teacher, or any guru, or any religion or any psychology; it won't matter, it will come to nothing. *How you seek is what you'll find.*

"If you can find your heart at each step -- you'll never get hard, you'll never get cynical, you'll never feel superior, you'll never feel invulnerable, you'll never feel insulated, you'll never feel better or separate from others. You'll just get more and more and more open.

"It's a big step to have even a little opening in your heart, because the situation that we've been presented with in this time is so strange. Things have gone very, very far off course. So finding that little opening is really only the beginning of the path to truth, but as far as I'm concerned, it's critical."

I told him that I would like to make that saying, *On the path to truth, at each step you put your foot down on your own heart*, the theme of our relationship. If I could retain it, I would certainly be sailing into uncharted waters.

It seemed to me that the greatest challenge to my remembering would be when we talked about methods, or ideas that sounded like psychology or self-examination, or when we talked about philosophy or spirituality. Even if it sounded like we were talking about those subjects, I had to remember that it was my open heart that was most important. I told him that I felt like the Tin Man in *The Wizard of Oz*.

He liked my comparison. "The Tin Man had no heart," he said, "and he went off in search of one. Well, you've got to find yours, and once you find it, there's no drug like a taste of your own heart. There's nothing that you can inhale, snort, shoot, or swallow -- there's no activity of any kind that has the intoxication of a touch of your own heart.

"Like that picture of the Hindu monkeyman, Hanuman, holding his heart open with his arms -- that's the story. You've got to find it, you've got to get it open, and you've got to keep it open. You've got to know what closes it up, and stay away from that. The intention doesn't come from your head. Yes, the ideas come from your head, but the intoxication that I'm talking about doesn't come from there. You've got to find that intoxication.

"Sure, romance may break your heart, but if you find what I'm talking about, it will break your heart open -- it will open it up. That's where you gotta start, because anything else is like all the games that people play. You'll just transfer all those games from the ordinary world and put them right smack into the spiritual world.

"People can have methods, meditations, teachers, people they call brothers and sisters, different colored clothes and incredible books, or whatever. But if their foot, at each step, isn't placed on

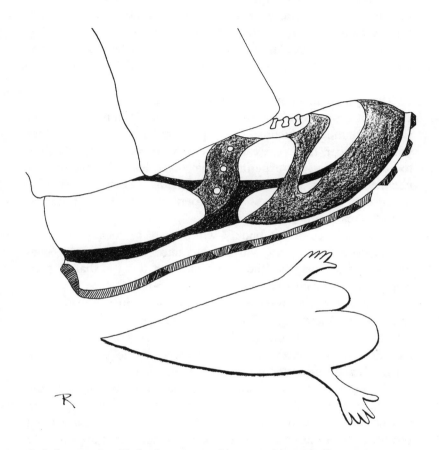

their heart, they'll do the wrong things -- things to be separate, to be superior, to be insulated, to be better, to be safe, and so it'll go badly. It's gotta start with one foot on one heart -- and follow the yellow brick road."

In the moments that I've been describing, the purpose of our relationship was clarified. Up to that point, I could pretend that we were poker buddies, or perhaps that I was hanging out with an eccentric philosopher. But now this was obviously no longer the case.

175

This extraordinarily unique man, who knew how to be a human being, was actually trying to teach me how to be one. From the beginning, he had no other reason to befriend me. He probably threw out his fishing line to many who crossed his path, but for some reason I bit on the bait, and with his help, didn't let go.

The rest of these writings must now take a different course. Our relationship was entering a new phase. In this new phase, Ray, the name by which my friend preferred to be called, and that you, the reader, have now earned the right to know, introduced me to an experiment. An experiment that could lead to removing the obstacles to what has always been with us -- something that he called our "innate goodness." An experiment that I was expected to study, learn, and put into practice.

In the balance of this book, I will attempt to convey the spirit of that experiment, along with some amount of its specifics -- remembering always, that the most important thing is that at each step, you place your foot down on your own heart.

From then on, he referred to what we were involved in as an experiment. According to Ray (as you now know him), the best way to avoid the hazards involved in this endeavor, was to try to look at whatever we did as an experiment. He helped clarify the spirit of experimentation with the following words.

"If you're going to experiment around, you have to leave the guidelines slightly open. You can't say, 'I'm going to experiment around, but I have to have this and this and this.' You can have a few 'this's,' but there have to be a few unknowns that are going to be the experiment part. When you get to the point where you'll try something new, because the way you are is no longer acceptable to you, that something new doesn't have to be so carefully devised, because you're just starting to search around."

The single most difficult part for me, in these first few weeks of learning about Ray's experiment, was struggling with my tendency to always get ahead of myself. My concept that the beginning was not the best place to be, frequently got in the way.

176

I confided in him about some doubts that I was having center-ing around my ability to stick it out through the basics, because my impatience often seemed to get the upper hand. I asked him if he thought that I had what it took to go through all this, what I called, preliminary stuff. Because in the past I'd been really weak with that.

I told him that when I was about eighteen, I had this fantasy of being a doctor in the Peace Corps. I wanted to save the natives in the Amazon and travel around healing the sick. I signed up to take the pre-med courses in college. I remember the professor in the organic chemistry class demanding that if we were going to con-tinue his course we would have to memorize the periodic table of elements, all hundred and whatever of them. All the other classes were like that too; you gotta memorize the anatomy, you gotta memorize this, you gotta be here, you gotta do this, you gotta do that. I hated it all. I couldn't study. I would just sit in front of my books and think, *I don't want to do this stuff. I want to heal the sick! Just turn me loose; I want to heal the sick.*

"I'm glad you've told me about this tendency of yours," he said. "I'm not surprised that it's hard for you to gear back and start from the beginning in our experiment. You had dreams of healing the sick and you've had dreams about this world of consciousness as well. You've absorbed a lot of ideas, beautiful ideas, incredible books. But how do you take the inspiration from these books, those flashes that you've had, those far-out people that you've met, and haul it back in, haul it all back in and start from the beginning? What you have to do now, is take all that and put it temporarily aside, not throw it away, because it's precious, but put it aside and start by memorizing our equivalent of the periodic table of elements."

As much as I may have wanted to avoid my normal tendencies, I fell into my usual pattern of becoming agitated when anyone told me the equivalent of 'be patient.' I told him that I followed him in theory, but that it seemed to me that I was ready for something that I could sink my teeth into (the actual phrase that I used), and if I had to start with memorizing tables or whatever, I might pack the whole thing in. He never reacted to my negative states with negativity of his own, just patience.

"We have to start off at the beginning," he said, "because there are some obstacles that you never even assumed existed. There are obstacles right here (he put his palm up to his face like there was a brick wall grafted to his nose). Get the picture? Obstacles right here at squish face level.

"You have some very wonderful aspirations, many people do. They don't always manifest them in beautiful ways, but people want specialness in life. So if you're really going to rediscover the lost connection to what keeps you alive, it's important you accept that you're going to have to start from the beginning."

"I wish it was as easy as that for me," I complained.

Ray wasn't about to give up without a fight. "Calm down a minute and let me give you an example," he proposed.

"If you're going to go to Paris, and you're in Miami, your first move has got to be in Miami. It's got to be there. You want to get to Paris, and Paris doesn't look like Miami -- it's nothing like Miami over there. You gotta cross an ocean, but you gotta start in Miami. If you live on Collins Avenue, your first instructions will contain the words Collins Avenue. I know that you don't want to think about Collins Avenue, you want to think about the Champs Elysees, but it doesn't matter. If you live on Collins Avenue and you want to go anywhere, including paradise, you gotta start off on Collins Avenue because that's where you are. It's not a good place or a bad place; it's your place. So you gotta back up and back up and back up, and that's what we're talking about."

He asked if I remembered a particular story that I had told him some time before. After repeated urging and cajoling, I begrudgingly told him the story again.

I was driving a Land Cruiser near Canyon de Chelly in Arizona. There was a river in front of me, and it was between me and our camp, which was on the other side of that river. I was very close to the other side, but I couldn't get there because the river was in the way. It didn't matter how close the other side was. I just couldn't get there. I had to drive for an hour up the road to the bridge, across the bridge, and down the road on the other side back to the camp. I sat there at the river for a long time before I agreed to drive all the way around. It was like worse than death. Anything but that. I didn't know what else to do, but what I didn't want to do was get back on that road and go all the way around.

He liked the story, and no doubt, sometime in the future would pull it out of me again. Telling it to him was good therapy. My resistance finally broke and I felt my impatience in the way that it should be felt -- as an obstacle that must be recognized, but one that can make big trouble only if it's taken too seriously.

He followed my story with some comments of his own. "You can't start from where you imagine yourself to be. It doesn't matter how close that imaginary place is to where you want to get to. Even though you can see the possibility of peace and harmony directly in front of you, you have to take a route that can be traveled by a human being. If you want to take on the experiment that we've been talking about, I mean *actually* take it on, then you're going to have to start from somewhere that's the beginning for you."

18

INNATE GOODNESS

I see... a new world stirring in the ruins, stirring clumsily but in hopefulness, seeking its lost and legendary treasures. And they will be here... hidden behind the mountains in the valley of the Blue Moon, perserved as by a miracle for a new Renaissance....

Lost Horizon, **James Hilton**

A person might assume that once this, what you might call, teacher/student relationship was clearly defined, that all other activities unrelated to that relationship would cease. That assumption couldn't be further from the way things went.

Actually, Ray and I became closer, more personal, and better friends. We continued to frequent poker tournaments together, in addition to involving ourselves in numerous other activities for fun and profit. Of course the main purpose of our relationship was always close at hand, and he continued to amaze me with his ability to make a lesson out of anything.

One morning quite early, there was a knock on my door. I was sure it was Ray, because he was the only person I knew that would show up in that way. I was in a semi-stupor but was still able to make my way to the door to let him in.

He came in, turned on the lights, and sat down. He encouraged me to splash some water on my face because he had to talk to me about something important. I did, and after I sat down opposite him, he started right off by suggesting that we take a little trip to meet some people that he knew.

In the past, we had gone many places together, and I had met a number of his acquaintances. On all of those occasions, these meetings were always casual and seemed almost incidental to whatever our main activity was, whether it be playing cards or whatever. It was too early for me to ask alert questions, so I just asked him where we were going. He rightfully ignored my stupid question and went on to say that since I was embarking on an endeavor that was by its nature a team sport, that I had better meet my team.

Needless to say, his "curveball" woke me up. I never really knew what he did when we weren't together, which was sometimes days and weeks. But for some reason, perhaps my self-importance, I had assumed that I was the only person that Ray talked to about these matters. I asked him what he meant by "meet my team," and he answered by telling me that he'd be back in an hour and we would go someplace where I could find out exactly what he meant. I of course agreed, and he left.

I hurky-jerkily twitched around my apartment trying to get ready to go, but really my haste was more purposeful than that. I was trying to quell the extreme anxiety that I felt caused by this "up-ing of the stakes" of the game that Ray and I had played for this past couple of years.

I was to meet other people that perhaps had met Ray in a similar way to the way that I had -- people that had heard similar talks and seen similar demonstrations of his skills. As much as I would like to conceal from you, the reader, the emotions that occupied me at the time, I feel it necessary to confess that there was, mixed in with my anxiety and anticipation, this ridiculously petty feeling of Ray's having been unfaithful to me. Can you believe that?

The hour passed. Ray returned, and we drove off to whatever was awaiting me. A "whatever" that couldn't have been more of a mystery had I been blindfolded and kidnapped. We drove into downtown San Diego and parked across from a medium-sized dark green house in a middle class neighborhood.

On our ride over, my head was spinning so fast that I never could get any questions out, and Ray never volunteered any information. When we parked, I finally asked, "What do we do now?" He told me to take it easy, and that if I had any questions I could ask them at any time that I wanted, inside or after.

We went in. I sat down in the living-room of the green house and Ray went into the kitchen, to, he said, "check out the contents of the refrigerator." There were six people in the house in addition to Ray and me. Although all of my attention was focused at trying to figure out who and what they were, I think it would be best to leave out both my observations and conclusions.

We did introduce each other, and I was the only newcomer. In other words, (ugh!) everyone knew each other except me. We spent about four hours there, and although I could not possibly recount everything that took place, there were several events that for me were particularly memorable. I will try to describe them accurately.

We eventually assembled in the living room and after two or three long silent minutes, during which I studied the threads of the carpet, Ray began to speak to us all.

"Children are beautiful. The younger they are, the more beautiful they are. Children are uncorrupted. The younger they are, the more uncorrupted they are. Children don't need methods to advance their consciousness. Methods are needed later on, only because these children have eventually become adults and have taken on protections to cover their beauty.

"In their view, in their peers' view, and in their parents' view, that protection is necessary for safety. But the coating that coats them for safety, coats their beauty as well. It covers them up and closes them up, so when you get to be as old as you guys are, you are completely closed. You're completely enclosed for your safety, and the beauty of that simple, vulnerable being has been lost.

"Grown-up people are also innately and naturally beautiful. I know that beauty is in there. So I've become what could be known as the best friend that you have in the world. Because I'm the only one that knows that there is something in you that's worth saving. Everyone else wants to do business with you. I only want to deal with the thing in you that's worth saving.

"I'm not interested in the preserving or the transcending of your personality. So I can joke with you at the most ludicrous times, because I'm not talking to that personality. I'm always trying to talk to that simple, beautiful being that you started off as. The one that eventually got covered up and covered up with all these obstacles, all stopped up by your protective covering, by your clouds.

"What's happened is that after awhile, you started thinking that all you are, are those clouds. And that beneath the deepest cloud there's a more firm cloud, and that's the cloud you want to set your feet on. You started off as innate goodness, and after a short time you got one step away, and then two steps away. At two steps away, you could still remember what was there in the beginning. But then you got three steps away and four steps away, and about the best you can remember is when you were one step away and how good it was then. Then when you get eight steps away and nine steps away, you remember the old days of five steps away. After awhile you get to be sixteen steps away, and the best moments that you can remember were when you were thirteen steps away, and your picture of paradise has become the days when you were nine steps away.

"Peace isn't any of those steps away. Peace is where it started, at innocent, beautiful, sweet, incorruptible, unpurchasable, innate goodness. Simple, not well-meaningness, not doing favorness, but innate goodness in its simplicity, like a baby. A baby means no one any harm; it can give pleasure, but it needs to take food. It doesn't make deals, 'Hey, I'll give you pleasure if you give me some food.' It just does its thing.

"You began as innate goodness and nothing has changed. You are still that innate goodness. It's in there, it has never gone anywhere. It has just been covered with protective devices.

"So, now I come along and tell you that if you can perform certain experiments, you can peek in under some of these layers. Maybe even get close enough that with some luck, you can start touching that innate goodness in yourself. But it's going to take peeling off some of this protective garbage that you have covered this sweet, beautiful thing with." Ray paused at length.

Not knowing the format of this get-together, I went back to my attempt at invisibility -- my rug studying. One of the six strangers was a lady in her thirties named Patricia who wore a lot of make-up. I didn't realize it at the time, but I had heard her speak at a lecture that Ray took me to long before.

After Ray paused, she asked a question, the details of which I have since forgotten, but I do remember the mood of it. She was "complaining," without accusing anybody by name, that she was having a hard time with methods of self-examination and confrontation that she considered harsh and negative. I thought her comments were petty and overly personal, but after listening attentively to Ray's response, I understood much more.

"Some people are so harsh," he began, "so dissatisfied with their faces, that they won't go out of their house without putting paint on them. None of *us* are dissatisfied with their faces. *They* are dissatisfied with their faces. How harsh can you get? When some people sit in a group, they won't say anything. They are so harsh with their thoughts, that they won't let anybody know what they're thinking. None of us could conceivably be so harsh with them that we wouldn't want to hear any of their thoughts. But they deny each of their thoughts. How harsh can you get? The same story with their feelings -- how harsh can you get?

"You say that my methods are harsh. *Your* method is the harshest possible method. It's total denial that there's anything beautiful within you whatsoever. A total denial marked by your insistance on lying, performing, acting, in every physical, intellectual, and emotional way. I can't imagine anything harsher than

184

that. There's no harshness whatsoever to what I put forth. I say, 'Hey, you're standing there sweating, take off your overcoat, take off your gloves, take off your hat, take off your sweater, take off something.' And you say, 'Too harsh!'

"You're the one who's being harsh. You're sitting there sweating, denying your whole life, not being able to say what you believe, not being able to look like you look, not being able to feel like you feel."

Patricia looked more than a little upset as a result of all this direct attention. I had no knowledge of the history of her problem, but it appeared that things were coming to a head after being hidden for some time.

"But it feels like you're all putting so much pressure on me," she said, her voice noticeably breaking.

"Pressuring you to what?" Ray broke in. "No one could put more pressure on you than you put on yourself. You are the ultimate pressure put-er on-er. You cause yourself to lie. I don't cause you to lie. Do you know the pressure you feel when you cause yourself to lie? It's really impossible to understand unless you take responsibility and see that you are the problem. No one is being harsh with you. You are the problem.

"What is that make-up doing on your face? It's okay to paint up for a party or an occasion, but you're a living statement that God didn't make you right. You're a denial of the existence of God. Not in your essential goodness, but in what has become of you. We each have what we've been given, and you're saying it's not good enough. You have the thoughts that you have, and you censor and protect them and only let them out in the safest places. Whether they're positive or negative, you have no right to keep such a close reign on your thoughts. Why would a person squelch their innate goodness? Do you think a person has a right to do that? I don't. That's like child abuse."

"I don't know if I have it in me to be as direct as you want me to be," she said as though beaten.

"Deep within you, there is an essential, simple beauty, a goodness, and everything that I'm steering you toward is to get to that goodness. It causes you trouble that you're in a situation geared toward removing some of those layers that obstruct your goodness. It causes you trouble because you're resisting it, trying to keep those layers on.

"It's like a tug of war. All you gotta say is -- 'Okay, tug of war is over. I lost.' And what would you lose? You'd lose one of the layers that obstructs your goodness. That's all I have in mind to take from you, one of the layers that obstructs your goodness, that's all."

"I can't help it," Patricia said impatiently. "It seems like all of you expect this to happen overnight. What do you want me to do? I'm doing my best!"

"How could it possibly be," Ray said calmly, "that we would be the reason for you to do anything? What's it got to do with us? Don't *you* want to get rid of the layers that obstruct your goodness? Because if you do, then you're in the right place.

"Yes, every once in awhile it's going to feel like something you've depended on is coming off. Because something you *did* depend on *is* coming off. It's going to be one of those layers that was obstructing your essential goodness, and it's going to be uncomfortable, but it's going to be good news.

"Listen, we've known each other for four years. If you're willing to take the heat that can sear off the covering to your innate goodness, fine. If that's not what you're into, also fine. But really -- get in or get out. We don't want to hear any more stories about your pain."

Up to this point, I was listening like this was a conversation between Ray and Patricia. I'd had so little experience with being in a group of people that I didn't realize that everything Ray was saying was as much for me as it was for her. This became clear to me when Karl, whom I had just met thirty minutes before, took advantage of a break in Ray's talking to look directly at me and ask, "Don't you think this applies to you too?"

My head snapped over in his direction and the words, "Who me?" were the only ones to jump out of my mouth. I had never before experienced being confronted in that way. My first reaction was embarrassment, followed almost immediately by a feeling that I couldn't have expected. I was in an exciting and dangerous situation, and it was thrilling. I imagined that all eyes were on me waiting for my response, but in actuality the baton had already passed on to Ray and he was continuing where he had left off, except he was facing toward me.

"That's not *you* that we're looking at," he said gently. "We're not revealing *you*. We're not embarrassing *you*. We're not seeing *you*. We're seeing another layer of covering. Maybe you could get rid of that one, maybe you could take it off."

He stretched his legs out in front of him and remained quiet for awhile. His eyes scanned the others, and I hoped that he was done with me. The intensity was scary, but it was magnetic as well. When my breathing approached normal , he resumed speaking (coincidentally I thought). It took a few moments for me to reconnect with his explanation.

"Think of how often some of you become defensive when asked a challenging question by one of the others. But once in a while, instead of defending yourselves, you say, 'I can't believe I was telling that lie the whole time.' Then everybody laughs and we go on to the next thing. It's like you've been oblivious, and haven't seen something about yourself -- then, all of a sudden, we all see it together, including you. Is it supposed to be a big traumatic embarrassing event? No! Everyone laughs and we're glad that it's behind us. Maybe it goes into the archives as a far-out story."

Was he referring to what had just happened to me? His eyes did glide by me on his last pass. I let it go and went back to his voice.

"So what's your story? Why lament? If you want to get to your essential goodness, then let's fry some covering! Let's do it! What's your alternative anyway? What are you going to do, keep pretending for the rest of your life?"

These last words were obviously rhetorical, but he still fell silent after them. I didn't know the rules and I didn't have a map, but I wanted to get into the game. I thought to myself, *What the hell! Here goes nothing!*

My voice broke in, sounding to me like it was coming from somewhere else in the room, and I asked, "What do you do when it's in your face and you want to run?" He accepted me as a player and took on my question -- and me as well.

"What happens at Nautilus when you start pumping iron?" he responded. "It hurts, but you tell yourself that this is what you're after. It would be good to tell yourself that now. I don't think that you have a good cheer for yourself. Why don't you try this cheer. *Is this me, or is this a covering to my innate goodness? This is a protective device. This isn't me. This is one of my deals, one of my stories. It hides me from the light. It protects me from what seems dangerous, but it hides me from myself. Is it worth it? Is it worth it?* Try that cheer for a while."

In his own unique way, Ray used this opportunity to introduce me to everyone. He asked if anyone else had anything to say in answer to my question. I guess I'd asked for it, and I figured that I was going to get it. Linda, a tallish blond lady in her thirties jumped on me -- I mean *it.*

"I'm in the middle of reading this book about the aftermath of a hydrogen bomb explosion," she began. "People couldn't breath the air, so they had to go live underground, deep in the earth. At some point they started to wonder if closing themselves up down there was worth it. You know, is it worth it to be wrapped up like this for fifty years, just because you still get food through a straw? Yeah, you're safe, but is it worth it? Maybe yes, maybe no, but at least you've got to ask the question."

It was a lot more painless than I had imagined, and a good answer as well. A few people took turns embellishing on Linda's science fiction story until Ray broke in.

"We live in a time when people are almost totally and completely numb. Lies are strewn everywhere, and people trade those lies, calling some of them 'truth.' One is a ten thousand degree lie and the other is a nine thousand degree lie. The person who tells the nine thousand degree lie feels superior, and what's more, he appears superior. You know what I mean? Like the difference between one politician and another. One of them seems honest and one of them seems dishonest. But they're both quadruple-digit liars. It's just that one of them is a little less of a liar than the other."

A young guy named J.J. asked, "It's hard to believe that this innate goodness exists in those politicians too -- does it?"

"Beneath the covering," Ray answered, "innate goodness exists within them and within us, and there's really nothing more worthwhile than to find it, or at least see how many layers you can remove in this lifetime."

The man sitting next to me had been silent for most of the meeting. Since our introduction an hour or so before, I had almost forgotten that he was there. His name was Phil, and he was older than I but younger than Ray.

His voice seemed strained as he said, "It's hard for me to feel responsible for having gotten so closed in. I think maybe that's why it's so hard for me to want to do anything about it."

Ray appeared to be looking equally at everyone as he proceeded to talk to Phil. "You gotta forget about your lament and forget about your whining and acknowledge that you dedicated a lot of your life to putting these layers on -- that's how they got there. You're not to blame, it's not your fault; you're not a bad person for it. You're this sweet little essence, this innate goodness, and you're covered with layers and layers of corruption.

"As they come off, you're going to feel a little bit more naked, a little bit more vulnerable than you're used to feeling. But if you can sit still for the operation, you'll find out that a little more grace came through that opening. Then after a few more coverings go, you'll feel more like shouting out, 'Wow! this is a wild and wonderful ride.'

"But not all in one shot. Let's not rush this -- a little at a time, a little at a time, and each time feeling more right. You know, there are some people that I've known for a long time, and they still haven't gotten into this cycle of things. They're still complaining about what's missing. They're still a victim and not a volunteer."

189

Ray asked each of us to say in our own words what our understanding was of what he had said. I would love to recount the various explanations, but I was so occupied with rehearsing (to myself of course) what I would say when it was my turn, that I hardly heard anything of what anybody said. Maybe not exactly the lesson Ray had in mind, but a lesson just the same. Oh well!

After a lengthy time spent having each person talk, we spent an even lengthier time eating some outrageous lasagna that Karl had made. Overeating helped calm me down (for better or for worse) enough to allow me to learn some of the details of the others' lives.

Phil was actually the owner of the green house, and Barnett had lived there for about a year. I liked the way that Karl moved about in Phil's kitchen. They all seemed to feel very much at home there.

After the dishes found their way in and out of the sink, we convened in the living-room. Before Ray had a chance to start talking, Phil asked him, "You seem to find it so easy to talk about these defects, these coverings. How do you do it?"

Ray smiled knowingly like he was going to say something profound. "It's easy -- they're yours, they're not mine." Ray enjoyed his joke so much that it took him a couple of minutes before he could go on. "But seriously," he continued, "you gotta hang in there and remember that what you're trying to uncover is what's beautiful in you, what you're *really* like.

"The only reason I can do what I do, is because when the smallest thing is uncovered, that pureness comes shining through a little more. It's not because I like to 'get people.' You know, I say something and you admit it, and I think, 'Yeah! All right! I got you.' No! I didn't get you. I helped you make one little crack in that covering, and now there's a little light coming through.

"You have to learn to hold still, because the moment those coverings feel threatened, they'll start to writhe in their attempt to get out of the light. They'll try with blame, with feeling bad, or even by saying, 'I'm confused.' You pay attention, and you'll see all that writhing and more."

"I think I know what you mean by hold still," Linda said, "and I even think I can do it some. But I know I have to get better. Are there any tricks that can speed up the process?"

"Anyone know any tricks?" Ray said half joking, half not.

"I think Alcoholics Anonymous has a good idea," Karl contributed. "I went to a meeting a few years ago, of course just to see what it was like. Their idea is to be honest about what's going on, like saying, 'Look what I've become.' They want you to look in the mirror at yourself -- you've just lost your job, you have a hangover, and you're vomiting. Get a good look, this is what you've become. I think you really have to learn to hold still to do that."

"Great example!" Ray applauded. "It's the same idea. That's why you have to sit still -- so you can see yourself as you are, and look at what you've become. Like you see on a TV drama, someone's arguing with their kids and they end up hitting them. Then they say, 'Oh no! Look what I've done. This has gone too far.'

"Well you've also gone too far. You're too separated. You've become too alienated from your essence, from your co-creations, and from your purpose, and that's no good."

"It seems so much easier to hear this from you (Ray)," Karl said. "It's much harder for us to point this kind of thing out to each other."

"I understand," Ray said. "It's difficult, but it's very important that you operate as a team and are willing to badger each other. But you must remember that you're not badgering the beautifulness of a person -- you're badgering that person's denial of their beautifulness. All that has to be relinquished is our denial that this innate goodness exists within us.

"So when you say to someone, 'What are you thinking?' and they experience that question as a challenge, they must be denying that they were thinking something. They must be denying that they had something to say. They were denying that they had feelings. They were denying that they existed. By asking them, you're saying, 'Hey, I see that you exist. I don't want to deny your existence. Throw yourself in the middle. Say what you gotta say. Do your life!'

"Some of you say that's harsh. 'Do you have to tell it to me like that?' But what are *you* doing? You're strangling yourselves! I'm saying, 'Hey, c'mon, take your hands away from your throat.' And as I'm trying to help you take your hands away from your throat you say, 'Do you have to do it so roughly? Can't you ask me if I would please take my hands away from my throat?' Well yeah, I could say that. If that'll work, I'll say that for sure. But then, what you usually say is, 'I didn't have my hands on my throat.'"

One of the others who hadn't said much, a young athletic-looking guy named Barnett, brought up that he never knew if what he observed about the rest of us was accurate enough to mention. He wasn't very smooth verbally, and it took a lot of patience to let him get it all out. What I got from what he said was that he didn't like to be confronting, so he was looking for reasons to avoid it. I thought that maybe Ray would say the same thing, but his answer was actually very gentle and supportive. I guess he saved the razor for wise asses like myself.

He said, "You have to be prepared to get in there and mix it up with each other and not be so careful about it. I think there have been little signs of willingness to do that, but it's not nearly enough. It's especially critical that you work as a team, because it'll start to happen that you'll feel that mirror in front of you. And when you do, there has to be somebody there to say, 'You gotta hang in there. Don't bolt now. You're getting a face full, but it's not of what's true and beautiful in you.'

"I'm talking about this now because it could be inspiring to you to recognize that in your interactions with one another, you are trying to get at something good, not something bad. You're not trying to nail the person in their evilness. You're trying to uncover that goodness beneath it. Even when you *are* trying 'to get' each other, it's only a covering to what you really want to do. Sure, I'm always after you, pointing out what's wrong with what you're doing, but I'm not criticizing your innate goodness. It's not criticizable. I'm saying there's an obstacle that you're putting forth, and if you want to have it, I guess you're going to have it. But I can see something beautiful beneath it, something worth uncovering."

After a short period of discussion, Ray asked me to wait for him in the car and he would be out shortly. I was removed from the feelings of awkwardness that one might have in a situation like that. I went out to the car, not even considering the usual departing politenesses.

I had just been part of a new, exciting, and purposeful interaction. What had transpired had taken me to a place of understanding that I had never been before. I strongly felt the presence, however buried, of my own innate goodness. I was prepared, I thought, to do whatever was necessary to uncover it.

The only criticism I had of what had taken place was what I perceived as an extreme amount of focus on petty personal stuff. I asked him about this when he got in the car, and his answer drove with us through the streets of San Diego.

"Once you know how to put your foot, or even a toe down on your own heart, you can proceed and be pretty sure things will stay on course -- but what course? Well, if you eventually want to see how it *all* is, which pretty much takes everything into account, the best course is to learn to see yourself more clearly as *you* are. You gotta start with how *you* are.

"Now years ago, when I got started with all this, I was attracted to the idea of seeing how *it* all is, without seeing how *I* am. It's cleaner, you know. But after a short while, I started to get the idea that there was something evasive going on. It wasn't going to work, because here I was taking this garbage dump that I called me, and trying to get the proper bus transfers to work my way up to the kingdom of the divine -- and arrive there as a garbage dump.

"Of course I didn't think about it like that, but that's what I was trying to do. It was an impossibility. I wanted to know *it*, as it was, but I didn't want to know *me,* as I was. It took a little time, but slowly I recognized that the way to know *it*, has to start with knowing *me*."

It seemed to me that some of the people I had just met in the green house weren't strong enough to go through the kind of uncovering that he was suggesting, innate goodness or not. I told him what I thought and then asked, "Isn't there something a person can do to gain strength -- then take on the heavy stuff later?"

"Some time ago," he said, "some friends and I bought this property in Oregon. It had two old houses on it. Before we bought the place, the plumbing drains had gotten stopped-up in one of the houses, but the people living there kept using it anyway. I don't know how long that went on, but when we finally moved in, it was really gross. Gross to the extreme.

"Now my idea for getting this place wasn't to shovel shit out of the toilets. My idea was for us to live in these houses, but there was no way that anything could take place until after that clean-up took place. Think about it. We couldn't really say, 'We'll get to that later.'

"Picture yourself in that position. You couldn't have said that either. You *couldn't* get to that later. There are some things that you have to deal with now. In some situations you have no choice, because the obstacle will obstruct anything that's going to follow -- it doesn't go away. It can change its form, but it won't go away."

"I understand," I said, realizing that there was no escape from this one. "But I really hate this petty personality shit."

"I don't like dealing with the ins and outs of the personality any more than I liked that episode. It's grubby, it's sticky, and it's tedious. That's the minimum. If you've been *really* successful at fooling people, it can be even worse than grubby, sticky, and tedious. So that's the down side. Think of the up side. If there were really some extraordinarily bright light on the other side of these clouds of fear and deception, wouldn't it be worth the effort to find a way to dissolve them?

"Disconnectedness, turmoil and covered turmoil, protective devices, these are all things that a person has to recognize. You'll never know anything real if you're oblivious to the cause of all your frantic scrambling."

I think I was surrendering to the necessity that he was proposing, in theory at least. A giddiness overcame me. I giggled through my description of what it was like when you get started on a trip, and the first thing you have to do is go down to the corner and get gas. You're travelling half-way across the country and you want to get started; you don't want to start with a stop.

"I was hoping that I could stop later," I said, summing up my sentiments.

He joined in with my laughing. I really felt like we were comrades in arms.

"It's unfortunate," he said, "that even on a deep, meaningful, internal, spiritual journey, you have to stop and take care of such banal business. I'll tell you this though, once you're able to cover that step, from then on it's cruising. Because if you can go through what's necessary to see yourself as you are, there is nothing that will cause you to say after that, 'God, that's really hard.' Because seeing yourself as you are -- that's what's hard. No, it's not equally hard for everyone, but it *is* hard for everyone."

I was so absorbed in his words that I hadn't realized that we were already parked in front of my house. I felt like an actor is supposed to feel after an opening night. It seemed like I would stay up all night winding down, and I certainly didn't want to do that alone. I told Ray how I felt and asked if he'd come in for a while. My other option would be to walk the streets for a few hours, get exhausted, and then I'd probably be able to sleep. He declined my invitation and suggested that I try a hot bath instead.

He said he wanted to explain how the process that he developed had come about, and maybe tomorrow would be a good time to do that. I calmed down a little, knowing that I would see him the next day, and we said good night.

Of course, as things happen, my priorities weren't as clear the following morning. As I walked around my apartment, the representatives of other facets of my life registered their votes for my time. It was actually three days before Ray and I had the talk that he had suggested. I realized that in his wisdom, he mentioned getting together the next day only to ease my departure. He knew that in reality, the other forces that moved me would have their say in the morning.

He waited for me to call him and when I finally did, a little sheepishly I might add, he proceeded talking to me about getting together as though it had been the night before that we had parted. He told me that he would be at his favorite local poker room, and that I should come by any time that it suited me.

I arrived in mid-afternoon to find Ray enmeshed in a special game that happened only once a month or so. It was a pot-limit game, which means that at any bet, on any card, you can bet as much money as there is in the whole pot. It's more a game of guts than it is a game of cards, and I personally have avoided such contests.

This type of game was an "event" at the casino, and I joined the small crowd watching over the players' shoulders. Ray had a huge stack of chips in front of him, and I hoped that meant he was winning. It also could have meant that he had bought that huge stack trying to get even for what he had lost.

When he spotted me in the crowd, he sent me a huge smile, and I deeply appreciated the inclusion. He took a break a few minutes later and suggested that we get some air. We took our traditional walk around the block, and after talking about the game (he was winning a bundle), he launched into his description of how his method came about.

"I've spent time studying methods that I was taught and developing additional methods while working with people. It's very difficult starting off in this area of clouds -- what I call the protective devices of the personality.

"I developed the practice of using myself as a guinea pig, because I'm always there. Everywhere I go, there I am. So if I felt like checking something out at two in the morning, I didn't have to make a phone call. By using myself in this way, I discovered more and more about the subtleties of these protective devices, until I knew so much about them that it was overwhelming. Paying attention to how we deal with our constant fear can make life very difficult. Without the right attitude, it can be really sickening to witness a thousand different styles of a nervous laugh.

"When I began to work with other people, I started off with these protective devices. It was very difficult, because very few people, if any, wanted to deal with them. Sure, somewhere in them they had the feeling that they wanted to know something beyond ordinary life. But how were they to avoid the attitude of, 'Yeah, I could think about how fucked up I am, but that's too depressing.'

"Well, since I understood this attitude, I knew then, and I know now, that this type of observation has to be done very differently than the way we usually observe. Each person has to discover in himself, the capacity for seeing himself 'as he is,' without flinching.

"I came to the conclusion that although nothing was going to make this step pleasant, still, some new attitude had to be developed that would allow a person to discover the obstacles that are there, without falling into the depression that usually comes with seeing defects about yourself."

I must mention here, that it never ceased to amaze me how Ray could change the focus of his attention without losing any enthusiasm or dynamic attitude. Just a short while before, he was playing high stakes poker, an extremely taxing and highly concentrated activity. Effortlessly, he had left all that behind, and he was talking to me about the development of consciousness, as though I was the only other person in the world -- remarkable!

"So what happened when you came to that conclusion?" I asked

"Unfortunately, nothing. Nobody could feel the perspective, nobody could see the humor. It didn't work. It was tense and pressureful, people got paranoid and self-conscious, you know

197

what I mean? People became overly careful of what they were doing. It became clear to me that examining the protective devices of the personality was not the first step -- even though it seemed like it should be the first step. You know, identify and remove the clouds that obscure whatever's on the other side, in order to feel Love, know God, know Truth, walk on water, all that good stuff.

"I saw that in the way we were proceeding, there was no way for that to happen. Some quality or capacity had to first be developed or discovered that could absorb this information, that could withstand this barrage of yuckiness and not take it personally. So I backed up again. I don't want to go through the whole sequence, but I backed up a few times, till I found the place where it was possible to begin."

I certainly understood his explanation, but I found it hard to think of myself as so sensitive that I needed all this training to see a few unpleasant things about myself. I asked him if there were some people (me) that, without all the preliminaries, had the ability to see these defects without flinching. "I might be fooling myself, but I think I could handle it. Hit me with your best shot," I joked.

He spoke calmly, as though talking to an idiot. "It takes a lot of patience to do what I discovered is necessary, though right now you think that may not apply to you. But my experience has shown me unfailingly, that there are many ways of 'handling it.' You might be able to handle it, but you won't see it as it is."

In the period that followed that surprise meeting at the green house in downtown San Diego, I got to know these six other people that were to comprise my "team." It was not an easy time for me. On numerous occasions, when I made attempts to ask questions of Ray, he referred me to one or more of these six. I knew that my independent and elitist attitude was being challenged, but knowing that didn't seem to make things any easier. They were certainly nice enough people, but I had such a long history of being a loner, that it was hard for me to incorporate anyone into my world that wasn't at least a Ray.

19

HOW ABOUT SOLITUDE ?

It knew that it had come home... but it knew also
that it could not stay. Beyond this moment lay another birth,
stranger than any in the past.

2001 A Space Odyssey, **Arthur C. Clarke**

There is a monthly magazine for almost every activity in which Americans are involved, and poker playing is no exception. It's simply called *Poker Player* and is published in Las Vegas. It can either be subscribed to or obtained at many poker rooms. In addition to feature articles of interest to devotees of the game, there are announcements of future tournaments as well as results of past ones. I read it cover to cover, mostly looking for the mention of players that I know, and primarily amongst those players, of course myself. I have also found the magazine useful for finding medium-sized tournaments at somewhat out of the way locations -- ones that the top pros would not bother to attend for lack of convenience. I have had most of my success at these kinds of tournaments.

It was October and just starting to cool off in the Southwest. I was sitting in a smokey, though well air conditioned casino in San Diego reading the current issue of *Poker Player*. A small advertisement about an upcoming tournament caught my attention. It was in Seattle, a place where I had once lived and to which I had often thought of returning.

The next time I saw Ray, I mentioned reading about this upcoming tournament, and asked if he had any interest in going there. He made some comments that I don't clearly remember. Something about what he called 'compartmentalization,' and also that he knew how to make use of most any circumstance, so he didn't have to be that careful about where he did or didn't go.

We agreed that I'd check it out further, and that if it still looked good to me, we'd fly up there. As he walked away, he casually asked me, without waiting for an answer, if I thought that being away from San Diego for a couple of weeks would negatively affect my team relationships. Recently I had been increasing the frequency of my contacts with the six people who were at that first meeting, but my attitude toward them was still very far from anything that could even be loosely described as a team spirit.

That night I phoned him -- partly because I found this dangling question of his disquieting, and partly because I actually was interested in hearing more of what he had to say on the subject of 'needing a team.' He suggested that we get together the next night with the other six, if they were available, because what he had to say would surely concern all of us. Ray suggested that I arrange for a meeting at my apartment because we had never met there before, and it could help me to avoid the pitfalls of (he used that word again) 'compartmentalization.'

The next night, we all gathered around my six foot round coffee table with Ray, who showed up with a big bag of pecans. He dumped them out in the middle of the table, and after about five minutes of cracking and crunching he began to talk.

"I've done a lot of traveling in the last, say, twenty years. On some of those trips I've gone with a bunch of people. I went on one trip to climb in the Andes with about fifteen people, and another with about a dozen into the Sahara. I'm telling you this because I've lived and moved around with groups of people, and I've seen what's possible if they have a common aim, one that helps the separateness between them decrease. Incredible things can happen.

"None of those trips could have been possible without that 'working together' happening. Maybe sometimes you can't see yourself as being part of a team, but my perception of this sport of 'finding truth' is that it's a great team sport. And as long as the quality is maintained, the bigger the team the better. It's my straight away experience, opinion, and conviction that anybody who says, 'Mother, I can do it myself,' has just never fooled with the realities of the challenge."

Ray picked up a couple of pecans and signalled with a movement of his head that we should feel free to eat the nuts while he talked.

"I was in a store on the way over here and got some of these nuts. I don't usually see pecans around here. They remind me of Texas. It's been a while since I ate a pecan from the shell, or ate them at all. I was looking at these things trying to remember how breakable the shell was. I thought I'd squeeze one and see. I didn't remember if it was like a walnut, or which variety of hardness it was. I was looking really closely while I was squeezing this pecan. I could tell that the shell was thin, but as thin as the shell was, I still couldn't break it by squeezing it in my hand. So I tried this trick that I learned for breaking walnuts, which are of course much harder. I picked up another nut and I squeezed them together in one hand, one against the other. Well, they broke real easily that way; they both broke. The shells were really thin but it didn't matter. I couldn't break only one in my hand."

Ray didn't have to suggest that we try it. The next few minutes were spent trying everything from Karate to isometrics. When the grunting and laughing died down, he continued, "You see, you can discuss how you think it should be, or how you would like it to be. You can think that the way that it's going doesn't feel right to you. You can discuss it, you can think about it, you can argue about it -- it doesn't matter. There are some things that it takes more than one person to do.

"Now in the world of things that man creates, very few such restrictions exist. If a person has powerful determination, he can perform an act alone that was originally intended for more than one person, like sailing alone around the world in a boat that was built to be operated by five people. But on issues where man has not been consulted, when the law says it takes two, like to make a baby, then it takes two.

"Well, the removal of these clouds, these obstacles to consciousness, can't be done by a person alone. It takes a team. That's it, that's all, that's the law. Man didn't set it up that way and man can't change it. It takes a team. It takes a male and a female to make a baby, whether you like it or not, and it takes more than one person to remove the obstructions that we've been talking about. One person can't do it alone."

As reasonable as Ray's message promoting working as a unit seemed to be, it didn't alleviate this tantrum-like squirming taking place in my stomach. I didn't want it to be true. It was too restricting, too definite, too absolute. If I truly accepted the implications of his words, it would mean my life would have to take a different course. I had no clarifying questions to ask; it was all right there in front of me. In fact, *they* were all right there in front of me.

Linda made some comments as though she was reading my mind and then speaking as my representative. She wondered about the books that had been written about people who have gone off on their own and sat under trees until enlightenment came to them. It seemed to her that sometimes teammates kept her back, and she harbored thoughts that she could do better on her own, with Ray's help of course. She did add that she knew she had this independent streak, and that she was never really comfortable around peers.

Ray listened to her carefully, as did I. I wouldn't have known how to answer, but fortunately for us, he did.

"It's an extreme advantage to be around people who think that it's okay to be foolish, when so much of the world is demanding that you be polished. Being honest is rough if you're around people that are demanding that you be smooth. They're acting, and they want you to act also, so as not to blow the show.

"I can't conceive of how this removing of obstacles can be done without a team. So I can tell anybody who feels like they're fiercely individualistic, that I've got no ideas for them whatsoever. God bless them and I wish them well.

"I grew up in New York, and I don't think there are more fierce individualists anywhere than there are in that city. In New York, everybody thinks everybody else is full of shit. That's about as fierce an individual as you can get. When you grow up there, you learn that everything is edible in some way or other. It's like, 'What can I make out of you?' You know, that's fierce individualism. And somehow or other, I became part of a team sport."

Linda broke in. "But how about solitude?"

"If you mean, is there natural solitude?" Ray clarified, "Yes! Absolutely! But there is no natural alienation. A person is, in himself, a complete world. But an interesting question is, how many people that choose to be by themselves are choosing that because they're complete? The answer is -- nobody you know, and nobody you've ever known.

"In my opinion, so much can take place, but one person alone can't do it. If a person loves what they might call their independence, then that person wouldn't even want to talk to me, because they're too busy loving their independence. I know people like that. You probably do too. It's too confronting for them to listen to somebody else who supposedly knows something that they don't know. Especially if it's about a subject that's not strictly tangible."

"What do you mean by a tangible subject?" Karl asked.

"If I was talking about astronomy," Ray answered, "it would be no problem for that independent person to accept that I know more than they do. That doesn't challenge their independence. But the possibility that another person could know more about being a human being, that's very confronting. So somebody who wants to be separate and special, more than they want to remove the obstacles that keep them from feeling the magnet of life, will resist the idea that it takes a team.

"What I'm saying is growth without increasing self-importance, removing obstacles without becoming bigger yourself, seeing the world as it is -- to achieve these things requires a team. There may be those that would disagree, but my experience has shown without exception, that is the case."

I guess Ray's answer didn't placate Linda's doubts. She requested that he clarify just how a person finds a team and knows when she's found one, and also that the one she's found is really her team. I guess that Linda wasn't too pleased with the rest of us. Ray made a joke about her high standards and then went on to talk about how a person finds her team.

"So, how does a person find their team? Well, all the dedicated chess players in San Diego found each other. How did they do it? Think about this for a minute. There are maybe a hundred good chess players in San Diego, and somehow, many of them often find themselves together in the same place at the same time. Now this city has hundreds of thousands of people. But even with that number, these chess players are still able to find each other. I don't think ads in the newspaper are the key, I don't think that's what brought them together. The chess club didn't bring them together. They found their way to each other. It might have taken longer if there were no newspapers and no chess club, but sooner or later, a person who really loves to play chess will find his way to another person who also loves to play chess.

"It happens. It happens in proportion to how much playing chess means to you. If you have that interest consistently, then when you meet somebody you won't be able to hide it. You'll tell them that you have that interest and you'll act like someone who has that interest. The word gets around. You all met me, you know. The wonderful thing is, when you're being who you are, after a while you look around, and you discover that you've found your family."

Before parting company from our 'family,' Ray suggested we bring some lightness and humor into the gathering, and of course he had an idea of just the way to do it.

Of the seven of us, Ray had only met one other than me at a poker game. The rest crossed paths with him through various other circumstances. We all knew that Ray had been a professional poker player, since he used analogies from card playing fairly often. Ray's idea for a little levity involved a deck of cards, which he took out of his pocket as he proceeded to explain a poker game that we were about to play together.

"This game is called *Lumfutz*. At least that's what we called it when I was thirteen. Everybody gets one card, and without looking at it, you stick it on your head facing out toward the other players. Just one card and you push it on your forehead till it sticks to whatever oil or perspiration happens to be there. If you're not greasy enough you have to hold it with your hand.

"Now get the idea, because you don't have to know how to play poker to understand this. Each of you has a card on your forehead. It's facing forward toward the other players, so you know the other peoples' cards but you don't know your own. The person with the highest card remaining after the betting is over wins the hand.

"Let's say you have a three on your head, a very low card, but you're looking out at your opponents, and some other player has a four. So you start betting. You think that you're a winner because they've got a very low card, but the other players are looking at you and trying not to laugh, because you have a three and you're betting that you're a winner. Take an even more extreme situation -- you both have two's on your forehead, and are both trying to play it cool because each of you thinks that he can't lose because your opponent has the lowest possible card."

After gathering as many pennies as we could find and dividing them up, the game began. I knew there was supposed to be some kind of lesson hidden in this game, but the amount of laughter that was produced was payoff enough for me. We played for about an hour, after which Ray said that he wanted to go and needed me to drive him home. On the way home, he talked about Lumfutz and our team.

"It's powerful to have a support group, because you get to see so much. If you're alert, you can recognize that some other guy is exactly like you. If you think he's not, then you won't get much. But people are really very similar, even though sometimes it's real hard to see."

"How is it that everyone on the team is supposed to benefit?" I asked. "I don't get that part. From my vantage point, it looks like some get and some don't."

"Unfortunately, you're right! But that's only because the ones that don't, aren't committed to the team. The one's that are, have a great advantage.

"For example, one time *you* might be looking foolish, not knowing of course how foolish you're looking. But *we* get to see. This time it isn't for *your* enlightenment, it's for *our* enlightenment. The next time we have to reciprocate by allowing ourselves to look foolish, and then you can get enlightened. It's hard to tell if your fly is open -- you're up here, you don't see it. It's hard to tell if your shirt is buttoned unevenly, because you're up here; you don't get to see it. It's hard to see if dirt is sliding down your nose, because you're looking past it. You don't get to see, others get to see. But remember, whoever does whatever they do, no matter what it looks like, no matter how foolish they sound or how much you assume that you know better -- they're probably just like you. If you remember that, then you really can click, especially if you work with a team."

When I dropped him off, he agreed that if I would make the arrangements, we would meet the following weekend for our trip to Seattle.

20

LITTLE DEATHS

*The Grand Old Trout usually shows
very little interest in watching the tombs being
put in. I guess because he has seen so many before.*

In Watermelon Sugar, **Richard Brautigan**

I've heard a lot of negative attitudes and opinions about airports and airplanes, but for me they're always exciting. I guess it feels like the possibilities for adventure are being increased. We flew out of Los Angeles on a non-stop to Seattle. We were assigned the window and isle seats with no one in the middle. I expected that Ray would probably take this opportunity to give a lengthy explanation on some subject or other, but instead he took the window seat and throughout the flight seemed to be engrossed in whatever he saw out there. It was typical of his aliveness.

I noticed that all the other window seat occupants were either reading, talking, or busying themselves with something. The few times that I attempted to start a conversation, he answered with a word or two (not his usual style). On my final attempt, he said that he never got enough of this perspective, and wanted to take full advantage of it.

As we landed, the flight attendant made the standard announcements and added in some humor. She said, "Please wait till the plane comes to a complete stop and the captain turns off the seatbelt sign before leaving your seat and moving about the cabin, so you won't suffer the embarrassment of falling down and looking clumsy in front of your fellow passengers." The announcement got a good laugh from the passengers, and was also effective in breaking Ray's silence. As we de-planed (what a ridiculous term), and through to the time we hit the freeway in our rental car, we talked about the phenomena of embarrassment.

"I once had a friend who was studying to be a stock-broker," he began. "This was maybe ten years ago. He knew a little about stocks, probably just a bit more than you and I know. So he got whatever license was necessary, and got a job in a stock brokerage business. You don't have to know much to do that. They don't pay you; you work on commission. They gave him a desk in a small office, and the man at the next desk happened to be writing a book. They got to be buddies, eating buddies, drinking buddies, some kind of buddies. Well the book that the office mate was writing became a best-seller about the money crisis. I don't remember the title.

"At the end of his book, he wrote a few lines that read something like, 'If you're interested in penny mining stocks, this is the person to call,' and he gave my friend's name, who, by the way, knew hardly anything about that stock specialty whatsoever.

"Believe it or not, my friend started getting calls and letters of inquiry, so he figured he'd better hit the library quick! He found a few books about penny mining stock speculation, read them, and became what's presently thought of as 'an expert.' Within six months he was on his way to riches and fame, publishing a newsletter of his own on penny mining stocks."

Ray always encouraged me to interrupt him if I was not following his ideas, or if I had any questions. This stockbroker story was interesting enough, but I was having trouble relating it to anything that had been happening. I told him that he was losing me, but he assured me that if I stuck with his explanation it would soon make sense.

He went on. "Herman Hesse once called this culture of ours the 'Feuilleton Age.' That's a nice way of saying the 'half-assed age.' An authority in our day is someone who studies a subject for three months through adult education at the community college, then is accepted as having an expert opinion. This is the age of mediocrity that has misplaced the concept of mastery, except maybe in the fields of high technology.

"Since the forces and energies that maintain life recognize our half-assedness in this age, they must understand that if we're going to receive help, they gotta come a hell-of-alot closer to where we are. They gotta make it easier for us, because none of us have the ability, in this Feuilleton Age, to jump any more than a little bit off the ground. Grace is going to have to come down a little closer to where we live our lives, and to how we live our lives.

"I'm saying this because at one time people made tremendous sacrifices. But now, because of the nature of our times, you know, the half-assed age, we might have to learn to take advantage of experiencing in microcosm, the lessons that a person from another time could learn only through great sacrifice.

"It's like a teacher going into a classroom and telling the kids that they're going to be learning something new, but the kids are too bored and restless to listen. The next week the teacher has to come back with some pretty pictures and movies to help them get into the subject, because he wants the kids to learn something. The teacher doesn't want to defeat them, he wants them to succeed.

"So if the forces and energies that maintain life want us to succeed in drawing closer, they're going to have to recognize the peculiarities of the time that we live in. Certainly if they don't want us to succeed, we sure ain't gonna draw closer whatever we do."

I started to interrupt him to let him know that I was falling farther and farther behind, but as I voiced the first word or two, he smiled and held up his hand for me to be quiet.

"So now -- what has this to do with 'wait till the airplane stops so you won't fall and be embarrassed in front of your fellow passengers?' The stewardess meant it as a joke -- but who wouldn't want to avoid looking clumsy in front of others?

"Embarrassment is one of those experiences that everyone is familiar with. Some people are embarrassed often, some not so often, but embarrassment is a known thing. If you're really cool, it merely means that you make sure you don't often get into circumstances where you might be embarrassed. But in the right (or wrong) set of circumstances, everyone can be embarrassed, and everyone has been embarrassed.

"Of course, we have ways of dealing with that embarrassment to make it go away, to make it like it's not happening. You have a lot of ways of being on guard, but still, you're always on the verge of being embarrassed. This embarrassment is lurking around every corner, and you have no idea how many actions you perform so as not to fall victim.

"The confusion arises because you're usually so successful at avoiding embarrassment, that you find it hard to believe that this avoidance is your moment to moment companion. What you don't realize is how busy you are, and just what it takes to be as good of an avoider as you've become. You're spending all that energy being on guard, and you don't have time for anything else.

"Embarrassment is an experience that feels like a little bit of death. Just a teeny bit, but like a little bit of death just the same. It feels like you'd do anything to avoid it because the loss seems really tremendous."

Finally, his last remarks were successful at bringing me alongside of the conversation. I realized the gravity of what he was talking about, and how the idea of the Feuilleton Age fit in. I had a flash of something that had happened in his presence, and I told him about my memories of the event.

"Remember the last day of the spring tournament in Reno last year? We were hanging around the casino getting ready to leave, and that creepy guy who won the L.A. tournament came over to talk to you. After you guys talked for awhile, he asked me what I thought of the poker games in England. I made up some opinions, thinking that was all I had to do to shut him up and get rid of him. Then it turned out that he had played all over Europe, and he started to ask for more specifics.

"I felt like I was really on the spot. One possibility was that I could have said, 'I've never really played in England; I made it all up.' But I couldn't possibly have mustered the guts to do that, especially considering what a creep that guy was. Or I could have started to bullshit more, but then I would have been in danger of getting in deeper and getting caught.

"That was one terrible feeling. At that moment it felt like I had lost the superbowl; it felt like everything was lost. This incredible scrambling went on in my head about how to recoup. How can I get back my footing? How can I work it out so that I'll stop sliding down this ramp into oblivion?"

Ray found this story so hilarious that I thought he was going to ask me to tell it again. He said that there couldn't be a better example of what he was talking about. After poking fun at me in some way or other that I can't (or won't) remember right now, he went on talking about embarrassment.

"Embarrassment is a moment of being out of control. It could be something momentary and even very small, when something happens where the control that you've learned to count on all of your life is suddenly not available. Even if you're out of control for one second, that moment seems like a moment of death, because death represents the ultimate of being out of control. It's really the only situation we know that is out of control for sure.

"The reason that I'm talking so much about embarrassment is because with our Feuilletonistic limitations, studying this phenomenon can be uniquely useful. Embarrassment is a microcosm of death, a 'little death,' yet a person can study it and still remain

211

light. It can be humorous, it can even be delightful, and we can all laugh about it.

"Unfortunately, embarrassment is rarely any of these, because we live our lives as though life and death actually were tied to so many things that happen to us. There's almost nothing that we take a chance on, almost nothing. It's all tied up with what we imagine as risking life and death. Not so much a physical life and death, but one that is almost more real to us than the physical one. The life and death of our image of ourselves, and what other people think of us. A life and death of the impressions that we make on other people, and what we feel we have to do in order that others approve of us. We proceed with the attitude that if we're not successful at making these impressions, it's all going to fall apart, and all will be lost, and there will be nothing left."

That brought up an interesting question to me. So since I had learned that it's better to speak up than to keep it to myself, I said to him, "That brings up an interesting question. How can a person take the chances necessary to see if there's anything there other than his own 'keeping it all going,' if that person looks on an experiment, of any kind, in terms of a life and death risk?" I think Ray liked it when I took on the part of an equal in these conversations. I liked it too.

"I have discovered," he responded, "that there are small ways in which a person can proceed with this experiment of seeing what might be on the other side of our frantic flailing. These ways are so small and non-threatening that there is a possibility of witnessing them with perspective and humor.

"As I said, at some time in the past, in order to discover his true self, a person might have had to give away all his possessions and change his life radically and traumatically. In our time, not only would such circumstances be traumatic, but so traumatic that our efforts wouldn't be sustainable, and besides, nobody is going to do that anyway.

"So if the forces that are operating us have in mind for this 'drawing closer' to take place at all, then those forces are going to have to give those of us who live in this age of indulgence a little more to work with, you know, cut us some slack.

"So embarrassment is actually a gift from those benevolent forces to us, and studying it is one of those ways that you can learn what you need to learn about yourself without having to go through the pains and pangs of depravity, torture, depression, and self-flagellation.

"I think I need an example," I interrupted, "of how embarrassment equals this slack we're being cut."

"But of course," he said, with a make-believe French waiter's accent. "I'm talking about little embarrassments, like yawning at an importune time, scrunching up your face trying to hide the fact that you're yawning because you don't want to be seen as a yawner. But you are a yawner; didn't you just yawn? Maybe you're bored. So what, so you're bored. What would you really lose if you were caught being bored?"

The image of a person distorting his face so as not to be caught yawning was funny enough, but the faces that Ray was making to imitate that person caused us both to break up laughing.

When I regained my composure, he continued. "You're laughing now and that's why I'm saying that this is a studyable example of the experience of death, in microcosm -- in embarrassment. A person can actually learn so much about death and keep laughing. You don't have to tempt the fate of physical death like at one time people did to experience loss of control.

"To experience the microcosm of death is more efficient, because if it doesn't go well, you can do it again the next day. In the old days you had one shot, and if it didn't work out, someone else had to carry the ball from there. What a great advantage it is to see some very necessary big things in microcosm, and still be able to get what's needed to proceed to the next step, while staying relatively light.

"I'm not saying it always goes like that, but that it *can* go like that -- relatively light with an amount of perspective and humor, and moving toward recognizing the only real cure -- the discovery of what it is that you're actually connected to. And you arrive there by diminishing this feverish propellor twirling and recognizing what was there before that twirling started."

I told him that I really appreciated it when he took the time to throw in a few words that tied what he was currently talking about, to the big picture. And I really did appreciate it, because as intricate as this jigsaw puzzle seemed to be, there was always a unifying principle. The times that I tended to become most confused or lost my way, were the times that I lost track of that principle.

We were in sight of the hotel where we were going to stay in Seattle. As we pulled up, Ray said there were still a few more things he wanted to say.

"What's equally important as the laughing part, is that after the embarrassment is over, you have evidence that you survived. That may be the most important of all, to see that you survived. Maybe you even found something in you that could thrive without that protection, that coat, that addition. You've discovered that something in you needs no protection, and doing so much to protect yourself may not be the way to live.

"When you fall down, most of your energy goes into not looking clumsy. Nobody tries to look clumsy, everybody tries to be relatively smooth. If you fall down and look clumsy, the first thing you do is look around to see who saw you, and the second thing, whether you recognize it or not, is realize that you survived. See, you knew that you'd survive the fall, but you weren't so sure that you'd survive the embarrassment. If this happens a few times and you survive, you can recognize, after awhile, that looking clumsy is not the worst possible thing that can happen to a person, because hey -- you survived. So you don't really have to be quite so careful.

"It's survival that I'm talking about here, and it's the same with seeing yourself as you are. You secretly fear that if you and others see how you really are, that you won't survive that seeing. It works the same as falling and looking clumsy, though. But always sticking with the little deaths, so you can keep it going.

Better to keep on chewing up small things so that the process doesn't have to stop. You keep on chewing and you keep on laughing."

Since you, the reader, know that the aforementioned happenings took place on the way to Seattle, even though it would be my preference, it would be unfair for me not to say something about our adventures there. Were I not writing all this down, I would have blocked such an unpleasant experience from my memory. As it was, in those few days, I had the worst losing streak of my poker playing career.

It happens that in Seattle at that time, there were laws that set a limit on how much a person could bet at any one time. These types of regulations cause the games to become less interesting and subsequently players would spend less time at the tables. Of course this translates into decreased revenue for the owners of the casinos and in this case inspired the creativity of those owners to redesign poker games to allow more money to get out onto the table without breaking the existing laws.

Up to this point in my poker career, I prided myself on the amount of discipline and patience that I brought into my style of play. Those two poker-important qualities allowed me to play and sometimes even win in games where players were far more skilled at the mathematical aspects of the game. On this occasion none of my strengths were in evidence. Not only did I play poorly and have atrocious luck, but I broke most of my own cardinal rules, including but not limited to, playing only in games with which I am familiar, and taking breaks to get some perspective when things are going badly. Ray's experience of Seattle must have been very different -- he never played and I never stopped.

I have no further conversations to report because we saw very little of each other for those three days. Even if we had, my receptivity to anything of a higher nature would probably have been non-existent. I'm sure he knew that, because he kept his distance. I expected that a lecture of some sort was to be forthcoming on the flight back to L.A., but the subject of my 'losing it' never came up, not then and not since. My guess is that Ray wanted me to make something beneficial out of the experience without his help.

21

HORIZONTAL & VERTICAL

Jubal called out, "That house on the hilltop --
can you see what color they've painted it?"
Anne looked then answered, "It's white on this side."

Stranger in a Strange Land, **Robert Heinlein**

I can't remember clearly whether it was the team's very next get-together after our return from Seattle, or the one after that. Whichever it was, Ray announced that he was going to use my inclusion in the team as an opportunity to start from the beginning with everyone. This announcement made me extremely self-conscious. Regardless of all that he had explained to me on this subject, I still associated starting from the beginning as a punishment. To my surprise, the others seemed extremely grateful for the chance to get back to the basics. Their positiveness alleviated my embarrassment over what I had imagined was the cause for this retrogression -- me.

Ray added the philosophical note, "The beginning is often the best place to be, because it's rare that we are ever actually any place else."

Curiously enough, those next several meetings, which took place at intervals of about four or five days and involved much discussion, interchange, and many questions, were some of the most dynamic that I can remember. When I tend to get ahead of myself, I often remember his words about "the beginning."

That first re-beginning meeting took place at Ray's house because he had a large blackboard on a tripod, one which he didn't hesitate to incorporate into his explanations. He wasted no time in getting down to it. "I'm going to start from the beginning and try to describe what a person must accomplish in order to get something going, not for themselves in a personal way, but to connect with movement in a direction that might be considered a little more vertical and less horizontal. If I'm not being specific enough in saying a little more vertical than horizontal, I should spend some time to clarify these terms."

He then drew a large crucifix-style cross on the blackboard and while retracing its lines, he went on. "What that cross says to me is that there's a part of life that goes vertically, up and down -- that's the part that's actually going somewhere. Then there's the other part, it goes horizontally, back and forth -- here to the right or there to the left. People think that it looks better to the left, or different to the right, but it's all on the same horizontal line.

"This aspect of life that goes up and down actually experiences different altitudes, different states. But the aspect that goes back and forth, let's say the horizontal level of life, is only one sameness with a lot of different colors on it, each of those colors claiming itself to be something unique. On that horizontal level exists everything that people think is better -- this is better, that's better, I'll be better, you'll be better. Whatever it is, on the horizontal line everything appears to be unique, but in actuality it's all pretty much interchangeable.

"There's so much variety, so many variables presented to us, especially in our culture and at this time that we live. There are so many different colors. It used to be that there was a little red, a little blue, a little green, but now there are so many colors. You know those Crayola boxes? When I was a kid, there would be one or two rows. Now they have rows and rows of magenta, lavender, burgundy, so many possible colors, so much variety.

"Our culture is very rich. The poorest of us is rich. We're rich in variety, we're rich in possibilities. We're not satisfied, but we're rich. So, when I say horizontal, I'm talking about all the possibilities that are ordinarily presented, like all the different professions, all the different relationships, all the different traveling, all the stuff. I'm not putting stuff down; a lot of it is beautiful stuff. But its beauty doesn't make it vertical -- it's still horizontal. It all has a kind of equality to it."

He asked if any of us could think of specific examples of what he was talking about. While I was playing with a few in my head, Barnett jumped in. What he said showed a clever side that I had no idea that he had. He started talking about tennis balls.

"You know the tennis balls that come in cans? They have numbers on them, like Penn-1, Penn-2. Let's say you open a can of tennis balls and there are Penn-4's in there. You wouldn't throw them away because you prefer Penn-2's. You'd never do that. It doesn't make a difference whether you have 2's or 4's. It makes a difference whether you have golf balls or tennis balls, because you're out there with a racket. But the difference between golf balls and tennis balls isn't what we're talking about.

"What's happening is people are opening cans and saying 'Penn-1 -- Damn! A Penn-3 would have really made it for me.' Can you imagine how ridiculous a person would sound saying that. Like they really think that if their tennis balls were Penn-3's, then they would have a different experience? It sounds absurd."

Amazing! Barnett with an example like that. Obviously, in my ignorance, I had already dismissed him as a less than credible person. A few of us gave other examples, but we all knew that Barnett had captured the spirit of the point. Ray commended our efforts and continued.

"That's exactly what's happening. That hope is ludicrous and unfortunate. I'm not making fun of it, I'm making fun with it. I sympathize, I know how real it can look. But there is something else, and I know that each of you has had inklings of that something else, that vertical something.

"What you really want to know is if there's some way to get onto that vertical line, because this horizontal line is looking awfully real and really awful right about now. It's not simple, because the groove of that horizontal line is very deep. You can get a lot of support for the reality of life on the horizontal line, so it's difficult to get out of that groove, but it is possible.

"I want to talk about the necessities for traveling on that vertical line as I see them and as I've experienced them. They're different than the necessities for traveling on the horizontal line."

I think that Ray sensed that we had a good participatory thing going, one that he wanted to encourage. He asked if we could come up with some examples of necessities for travel on the horizontal line. Everyone gave examples ranging from appearance, connections, and personal style, to talent, possessions, and intelligence. He acknowledged that those were some of the horizontal biggies and then proceeded to talk about the vertical line.

"There happen to be a full set of different necessities for traveling the vertical line. When I refer to this vertical and horizontal business, I'm not patenting a term that I've used before. I'm using an interesting way of expressing this idea, this analogy of the cross, a vertical line and a horizontal line. So I'm going to talk a little about what I see as the requirements for that kind of vertical travel.

"It would be dishonest for me to say that understanding your condition is not a prerequisite for any kind of vertical travel. It is very definitely a prerequisite. You've got to see the nature of your own existence in a very immediate, very moment to moment way. So as I say, I put a lot of energy into method, time, effort, and concentration in that regard.

"I can help you to develop a mirror that's clear enough to look in and see that what you imagine to be 'making it' may not be 'making it' at all. Not by my interpretation or in my opinion, but in your own. I can help you to learn to clean the cloudiness from the mirror that you ordinarily look into, the one that allows you to imagine things like: 'Everything's okay enough, and anyway, nobody else is in better shape,' and 'what else can a person do?'

Without the burden of those imaginings, you can learn to see that the present situation is actually catastrophic, disastrous, going nowhere, and in need of immediate remedial action.

"That's an extremely confronting view, not something that you can easily shove in front of somebody's face. Of course you can do a little shoving if a person is willing, and has an inkling of what his life has become. Then you can learn to develop that new kind of mirror for yourselves, so that you can look in that mirror and see how it really is, regardless of what kind of performances you're putting on for other people."

Karl raised his hand. It wasn't the usual method of jumping in, but it seemed appropriate at the moment. Ray called on him, keeping with the spirit of formality of his gesture.

Karl said, "I can't see how it is really possible for us to develop a mirror that can show us that our life is a loser. My life seems to be a sequence of activities that exist only for the purpose of diverting myself from that painful possibility."

"We must adopt a new attitude," Ray answered. "If not, we'll continue to think that we don't want to look in this mirror because it's just too painful. After all, we're barely keeping it together. Somehow it all fits itself together, then we go to sleep and don't have to think about it.

"You understand, something new has to come into a person's ordinary way of dealing with life so as to allow the possibility of developing this mirror which can show how it really is with them. I hope I'm being clear here, because I'm talking about something very precise. Before this mirror gets to be polished and presented and looked into, even though you're the polisher, presenter, and the looker-into-er, before that, something must develop in you which has the ability to look at this mirror without turning away or distorting what you see, because this mirror in itself has no more power than any other mirror does. A mirror is an inanimate object; it doesn't do anything and it has no opinions whatsoever. It sits there and reflects exactly what's in front of it. This mirror is one thing, and then the viewer of this mirror is quite another. Do you grasp the importance of this point that I'm making?"

Patricia (with the make-up), obviously being an authority on mirrors, wasted no time in reassuring Ray of her understanding of the subject. She explained her views.

"I can see that what we seek is really the important thing. Because a mirror can be used for what you've been talking about, but a mirror can be used for other things as well -- to improve your appearance, slit your wrists, start a fire or even burn down a forest."

The tone of the meeting lightened for a few minutes while we fooled around with all the possibilities of how mirrors could be used. My contribution was -- a mirror can be used to send a signal to rescue boats at sea.

Barnett, obviously excited about his potential contribution, capped the subject of mirrors with the following story. "I remember when I was a kid, we used to sit in the back of the classroom with these little mirrors and shine them on the blackboard. The teacher thought that they were spots on the blackboard and would try to erase them. We'd move them when his eraser got near, and then the teacher would chase those little spots till he realized what was going on."

We all looked at each other with the common recognition that Barnett had just re-established his pre-tennis ball story reputation.

"You have to back-up," Ray interceded, "and before starting this self-revelation process, you must develop the unique ability to see things as they are, without flinching.

"You may think that you're objective, you may think that you're stoic and an evaluating kind of person, but when you see something about yourself, and you counted on that something to be the way you always thought it was, most of your calm and objectivity won't be there. But since it's really important that it *be* there, there must be a training period to develop the ability for real impartiality. Not impartiality in an ordinary sense, because impartiality in an ordinary sense requires that you don't care."

I had heard him use the word impartiality before, but had never really pinned it down. I asked if a judge in a courtroom was an example of impartiality in the way that he used the term.

"If a judge in a criminal case has his own son come before him, he's not going to be able to be impartial. If he has to pass sentence on his wife, where's his impartiality? He doesn't have his impartiality, because he cares. Of course if he's trying the case of a stranger, then he thinks he can be impartial. That's not impartial as I think of it, because he's not deeply interested in the life of that person -- he sees a lot of people.

"The person you see in this mirror is you. You're not intimately involved with anyone more than you are with yourself. So this quality of impartiality must involve caring, because of course you care tremendously about everything affecting yourself. At this point, you don't really care about very much else."

Ray asked if anybody had any questions or comments.

"Did any of you ever see the movie, *Dr. Lao*?" Phil asked, *The Seven Faces of Dr. Lao*? It's about this man who traveled with a magical circus in the Old West. One of the attractions in this circus was a collection of creatures that took on the personality and character of the person who was looking at them. So the creatures became snakes or spiders or whatever, according to who was standing in front of them. When people came over and started talking to them, the people had no idea that they were talking and looking at themselves. They thought that they were looking and talking to some repugnant creature."

We had some good laughs together, talking about what creatures we each were (no, I won't tell you), and eventually Ray got us back to the subject of impartiality.

"So you have to develop a unique type of impartiality, one which includes both the capability of caring, and of seeing things about yourself without flinching. The training period for learning this is very gradual, very precise, and very necessary. Because right now, believe it or not, your capacity for impartiality is very, very small. I'm not saying it's nonexistent, some of you have a little more, some a little less, but it's still very, very small.

"As I've said before, we're talking about fixing broken auto-mobiles. And when you're talking about fixing a broken automobile, the first thing that you have to see is that the automobile is broken. Everyone who rides in the car hears a clanking. Why don't we hear the clanking? We're driving the car. It's our car but we don't *want* to hear the clanking.

"We know we just fixed it last week, so we don't want to know about that clanking. We think, 'There is no clanking, the brakes are fine. He told me that they'll squeak a little, but they're perfect. It's not the brakes, it's some living organism that's growing on the tires that squeaks. All I have to do is feed it. It won't keep me from stopping. The car is safe. There's no problem.'

"*Riiight*! You don't believe it for a minute, but you want to believe it. Well that`s the story, and that's the problem."

Ray paused a moment and then asked what we thought about what he was saying.

Up to that time, my contact with my teammates had been isolated to meetings of this kind. I had not yet gotten together with any of them individually, or as people normally get together with each other. For that reason, but not only for that reason, I was unaware of what the others did with their time. I was about to find out that Phil was a house painter, by way of some personal experiences he recounted in response to Ray's request for feedback.

"A couple of weeks ago," Phil began, "I was hired to paint the inside of this house near Mission Bay. After checking out the job and giving an estimate like I always do, I took two helpers and we finished the job in three or four days. Then a week later I was called to come back, but in the meantime we had already started another paint job. I went back to Mission Bay to see why we were being called back, and the person who hired us told me that there were a few places where defects showed up in our painting.

"I suspected what might have happened there, and of course I didn't want to do any repainting. I was already on to the next job. So when the owner had me look at some spots on his walls, I heard myself saying things like, 'No, that's not a defect, that's a shadow.' I made a bunch of excuses like that, and maybe I even partially believed them. Because I didn't want to see what was there. I didn't want to repaint the place."

I was really impressed with Phil's story. Not so much with the story itself, but with his ability to be so honest with us. I wondered how long he had been at this, to be able to disclose that kind of deceptiveness on his part. That was sure out of my range. I eventually got to know Phil pretty well, and it all started for me with recognizing his ability to tell that story and wanting to get to know somebody with that kind of strength.

Ray acknowledged Phil's super example and added, "So that's where it starts. It starts with recognizing that we don't want to see what's there. It's too disruptive to see what's there. But even though we're in a desperate situation, not meaning desperate in the ordinary sense, but we're in a despairing situation in life, we have a lot that we're already keeping together. We don't want it thrown into chaos. So we look at this wall and don't see what's there. We're looking in the mirror and seeing what we want to see, rather than what it's showing us.

"There's a considerable endeavor ahead for those of you interested in learning to see the creation as it is. But to start, you've got to see what's happening with yourself, not as you would prefer it to be, not as you wish it was, not as you hope it is, but as it is.

"Maybe when we were very young, we saw the world in that way. If you've ever been around kids, you know this. But we've become incapable of seeing things like we once could, because so much has been added on."

"Am *I* ready to start learning this special kind of impartiality that you're talking about?" asked J.J. "I think I am. I'm already pretty good at seeing things about other people without flinching."

We all had a good laugh over that one, and soon even J.J. caught on and joined in. I thought of what Ray had said about looking foolish. If I could learn to see myself in J.J., that would truly be an accomplishment.

When the laughing died down, J.J. said, "Well, I guess I survived."

That really shut us up.

After a few quiet moments that I filled with thoughts of how I underestimated J.J. , Ray began to answer his original question.

"I know a lot of potentially helpful gimmicks that I call tools. You know what I mean by tools? Something that you use to make sweet intentions happen. Some of them are very effective, but they work in a strangely diabolical way.

"If you're a good chef and you have a very sharp knife, you've got something going. But if you're a poor chef and you've got a very sharp knife, you're probably going to cut your finger. So you're almost better off with a slightly dull knife, because if you've ever seen a chef's knife, you know they're really sharp. Patricia was right, the tool is really not the important thing, it's the person that's holding it that's important -- not the size of the person or the sex of the person or the age of the person, but the intention of that person."

Ray paused for a while, then suggested that we all take a walk around the block together before getting into some specifics. It was difficult for me to break away from the ideas that had been presented and appreciate the outdoors. I ended up walking behind Ray and J.J., who, I found out, had gotten together with the team just shortly before I had. Since the starry night couldn't capture my attention, evesdropping on Ray and J.J. did. As we were walking around the block, Ray was responding to J.J.'s question about something he called 'shortcuts.'

"Ram Dass took tons of L.S.D.," Ray said -- "traumatic disruption to his system. Yogananda had visions, Carlos Castenada had his sense of reality turned upside down by Don Juan. We've been exposed to these types of stories, and whether you know it or not, you've built up a picture of how it can go. I don't dismiss the value of traumatic disruption; there are even times that I've suggested exploring specific semi-traumatic experiences, but there's trauma, and there's trauma.

"I'm saying this because the idea of having an experience that can give you a picture of what's on the other side of one of your obstacles is a fascinating, attractive, and scary idea. An experience of this kind can't remove an obstacle, but it can give you a picture of what's beyond that obstacle. Some drugs obviously can be effective in doing this, as can certain altered states of different kinds and certain extreme ordinary experiences."

J.J. said something about wanting to travel in foreign countries, but his voice was a lot quieter than Ray's so I couldn't hear too well. I put together what he must have said from how Ray responded.

"Let's say that you do travel in a foreign country," Ray continued, "one with a very different culture -- now that's trauma, you understand, that's severely different. You find yourself being a different kind of person. Your possessions mean much less to you, your schedule means less to you, time means less to you. Through this traumatic experience, you get a picture of what's possible. Then you go back to your life, and in a short period of time, what usually happens is you revert back to the way you were before your trip. Even though this reverting happens, I have found that those kinds of activities that give a person a picture of what's possible are very necessary, very effective, and even precious. But the idea that those experiences are going to change you is absurd. Anybody who has experienced what I'm talking about, knows that those things aren't going to change them at all.

"Do you understand what I'm saying? The use of traumatic experiences that turn a person's life upside down in the hope that they'll be so affected that they'll become a different person, are worthless. What will usually follow a person's traumatic experience, is they will feel the need to re-establish the way it was before. There's only a certain amount of energy that a person has for anything. If they feel the need to use that energy to re-establish their okayness, then they're not going to have the energy to gain any new ground. So for that reason, turning life upside down is rarely worthwhile, and even then, only for the purpose of giving a person a glimpse of what life would be like without some of that person's obstacles in the way."

They walked along silently for awhile until J.J. said something (*inaudible*).

"It's best to start with smaller things," Ray said. "Little things that you imagine about yourself. There are actually very precise methods for doing that. You can start with things that are so small that you can develop this impartiality and not get assaulted so quickly with psychological challenge -- like thinking that you're an evil person."

Ray asked J.J. if he was still taking classes at San Diego State. I was pretty sure that his answer was yes.

"Let's take an example -- a person walks into a classroom filled with seated people. If he comes in late, he'll probably sit in the back rather than walk up and sit in a seat up front. Let's say you ask this person, 'Why didn't you sit up front?' Well, whether you ask him in a confronting way or a non-confronting way, it's still confronting, because you're threatening to uncover some inconsistency. That person would probably explain with all reasonableness, that he didn't want to be disruptive to other people's concentration.

"Now, if this person develops the impartiality that we've been talking about, this ability to see himself a little bit more as he is in this matter, he might know, after awhile, that he didn't really give a shit about being disruptive at all. If it would serve his purpose, he'd be disruptive in a minute. He was afraid to call attention to himself in that circumstance. He was not acting in consideration of other peoples' concentration. He was acting in consideration of his own reluctance to have fingers pointed at him. He was concerned that he would be seen as one who disturbed others' concentration, because then perhaps others would be annoyed with him. A self-serving action veiled as a considerate gesture -- that's not a heavy traumatic realization, like finding out that you don't really care about your wife and kid. It's a small thing, not a teeny thing, but small enough to look at without flinching in this newly developing mirror of impartiality."

The desire to participate in their conversation overtook me, and I sped up to overtake them. "Is that what you mean when you refer to 'anomalies,'" I asked, pretending that we had been three all this time.

Ray laughed knowingly without looking over at me. "Exactly!" he said. "Things that don't quite fit together, and everybody, including the culprit, can laugh about them. The person can very clearly see that he or she assumed something about themselves that was not the case. If you start training on the little things, sooner or later, the strength of your impartiality and the clarity of your mirror will grow, and then you can take on those bigger things.

"There's no real benefit in causing a big reaction, because a big reaction is a big disturbance, and a disturbance only feeds itself. Humor is much better, lightness is much better. Eventually, you have to see yourself as you are. That's it! But if you take it little by little, then you can get hooked on the process. The rest of the world begins looking a little silly -- a silly game of people pretending that they're something they're not."

I think that I may have eavesdropped as attentively as J.J. listened to the answers to his question, because I wasn't aware of passing the house for the second time around the block. Ray suggested that we go back in and have some tea. We did, and as we sat in front of the blackboard sipping, he continued from where he had left off before our walk.

"I'm going to tell you about four specific components that are necessary in order to get to know yourself as you are. Of course they will be helpful to you only in proportion to the purity of your intention, but here goes anyway.

"This first component, 'surprise,' is not one which you would expect to be part of self-observation, but because of our nature, surprise is a critical element . When we're trying to see ourselves as we are, we have this way of getting prepared. Do you understand *preparing*? Some of us are very good at it. Some of us are expert at it, and some of us aren't so good at it. But everyone has had a lot of practice preparing. Preparing means that the moment you try to see something about yourself, you'll already have had part of that moment to smooth over that something so you won't really see what you were trying to see. In order to really see that something about yourself, you have to be surprised. Now obviously, in order to be surprised, you need someone to surprise you. Or better yet, *someones* to surprise you. So I describe this work that we're involved in as a team effort. In my opinion, a person cannot surprise himself -- so if surprise is critical, which I consider it is, you need help.

"Do any of you remember when McDonald's or Holiday Inn or some chain's advertisements had the theme, 'No Surprises.' Some people might think, 'Who wants that?' But we've learned to like it when there are no surprises. There are a lot of things in your life that you don't want to be surprised about. But without surprise, all you would learn about yourself is what you already know.

"Try to follow this. Imagine that you're behaving in some way that you don't know you're behaving. If you discovered that you were acting in that way (unless it was some way of acting that presented you in a favorable light), you would make sure that nobody else knew you were acting that way. So surprise is what you need, and you need help to be surprised."

There was considerable discussion that followed this riddle, as well as after his presentation of each of the other components. I am electing to omit that discussion so that you can appreciate the continuity and completeness of what he explained.

"Next, there's the component of 'willingness.' Now if you don't have willingness, even if you live on a roller-coaster of surprises, it won't matter; you'll find yourself being an adversary in the proceedings. Everything will have to be forced on you. You'll have to be constantly tricked into any progress whatsoever. Defensiveness and fear will be your constant companions. If you're willing, it's possible that you can see yourself as you are. If you're unwilling, you don't even *want* to see yourself as you are. People rarely have questions about willingness; it's a pretty obvious necessity for any new undertaking, so we can move on to the next component."

"Before we move on," Linda interrupted, "can we take it for granted that because we're here, we're willing?"

"The only thing you can take for granted," Ray proclaimed soberly, "is resistance. It will be with you at every step. So the answer is no! You can't!"

After the appropriate pause, Ray continued. "Ready for the next one?" he joked. "Okay, when you think of the way nature manifests, you can see an incredible preciseness there. For me to call it incredible is a ridiculous underestimation. We've all heard about and witnessed the preciseness in the way each leaf is made, each snowflake, not to speak of all those little black obelisks traveling around the universe in *2001, A Space Odyssey* -- all that preciseness.

"And then we study human consciousness and we say, 'Oh, I feel this and I feel that,' and we imagine that we've in some way embraced the truth. In actuality, learning to see ourselves as we are is as precise a science as any science I've ever come in contact with, and I've come close to a few of them.

"In other words, if we wrote down a mathematical formula, we could say that there is a precise way to deal with it, there is a more precise way to deal with it, and there is the most precise way to deal with it. There's a precise way to fix a car, a precise way to build a building, or make a clay pot -- we can relate to that. But preciseness with seeing yourself as you are -- ahhh! -- people think that that's another thing. They expect that in order to accomplish seeing yourself as you are, the components employed would be more intuitive and indefinite than precise. But no! 'Preciseness' is intimately linked with learning the art of seeing yourself as you are.

"Preciseness in seeing yourself as you are requires the use of practical examples. Examples in other sciences can be theoretical, but theories are not sufficient here. The preciseness, the exactitude of what you have to see is extremely practical and non-theoretical.

"When we see each other, we see something very precise. When we look at a person, we see the color of their eyes, the size of the pupil, the nose, the earring, their hair; it's all very specific. The eyes see things as they are in a very specific way. This mirror that we're talking about for seeing yourself as you are has to have that capacity of preciseness. Since that picture of yourself as you are is not necessarily only physical, there is special training needed in order to wield that preciseness.

"The bottom line is, in order to see yourself as you are, your observations can never be general. There always have to be specific details. A person can describe the meal they ate in retrospect by reporting that they had dinner, but as a person is actually eating, they take one bite at a time, one fork-full of potatoes followed by one fork-full of salad -- never dinner, always specifics. Eating dinner is a *story about* precision; a story about precision can never be precise.

"The required level of precision needed is beyond what anybody could possibly suspect. An expert is needed to teach the development of this component, because a person is not born with, nor does he normally develop that preciseness on his own.

"A brilliant mind can figure out aspects of chemistry, aspects of physics, aspects of biology, but no one is going to put the whole thing together from beginning to end in his lifetime. You need to be given something and then you can build on what you've been given, and then you can pass on your conclusions and somebody else can build on that. That's the way it works in computer science, library science, and this science as well. You need to learn precision, and you need an expert to get you started.

"So far we've talked about surprise, willingness, and precision. The fourth component of learning to see yourself as you are is 'presence.' The element of presence is a very curious addition to the rest of these, and I would say it is the one of these four components that gets ignored most often. It's the easiest one to leave out because it's the one that people really know the least about. It doesn't fit very well into contemporary life, whereas the other three have their obvious counterparts in life.

"Let's look at those counterparts -- precision has expertise, surprise has spontaneity, and certainly willingness has willingness. They all have their counterparts, but presence doesn't. The quality of presence isn't something that you learn about in school;

it isn't given much value there. When a politician talks about issues and makes promises, that's not one of the things he promises. Neither The Declaration of Independence nor The Bill of Rights mentions presence. It's a very hidden and a very subtle something, very easily lost, like right in this moment.

"So if you can follow what I'm saying now, there's the meaning of the words, and then there's also the sound of the words in your ears. If you follow the meaning, you'll lose the sound, and if you follow the sound, you'll lose the meaning. This component of presence requires that they be simultaneously appreciated. Presence, if it is ever found, which it rarely is, can be lost so easily that if you had it when I began this sentence, by the time I finish this sentence you will have lost it."

J.J. interrupted, "It sounds like what you're describing would take paying more attention to what's happening than I'm used to. Are there ways a person can learn to pay attention better?"

"The route to presence is through relaxing," Ray answered. "It's not through paying attention. You can't pay your way into presence. Presence is like the state of trees and flowers, the state of animals. Presence is really a very simple state. It means not thinking about the past and not thinking about the future. It means that you're not planning and you're not rehashing. You're where you are. If you want to bring it down to the very close -- you're right here.

"In order to be present, you need only to possess the qualities or capacities of these other beings that I've described, like trees and plants and animals. If they can be present, then in order to be present, we have to use some quality that they also have. If we use something additional that only we have, then we're not going to be doing this simple thing that they're doing.

"We can do things by concentrating, but being present is not one of those things. Being present requires what you might call a non-effort rather than an effort. *Becoming* concentrated, to use these complex words, is a non-effort. *Trying* to concentrate is an effort, and you will not experience presence by trying to *pay* attention.

233

"Let's say you like to listen to music, the kind of music that's like poetry. So you're listening to this music and there are a bunch of words, a jumble of poetic phrases. Then somewhere in the middle of the song you become relaxed -- you're not fighting to go anywhere or thinking about other things. You find yourself agreeing to be there with that song, and right there and then, a phrase comes through to you. You were there and it was there. When you try to listen, that's doing something called trying. Your experience is something completely different. But when you become relaxed, you're lulled into this okayness. You're here for a second and that song gets through to you. In a sense, presence is a gift, and you can't pull it to you. If you're pulling it, you're not going to get it.

"So these four components all taken together can show you that there's something considerable to be taken on if a person is going to begin to see themselves as they are. You're starting with learning something about where that warm spot is in your heart. You must become responsible for finding that spot. Soon you'll discover that there's something in you fighting against finding that warm spot. That something must be dissipated, whatever it takes. The intention of finding that warm spot in your heart must grow, and with that expanding, you have the chance as you start to walk, to put your foot down on that heart, on that warm spot. And as you put your foot down on that warm spot and start to see yourself as you are, you begin the sequence of being able to see it all as it is."

It was Ray's usual custom at the close of these group meetings to ask if anybody had any questions to clarify what had been talked about, or anything else. During the lengthy exchange of questions and answers that proceeded concerning the four components, I realized that I had been harboring some questions concerning what I should do about pursuing this non-profession profession of mine. This question arose for me consistently in direct proportion to my success, or lack thereof, at the poker tables. After the Seattle debacle, it was my constant companion. Since I seemed to have regular access to Ray's ear, I thought that I'd hold the question for a more private moment. This was, I learned later, my sneaky way of keeping myself separate from the team.

My teammate Linda, not suffering from that particular short-coming, asked my question, by coincidence, in relation to the details of her own life. Ray's response, though brief, was one that I hope I'll never forget.

"We each have different jobs in our everyday lives, and we each aspire to different things. Many people have lofty ideas about how important it is that they do the things that they're 'meant to do' and discover their 'this' and their 'that.' I have a very different attitude about vocation, very different. My attitude is -- get a job, then go on to the next thing.

"People like to think that destiny involves some skill or talent. To me, destiny doesn't involve any skill or talent. Destiny is discovering our connection to the creator and seeing where that connection leads. Remember that movie *Oh God*, the one where George Burns plays God? Well this guy asks God if heaven is pretty empty these days, and God answers that there are just a few cleaning ladies up there. And I sincerely and absolutely believe that to be the case.

"All the paths of glory and fame and skill and talent and recognition, none of them are worth anything on the path to truth. The finest most talented writer, artist, dedicated civil servant or whatever, it doesn't matter, it's all a bunch of ordinary stuff.

"When we look at the beauty of a little child who hasn't quested for or accomplished anything and has no aspirations for anything, we see the eyes of the creation are there. So much focus on all that other stuff reflects an incredibly distorted picture of our own importance. Do people actually believe that somewhere out there beyond the Milky Way Galaxy they're going to care what kind of pictures we paint?

"In my world, the true love that comes from experiencing our actual connection is the only thing that counts. That is a different level of experience, and it's all that really matters. So if a person suspects that this could be true, then he should take care of what he's gotta take care of, and take care of it simply -- then go on to the next thing.

"No decisions that you make about any details of your life's problems, plans, and relationships are significant. Get them taken care of simply and directly so that you can start to find out how to become a servant of the energy that has put you on Earth."

Ray ended the meeting with the surprise announcement (at least it was to me) that he would be away for a few weeks. He suggested that we try to get together as often as possible to discuss our understanding of the four components that he had presented. He added that since we were starting from the beginning, we should remember to avoid any overcomplicating.

22

NATURAL VS. NORMAL

"Speaking of livers," the unicorn said. "Real magic can never be made by offering up someone else's liver. You must tear out your own and not expect to get it back. The true witches know that."

The Last Unicorn, **Peter Beagle**

The next few weeks were such a flurry of new impressions that it would be hard for me to present their contents in any organized way. Our team had numerous meetings at various locations -- day meetings, night meetings, at my house, at each of their houses. Several of those meetings are especially memorable to me, but the most significant was the last one, which I'll try to describe.

Ray often encouraged us to try to answer each others' questions. I usually played it safe and either waited for someone else to speak up, or for Ray to give the authoritative answer. He often made a point of assuring us that there were no right or wrong answers, but only right and wrong efforts. I believed that in theory, but it rarely inspired me to overcome my reticence. Since the authoritative answer was not presently accessible, a new situation and potential experience was becoming available. I wondered if I would take advantage of it.

Linda, who had known him the longest, was also the bravest in terms of sticking her neck out. Over the past weeks, watching her take those chances that I backed away from, and seeing that she had developed, through practice, the ability to give some pretty good answers to other peoples' questions, was beginning to inspire me to take some chances of my own. I had given myself a pep-talk before this particular meeting, so when the opportunity arose, I was primed.

When I arrived, only Linda and Patricia were there. I missed the first part of their conversation, but I surmised that Linda was talking about certain efforts that she was making and that she realized that much more was necessary.

Patricia interrupted in a sing-songy saccharine tone. "But don't you feel that we can just allow ourselves to receive all this wisdom in time? What about receiving things in the natural order and then progressing as we follow what feels most natural, or are you saying that we should do more than that?"

Linda waited a moment, I think to make sure that Patricia was finished with her ballad, then she responded. "The only relationship whatsoever between what you're saying and what I'm saying is that they are opposites. The way I look at it, there is no natural. Natural is a nice word, but normal is a more accurate word. I think that if we were natural, then everything you said would be so, but we aren't natural. We're normal for our time, but there's nothing natural about us. To use the word natural, which is the key word here, as I see it, leads to assumptions -- but naturalness is no longer in existence. Natural was left behind when we stopped feeling the connection that Ray talks about.

"You and I don't feel that vibration behind our breath that keeps us alive, nor probably have we ever felt it, so we aren't natural. Natural is a chimpanzee or a giraffe or a rhododendron plant -- normal is us. So if you replace the word natural with the word normal, then you can ask, 'What normally happens?' My answer to that is what normally happens is that we fear. And that fear drives us to lie, to deceive, and to cheat. That's what we do."

I was blown away, to say the least, by the power and authority of Linda's words. I didn't know where she got the courage to be so bold, but I figured that if I were going to listen to my own pep-talk, I'd better jump on this opportunity and get into the conversation. These ideas of hers were in no way new to me. I had, in fact, studied certain parallel phenomena myself and had made some startling discoveries. I had a momentary flash of the rules about raising our hands in elementary school, but opted instead to dive in. I took a deep breath, suspecting that I had a lot to say and that it all might even come out -- and it did!

"This issue of natural versus normal that you were talking about seems to me to be related to another issue, one that I've been thinking about. It's the ideas of sharing versus using -- what we imagine about ourselves versus what's really taking place. Something happened to me the other day that I think might have something to do with all this.

"Ray asked if while he was away, I would do him the favor of picking up his thirteen year old daughter, Laurie, from school and dropping her at her dance class at the Pacific Beach Center. Of course I agreed.

"So there I was, driving down La Jolla Blvd. with Laurie. Now you've got to picture this. We were going south on La Jolla Blvd., toward Mission Beach. We were passing the Pacific Beach Center and were about to make a left from the right side of La Jolla Blvd. into the parking lot. There weren't any cars coming the other way, so we crossed La Jolla Blvd. and started to pull into the parking lot. Well, there was this car right in front of us in the entry driveway who hadn't decided yet where he was going to park, so some of my car was sticking out onto the road. There was no real problem because there are two lanes coming this way, so anybody who might be coming down would have plenty of room to go around me.

"Anyway, this person came speeding down the road. He was coming fast because he saw a chance for conflict. I was sticking out a little, so he wanted to rush, just to make sure that I didn't get out of the way before he got there. That way he could beep his horn and make a little trouble. He was rushing down and started beeping his horn. Both Laurie and I looked over as he drove up. He screeched to a stop about a foot from my car and with all the anger he could muster in one glare, he proudly held up the middle finger of his right hand in a familiar gesture of vehemence.

"Laurie looked at me and started to laugh, and I laughed too. We were laughing with each other, not at this person who was obviously in pain, but at how absurd this situation was. Here was a set of really benign circumstances, and this person insisted on expressing tremendous negativity. He was looking for a fight, and he didn't even need somebody else to take the other half of it. He just needed a little bit of imagination and he found what he thought he was looking for."

"That sounds like a great story," Linda said mockingly. "But what the Hell does it have to do with natural versus normal *or* sharing versus using? Hey!" she said looking toward Patricia, "Maybe he's just using us -- that seems normal for him."

They joined in a laughing binge, and as they did, I imagined that I was being reduced to a lower form in their opinion of me. After telling the story, which I probably did only for the purpose of participating -- I, myself, couldn't even remember what it had to do with anything. My normal response to an assault of this kind would be either to fight back or get defensive. I decided to put some of what I had learned over the past year into action and try a different road.

"Let's forget about what happened on La Jolla Drive, okay?" I suggested. "At the moment I can't see the connection either. When the two of you were talking I got really excited about the subject. I just didn't know how to participate so I brought up that thing about Ray's daughter. I guess I figured that it would get your attention. What I'd like to do is try again *sans* bullshit because I really do think that I have something to say about the subject."

I could tell by the looks on both of their faces that the method of response that I opted for was far superior to the ones which I usually chose. Linda encouraged me to continue, and Patricia even gave a guarded conditional okay.

"Just because people can say the words sharing and natural, they imagine that they have those experiences. S*haring, I shared, I am sharing, I would like to share, Sonny and Share*. But I happen to have discovered, of course with Ray's help, but also with a lot of checking it out myself, that there is no more sharing than there is naturalness. What there is, is commerce, and what there is, is using, and that's what's normal."

I guess Patricia could handle a lecture from Linda, but she was not about to lie down for a freshman like myself.

"That's all very clever," she said, "but are you saying that you think that sharing is impossible?"

I tried to resist the feeling that I too was in a battle, even though no middle fingers were raised. I tried to keep calm. "I'm not trying to prove that there is no sharing possible," I said, "or that everything is degrading and that all there is, is using. I'm saying that there is no sharing *as we are now,* and all there is, is using. I believe that sharing is possible, but it's only possible if we recognize that we aren't capable of it now. The way I see it, we are all what Ray calls machines for self-gratification -- using machines. That's really all we can do. There's no blame about it."

Patricia looked as if she was facing an open pair of aces with a hidden pair of kings. She was not encouraging to look at, so I rotated my neck to the left. Linda had a big smile on her face. I didn't know if it was caused by having found a confederate for her position, or realizing that she had found an ally in the quest for which we rallied around Ray. I didn't try to figure it out in the moment, but simply used that smile as a springboard to re-launch from.

"It's even understandable why we've become using machines," I continued. "We're tremendously insecure because we have no connection to anything. Once we recognize that we're using machines, then we can aspire to something else. Most people imagine that they *are* natural and they already *can* give. That's why *we're* going through this process of being sanded down with forty-grit paper. Because when we stop imagining that we can share, and give, and be natural, we'll start to see impartially that we really aren't capable of giving -- that we're using machines, and that everything we do is self-serving and for personal gratification. Then maybe we can start to build towards what's possible.

"We're not able to share because we're always in so much need. We have to learn to fill up from within. It may be the most natural thing in the world, but we've forgotten that. Unless we become filled up from within, we'll be in need from without. And everything will become fair game for us to use for that need. And that's understandable. A starving person grasps, a drowning person grasps for stories about the boss's daughter. There's a lot of need there."

Patricia had reached her limit. I knew the experience well. It wasn't that she was on the verge of charging out the door, but she wasn't going to let me go on without getting in some views of her own. I realized when I glanced up that I hadn't had enough exposure to her to know if I liked her or not, but my impressions of her consistently seemed to fall in the category of Martian. Martian is a category of female that I keep reserved for airline stewardesses and show business people. They're usually large (not fat) and blond. Patricia was neither -- go figure it out.

I yielded the floor, as I always did with aliens. She spoke for a few minutes about how both Linda and I were too cynical, and that she could think of a lot of examples of sharing and naturalness. Linda must have understood that something big was getting worked out in Patricia, and that to challenge her to give examples would only cause her to become more entrenched. I was more from the challenge-her-school, but fortunately for everyone present on this occasion, Linda prevailed and asked me (in a similar manner to the way in which she would have asked Ray) to say more about my ideas of getting filled up from within. I knew I was in the presence of someone who had truly grown from her involvement with Ray.

I went on, "When we become filled up from within, then we're in the position of not needing. And being in the position of not needing is very different from being in the position of needing. Because if I meet you on the street and I'm in need, every action that I take will precipitate from that need: I need you to like me, I need you to recognize me, I need you to be impressed by me, I need you to accept me, I need you not to be mad at me, I need you to go away thinking well of me. I need so many things -- so my actions, which will precipitate from those needs, will be distorted and perverse. I might give you gifts of all kinds, but my giving is only to get what I need. I can't really see you clearly."

"What do you mean by, I can't see you clearly?" Linda asked.

"If I don't need, then I can see you clearly, rather than through the clouds of my need," I said, feeling as though we were dancing and I was finally getting a chance to lead. "I know you need a pat on the back, or a slap across the face. I know you need a good word. I know you need some money. I know you need some food. I know you need not to get some money. I know you need not to have food. I can even let you walk away, or I can try to bring you closer. Not because I need you to be there or I need you to go away, but because I can see what *you* need. I suspect that it's an incredible experience to see, hear, and feel through something other than the clouds of my own need, and from small flashes that I've had, I know that it's definitely within my capacity."

Several minutes before this point in my discourse, Ray and two other team members had arrived and were all seated facing me. In the moments that I could muster the courage to look over at Ray, I noticed that his eyes were sparkling. I didn't have time to analyze the situation then, but I suspect now that he was both proud of me and pleased that his efforts were showing results.

When I had occasion to pause (after stating my opinion that 'giving' was within our capacity), my nervousness filled the lull. I attempted to regain my level of confidence by making a joke. I asked, pretending I was Ray, if anybody had any questions about anything that I had said. Ray ignored the nervousness which prompted my asking for questions, and put a question directly and respectfully to the person who had just given that inspired talk.

He asked me if I thought that people could actually hurt each other. It was the perfect question, because everything that I had said was leading in the direction of what I had learned from him and from my own experience about this much misunderstood subject. With the help of Ray's vote of confidence, I continued with renewed courage.

"Well the way I see it, people are trying to make themselves safe, and in order to do that, sometimes they seem to hurt each other and sometimes they seem to help each other. Sometimes at the benefit of each other, sometimes at the expense of each other.

"There's a line in a Bob Dylan song:

> *I didn't mean to make you so sad*
> *You just happened to be there, that's all.*

"Nobody was trying to help you and nobody was trying to hurt you -- *You just happened to be there, that's all.* We're considered fortunate when in our interactions we cross paths with the help part, and we're considered unfortunate when we cross paths with the hurt part, but all that's really happening is everybody's trying to do the best for themselves. There's a lot of people feeling afraid, trying to be okay, trying to protect themselves from their fear -- and sometimes that protection manifests as friendliness, sometimes that protection manifests as hostility. Sometimes somebody else gets in the way of a person trying to protect themselves from an imagined danger. But whatever they're doing -- *You just happen to be there, that's all.*"

It was Ray's first meeting with us in about a month, and he wasn't about to take over until he saw what kind of show we had put together for ourselves while he was away. There were a few moments of awkward silence, and as I was about to answer my own semi-rhetorical question (which at this point was okay with me).

Phil spoke up. "Leonard Cohen said it also in one of *his* songs:

> *When all has come to dust,*
> *I will kill you if I must,*
> *I will love you if I can.*

That's the story. Sure, there's love, but people in ordinary life aren't capable of manifesting that love. They're capable of feeling that love, but it doesn't come out. Fear gets in the way. It's a source of tremendous frustration in life. People in ordinary life aren't capable of helping. Even though they feel the desire to help, they're not capable of manifesting that help. It doesn't happen; fear gets in the way. Sometimes we get what we want, and another person seems to have played a part in it. Still, that person wasn't capable of helping us. Only by coincidence did we get helped. Because if they, in order to protect themselves, had to do the opposite -- we would have thought that we didn't get helped.

"You know, this isn't all just theory to me. I'll give you a good example of what I'm talking about. For a while I worked on a job over near Jacumba by the Mexican border. The road there was almost always deserted. Some days when I was driving home, I would see somebody walking, but I wanted to be alone, or maybe I was afraid they were smuggling, so I wouldn't pick them up. Other days I was feeling lonely and wanted company, so then I'd stop and give them a ride.

"That hitchhiker would say (in Spanish usually), 'Hey, thanks for helping me out.' But I didn't really help him out. He may have gotten help, but I was just doing what I needed to do. It could have gone the opposite way as well.

"When I first met Ray, he told me that the only way a person could hurt me is to pick up a stick and bash me over the head. I disagreed. My point of view was that people have relationships with each other; they become vulnerable and fall in love; they do all these things, and become devastated. That's emotional damage. It's not like a whap over the head, but it's as real as a whap over the head. Ray completely and absolutely disagreed with that point of view, and now so do I.

"My point of view has changed because I've seen Ray in numerous interactions with people -- like one time we were in the supermarket and he took some lady's cart by accident. The lady looked at us enraged. She said, 'I can't believe you're so inconsiderate that you'd do that. Why don't you get your own cart instead of stealing mine.' I know the options that I would have had open to me in that situation. I would have either gotten scared, felt bad, or gotten angry back at her. I learned from Ray's response that

245

there's another option. I could look at that person and think to myself, 'This person has had a rough day. I wonder what I could say or do to smooth her way, because I know that she's not mad at me. I just happened to be there, that's all."

"That's the most ridiculous thing I've ever heard," J.J. interrupted. "Sure, I agree with the part that you can show a little compassion even if someone is getting heavy with you. But to say that people don't do emotional damage to each other is baloney!"

"You may think that now J.J.," Phil said with surprising patience, "but you're wrong! Sticks and stones can break your bones, but nothing anyone else feels, thinks, or says, can do anything to you at all. You can give plenty of trouble to yourself by making something personal out of it, but they can't do anything to you.

"Nor in fact, is there anything anyone *wants* to do to you. No, everyone wants to get people to like them. People try to influence other people and take advantage of other people because of their insecurity. Everybody's trying to get to feel loved and secure and okay -- everybody, even the worst of us. Some people have very strange ways of doing that, but there is no doubt whatsoever -- that's what they're trying to do."

A few more minutes of discussion followed Phil's remarks until Ray said that he had to leave. He stood up, said it was great to see everyone doing so well, and gave a letter to Linda, asking that we read it aloud after his departure. As he walked through the doorway, he looked back and told us that we could discuss the contents of the letter at our next get-together.

I had been so involved in the proceedings that I never suspected that an announcement which would so greatly affect my life could be anywhere nearby. I was wrong to be so naive.

23

WOLVES & MEN

Just do the steps that you've been shown
By everyone you've ever known
Until the dance becomes your very own
No matter how close to yours another's steps have grown
In the end there is one dance you'll do alone.

Jackson Browne

We all seemed to be sitting unusually close to each other as Linda began to read.

Dear Friends,
At the end of the month we will have completed our re-beginning.
It is my intention, at that time, to leave you to yourselves and to each
other, so that you can develop as you individually see fit. It will be an
extended separation, not one that can be survived by a holding of the
breath. Until such time in the future as it appears appropriate, I will
be suspending any and all contact with each of you. Not only will I be
away from this area, I will be out of the country, and consequently out
of reach for consultation of any kind.
My decision to leave you to yourselves and (I hope) to each other,
represents the greatest compliment that I could pay each of you. It is

my assessment that you are ready, as a team, to take the next step without my supervision.

In the months ahead, those of you who feel the necessity to commit to working together will find yourselves establishing your own dynamics of interaction. Whatever those dynamics are, compassion must be one of their components.

Of course, sooner or later, everybody knows it's going to get dirty. If you had a rotten tooth and went to the dentist, when you first sat in the chair and he sat opposite you, and you were only discussing the problem, you might think how silly you were to have worried so much. But in your head you'd know that sooner or later the blood was going to pour, and the burning bone and tartar were going to fly. You know in there somewhere, in your thoughts and in your feelings, that sooner or later you're going to have to get down to it with each other. Sooner or later, if you want to get clean, you've got to wash off the dirt.

But you can't shovel through this stuff and get wrenched by everything that happens. I hope you will use the ways that you've learned to develop perspective and even humor about what's happening. Since some amount of shoveling is inevitable, it's best, in the beginning, to focus on things that are so small and of so little consequence that it's easier to see them with that perspective and humor.

Remember, I'm not suggesting now, nor have I ever suggested that you be any different than you are. I'm suggesting that you see yourself as you are. That's all you have to do. There's nothing about you that's too bad, that's too evil, or too anything.

The formula is for each of you to start from where you are, be calm, and stick with small things. It can be interesting and even entertaining, and there's no reason for it to be more than mildly disruptive. It can be mildly disruptive, that's all right. A few of you could use a little mild disruption.

Let's make sure that we make use of these next few weeks together.

Ray

The details of our individual reactions and any talking that followed the reading of the letter are best kept recorded in each of our private memoirs. The only words that I will disclose were J.J.'s, and in their simplicity they sum up a common denominator that ran through all of our reactions. He said, "What'll we do now?"

We did meet together with Ray several more times before his departure. In addition to those times, I was grateful to get to spend some private time with him (as did all the others).

Other than that, the only substantive communication that any of us has had with him was a letter we received a short time after his departure. It was from San Francisco and was in response to a letter written to him by Patricia. Somewhere between here and the conclusion of this book, I intend to include the text of that letter, which, in a way, is also written to you, the reader.

Aside from that inclusion, it is my aim to use the balance of these pages to describe the contents of the second of those last three team meetings with Ray. I'm separating that one out for presentation to you, because the subject matter of his talk on that occasion was, as he described: "A missing piece that if ignored could render meaningless all the rest."

That meeting took place during a sort of farewell dinner at a Thai restaurant downtown. We were all seated at one of those big round tables that has a rotating center. Ray seemed pretty knowledgeable about Thai food and even said a few words in Thai to the waiter, something that sounded like 'popcorn cob.' After the eating subsided and before the overeating began, Ray had some things to say to us.

"When I leave," he began, "Phil is going to look after my car. So this morning I took it to the mechanic to have it checked out. He's one of the best car guys around and I've known him for a long time.

"While I was there, somebody drove into the shop wanting to have his motor looked at. The mechanic picked up the hood and after using whatever gismos he needed to do his analysis, he realized that the engine was shot. While he was checking the motor, he happened to look in the back seat of the car and saw that there was a new can of car wax in there, along with a bunch of stuff to make the car look real spiffy.

"When the customer went into the office to make a phone call, my mechanic turned to me and said, 'This car probably isn't even going to make it home, and he's got all that wax in there to shine the skin. How can I tell him that those things he has in the back seat are a waste of time? He's not even going to have a car after another few days, and he's certainly not going to rebuild the engine. That car's not worth it.'

"From my friend's perspective, the whole thing looked ludicrous. He had the expertise which allowed him to know something that the owner of the car couldn't know.

"Situations come up pretty often where one person's knowledge and ability gives them the perspective that another person doesn't have. Can any of you think of an example of what I'm talking about?"

I certainly knew what Ray was talking about, but the only examples that I could think of had to do with poker games, and I didn't want to talk about cards. Fortunately J.J. bailed us out with a good one.

"If you work at a flower stand (J.J. works at a flower stand), after a while you learn some tricks to make flowers last longer. So yesterday a lady came up to my stand and asked for one of the bouquets. I cut the stems, and as I was wrapping some plastic around them to put some water in, she said, 'No, I don't need that. I'm just going a few blocks from here.' Well, I looked at the Sun, and since I knew that she was going to be keeping these flowers in her car, I also knew that by the time she got to where she was going, all that would be left would be a bunch of shriveled weeds. What could I say to her? She didn't know what I knew, because I've been doing flowers for a while."

For the next ten minutes, Phil, Linda, and I talked about the flower incident. Ray listened but didn't say anything. The discussion centered around the question of who's responsible, the person who thinks he knows or the person who really knows. Opinions were really flying back and forth. Before things got too theoretical, Ray came in on it.

"So here I am," he interrupted, "listening to what's going on, and thinking, *Wow! that's really incredible. This discussion has no chance whatsoever of going anywhere. Here are seven sincere people who are imagining that they're figuring something out. Seven people who are talking about a subject that could be genuinely important to them, and they're imagining that they're in some way going to become more clear about it.*"

Hearing Ray say this was very surprising to me, because I thought that I was even impressing him with my dexterity of mind. Since I was obviously wrong, I figured I'd keep a low profile. Sometimes it's safer that way.

He continued, "Now from my perspective I know that there is nothing constructive going on here; it's like pouring water into a cup with a hole in the bottom. Sure, all the words were accurate and all the attitudes were correct. True, nobody was meaning to do harm or cause trouble. Still, it was just like that person who was buying the flowers. She didn't happen to know that you can't leave flowers in a hot car without something to keep them moist or they'll wilt. Maybe she hasn't been around flowers. And how about the customer at the auto shop? He didn't know that his rings, or his valves, or cam shaft, or whatever was shot. He didn't have the experience or the knowledge to know that. So he was getting ready to shine it up, even though the car wasn't going to last through the week. He might not even be able to get it home.

"And here I am, in the same position as J.J and my mechanic, knowing from my area of expertise that as credible as your intentions are, your discussion isn't going to get you anywhere, and what's more, knowing why."

At first, it appeared that Ray was going to proceed to tell us why our discussion wasn't going to go anywhere, but he fell silent and seemed to drift away into some private thoughts. J.J. spoke for all of us when he asked Ray to please drop the other shoe.

"Can you tell us why?" he asked quietly.

"Sure I can," Ray answered in a cheerful tone, one which acknowledged J.J. for saying what he was thinking. "I'll do even

251

better. Since I have the expertise, I think it might be good to talk about some specifics tonight, so that's what I'm going to do.

"Sooner or later you get to know that you're not really getting anywhere, and sooner or later you start to wonder why. If you still think now that you're getting somewhere, then you're not at *later* yet, you're still at *sooner*, but sooner or later you'll see that you're spinning your wheels. You're sincere and you want something, and you hope and pray for something, but somehow you always end up getting in the way."

Linda chimed in that she felt she was at *later,* and still couldn't see what was wrong with their conversation.

Ray held up his hand for her to be patient and then resumed his explanation. "I'll tell you how you can check out one of those specific obstacles that causes you to imagine that something is going forward when it isn't.

"Some of you, I know, have read a book called *Steppenwolf.* It was written by Herman Hesse about seventy years ago. If you haven't, it's about a man named Harry who's having a really hard time with life. He has discovered that he actually has two halves, one that he calls 'the wolf,' and the other 'the man.' The wolf has its wolf's nature and the man has its man's nature. The wolf is a wild thing; it likes to drink the blood of freshly killed animals. It likes chaos and abandon, noise, severe temperatures and unknown situations. The wolf is territorial; it grabs its food and doesn't wait its turn. The wolf is rude and crude and urinates in places to mark its territory, and sometimes just urinates for the hell of it.

"The man is very different from that. The man feels the pull of the unmanifest, the divine. The man feels the urges of saintliness and goodness and giving, and sometimes even acts on those urges. Harry is living with these two forces existing in him, and it isn't working out.

"When the wolf goes out to eat, drink, and be merry, as he's eating, drinking, and being merry, the voice of temperance comes in, the voice of other people's need comes in, the voice of spirituality and wholesomeness comes in. Likewise, when the man tries to read his esoteric books, think his uplifting thoughts, and embrace the spiritual music that means so much to him, lust and restlessness enter and he yearns to prowl the streets and drink his fill.

"It's an untenable situation. So he gives himself till his fiftieth birthday, and if things don't work themselves out, he's going to end it all. Because these two parts of Harry are not living well together, and there is no peace.

"So let's leave Harry for now and talk about these three and their conversation about responsibility. Each of them was describing their opinion, 'I think this' and 'I really believe that.' Throughout their discussion, the views of the man came out in beautiful, sensitive, and esoteric terms, the wolf being in absence. The wolf was being hidden; his existence wasn't being acknowledged."

Ray looked directly at me. "You weren't presenting that the wolf was biding his time in the wings, that some other part of you was waiting for its turn, feeling restless and territorial and competitive. This entire discussion took place and there were no wolves. It's a tremendous illusion that we are all *men* in this room, because we aren't. True, there are eight humans here, but there are eight wolves dwelling among those eight humans as well as eight men. And in your conversation, only the men were represented; there was no representation of the wolves."

I didn't feel like I was trying to conceal any wolf, nor could I see why a wolf would have any interest in the subject of responsibility. I told him that, and asked when the wolf gets to do *its* thing.

"These days, special situations have to be set up so the wolf can have a turn. I'll give you an example of what I mean. Some years ago, I was in a stadium watching the Baltimore Colts play football. At that time, the Colts had a defensive tackle named Bubba Smith, a three hundred pound lineman, one of the first really big guys in the league.

"There were three fans sitting in front of me shouting, 'Kill Bubba, kill.' That's all they shouted for an hour, 'Kill Bubba, kill.' 'Kill Bubba, kill.' That wasn't only their cheer, they wanted Bubba to kill. I don't know what Bubba wanted, but that's what they wanted.

"Same with the people who watched the Roman gladiators. They didn't deny the wolf. They denied the man and learned to hide their sensitivity. How would a person at that time be looked on if he spoke out in support of non-violence?

"Think of the wolf in you, and in the people you know. When does this wolf get its voice heard? We eat with forks, our fingers well removed from the food, taking little bites, holding napkins to cover our mistakes. There are even restaurants now that advertise small portions. Compare that to the days when bones were thrown over shoulders to the hounds, times when the wolf was more acceptable.

"Now, except for a war here and there, the wolf has to operate in the shadows. Does that make us any less wolf? Maybe so, but probably not. Sometimes in very private and guarded circumstances, we get to be a little wild. But the rest of the time that wolf is denied, and we pretend to be something else."

"It sounds to me," Barnett commented, "that if everybody let their wolves do whatever they wanted..."

Ray knew that there was no reason to let him continue. "I'm not suggesting a course of action in which chaos reigns. What I'm suggesting is that we have a severe illusion about ourselves; it can't go well for us with this illusion and denial. There are things about ourselves that we must learn, because some of them are obstacles to what we seek."

Karl, who was usually a proponent of "letting it all hang out," asked Ray if he was saying that the wolf was an obstacle.

"I'm not saying that," Ray explained. "I'm saying that denial of the existence of the wolf is an obstacle. I'm saying ignorance of the existence of the wolf is an obstacle. I'm saying that the illusion that we are one thing is an obstacle.

"Denial of the wolf doesn't create a good situation for the elevation of the man, because it is the denial of the totality of ourselves. Denial that we are many, many, many selves leads to imagination. Even if you're fortunate enough to know about your condition theoretically, you don't know what's happening in the moment. You have parts -- parts with vastly diverse interests, and as they come forth they all claim to speak for the whole.

"I'd like to ask all of you a question. Why did you come here today?"

Everyone but Linda took a crack at the question. The answers, though somewhat different, all contained the component, 'I came here because I don't want to miss these last couple of meetings with Ray,' or some such thing.

He nodded knowingly. "Of course that's one reason, but none of you mentioned your ravenous appetite for food and the possibility of gorging at a Thai restaurant. That particular wolf in you that has only one interest, to get its food, was not represented in that answer. It was totally unrepresented along with all the others, and others, and others. It's not just one wolf and one man, but a thousand wolves and a thousand men, all lumped together in this package that you have one name for -- your name.

"You expect consistency. You expect life to reflect homogeneity. You expect that your actions should proceed along one line, and you wonder why they don't. Well they can't, anymore than you can say that we are a group, you understand." He held up both his arms in a gesture that included everyone at the table and asked, "So tell me group, what are we going to do after we leave here?"

Most of us laughed. The idea that we were one entity which was going to slither in unanimity from the restaurant to some other location seemed ridiculous.

Ray laughed too, probably because of a similar mind picture. "But when you say, 'What am *I* going to do after,' you don't laugh. *Actually, there are fewer of us at this table than there are of you, in your body.* There are only eight of us here at this table, but there are hundreds, maybe thousands of you alive in your body. Each of you has a plan for what you will do when you leave this place, and similarly, each wolf and each man within you has its own plan -- one that it will try to make into 'your plan.'

"Eventually you will leave this restaurant, and soon after, you will start talking to someone else -- five minutes, five hours, tomorrow, whenever. In that conversation you will imagine that what you're saying means something, and you will imagine that the words of the other person mean something. What neither of you will recognize is that represented amongst the two of you in that conversation, there is only one wolf of many in one person, speaking to only one wolf of many in the other, or one man of many to one man of many, or one wolf to one man, or one man to one wolf. How can your conversation be meaningful if so many unrepresented interest groups alive in you both are not heard from?"

Patricia had one of her rare moments of humility. She must have really been taking in what he was saying. She looked down as she said, "It sounds like we're that man who drove his sick car away from the shop. If he knew he would never get to drive the car again, he would feel pretty ridiculous; it was dead, and he was waxing it. Is that really what *we're* doing?"

"You may feel the desire to live more spiritually," Ray answered, "and maybe you even want to learn to meditate, but how are you going to deal with the wolf? Have you ever seen a wolf meditate? Wolves don't meditate. They pace up and down in their cages. Did you ever try to meditate and feel that even though you're sitting still, you're pacing up and down the cage? Only one of *you* agreed to try to be still. But there's not only one of you; there are all the others brought along without their consent. Like the wolf, they never stop till they're exhausted, or till they have eaten so much that they fall asleep. The wolves in us do likewise.

"Or maybe you come to church thinking that you have some religious aspiration. And during the service you find yourself looking over at some guy who owns a store. You think, 'Maybe I'll talk to him afterward and see if he can get me a good deal on a ... whatever.' Do you understand? The man comes to that service; the wolf appears -- over and over again, someone's always denied. 'Oh hi, yeah, you're the guy with the store down at the corner?'

You pretend like it all fits together, but it doesn't all fit together. It's completely discordant.

"Each one of us contains thousands of interest groups all in separated pockets, all looking for their segment of life so they can arise and say, 'This is my thing!' All the rest of the time they're waiting, waiting, waiting for that moment to jump out and be alive."

J.J. asked, in what was for him, a very subdued voice. "I feel like I'm really aware of what you're talking about a lot of the time. Am I fooling myself?"

Ray responded with intensity. "You aren't aware that each time you speak, even in this very question, you think you speak for the whole! You certainly put forth to others that you speak for the whole of you. When you make an agreement with somebody, you don't say, 'Well, there are a thousand of me, this one agrees with you, but tomorrow, who knows?' Can you imagine that happening? We wonder why the divorce rate is so high (J.J. recently got separated), but it's really a wonder that a marriage lasts even a day."

Usually, when new ideas were presented and a good deal of group input was happening, Linda became very animated and involved. We had been talking about this subject for a while, and though she had been listening attentively, she hadn't said anything for some time. Ray must have noticed also, because he asked her what was going on with her.

She looked up, and while shaking her head from side to side, she began to speak. "I can't believe it. I've known about this idea for a long time and this is the first time that I've really gotten it. Something that happened to me yesterday ..." her voice trailed off.

"What happened? You should tell us what happened," Phil said like he was unearthing a buried treasure.

"Okay, okay, it's really no big thing," Linda returned. "I've been getting a bad deal at work and I finally decided that I'd had it. I got myself stoked up to go right into the boss's office and tell him that if I didn't get this promotion, I was leaving. 'I'll tell him whatever I have to tell him, but I won't leave without it.' That's what I said to the guy I share an office with. And the wolf trots on over there. And as she puts her hand on the door handle and starts to open the boss's door, the man(woman) arises and walks in, and the wolf is left standing outside the door.

"The man says politely to the boss, 'Excuse me, do you think if you're not too busy, maybe I could have a moment of your time?' The wolf plans and the man acts it out, and nobody gets what they're looking for. I hope I never forget this one -- it's almost funny."

"Did you get the promotion?" Barnett asked.

Everyone looked at him incredulously. I assumed he was joking, but I couldn't say for sure. A silence of several extra seconds followed, then Ray took up where Linda left off.

"If you can begin to see this distortion, life will become a tremendous comedy if you have the right attitude, or a tremendous tragedy if you don't -- but certainly tremendously different than you assumed it to be. So many understandings that you have are based on the assumption that you are one thing. All the questions that you ask and all the statements that you make reflect your understanding of yourself to be one thing. You always refer to this person as 'I', 'Me' -- always!

"Now you know the tip of the iceberg of the problem. You know the description of the problem, and some of you may have even checked it out to some degree. Still you only know the tip of the iceberg. I say this from personal experience, because I know that I've checked it out more than you've checked it out, and always it expands. It's unbelievable how huge this distortion is, and how consolidated our agreements are that allow this distortion to continue."

Ray had given us much to digest, not to speak of all the Thai food that was left on the rotating center of our table. We took a break from the discussion and ate for a while. Sometime during that half hour of eating and food talk, Ray told what has become one of my favorites of his stories. Here it is.

"We raised sheep on our farm years ago. In early fall, when mating season came around, we would borrow rams for stud.

Since we didn't know much about sheep, our first year we went to a neighbor to get some rams and to learn the ropes.

Neighbor: *How many ewes do you have?* (A ewe is a female sheep.)

Ray: *About thirty five.* "I was thinking I'd need about a half a dozen rams, my frame of reference being -- relatively personal. I knew that rams have a reputation like bulls, so I figured I was looking for a half a dozen rams for thirty-five ewes. I had read somewhere that they have to have intercourse around six times before you can be pretty sure. You don't want to take a chance, since mating season only happens once a year. You want to make sure that it's working out. The arrangement is supposed to be that we get to keep the rams for a week, and they have to do it with all of the ewes every day, so I'm figuring half a dozen rams."

Neighbor: *Yeah, I got a ram.*

Ray: *No, I think I need....*

Neighbor: *How many ewes?*

Ray: *Thirty-five.*

Neighbor: *No, Fred will take care of 'em.*

"So I looked over at Fred the ram. Well this guy was the farmer and I wasn't, so I took his word for it. Well Fred had no problem. He was busy, but he was competent, and all the ewes got pregnant."

We joked about Fred for a few minutes, then Patricia asked uncharacteristically (I guess it was her wolf), "Why did you tell us that story? What's it supposed to mean anyway?"

Ray appreciated her departure from usualness and answered with a smile. "There are animals that are monogamous and mate for life, and there are animals that have very different habits. There is a wolf inside us that has laws by which it lives, and then there are all the societal regulations of our time. We know what the rules are, but we don't know what we are.

"Now here I thought I knew the rules for rams, but I was wrong. If Fred were a different animal, I might have been right. So what animal are we? We don't know. We only know what society's rules are. We only know how to pretend. We eat daintily; then after everybody leaves, we go to the refrigerator and stand there scarfing everything off the shelves with a stuffing in the face motion. We don't know the animal that's alive in us, and likewise, because we're so busy squelching that animal and causing it to obey the rules, we don't know the man in us either."

After taking Ray's answer in stride, Patricia came back with a follow-up. "So how do we get all these wolves and men that are trapped inside this body to get along? How do they get to agree? How do they proceed?"

Ray said some words applauding the directness of their exchange, and then went on. "Up to this point, the way it has been resolved is that you will present yourself as one thing even though you're not. Then what will follow, is you'll have to substantiate and defend to yourself and to others that you are that one thing. In order to do that, you will have to lie. But then after you lie, you'll become insecure and afraid, because in you somewhere, you know that you lied and you're afraid of being caught in that lie. So then you'll have to lie again, to cover the first lie and try to alleviate that fear -- and so on and so on and so on. All starting from this misrepresentation that we are one thing -- the agreement that we are one thing, and the accepted demand that we have of ourselves and each other, that we present ourselves as one thing."

"Sounds like something's got to give," J.J. said.

"Something *has* got to give!" Ray accentuated. "The wolf is not going to go away, and the man is not going to go away. That's the experiment that was put on us, and it's not ours to change. Each of us is a unique experiment on the part of the creator, and in that unique experiment there are men and there are wolves. You can like it, you can not like it -- you can go to a monastery, you can go to Tahiti. This experiment that we call 'our lives' contains the man and the wolf. Our challenge is -- can we see how they fit together? Can we work it out?

"If you've read *Steppenwolf* you may remember how it began to be resolved in Harry. He was condemned to enjoy the 'radio music of life' and experience lightness and humor. Because, obviously in this ridiculous situation of many selves and one body, without lightness and humor, we're lost."

Ray asked if we were approaching overdose. All of us were game for more, so he offered to tell us about a specific experiment we could try.

"If you want to study this phenomenon that I'm describing, one interesting way is by noting situations in which certain common phrases are used. *I forgot* is one of those phrases. When a person uses that well known expression, he is presenting a microcosm of this entire (many selves in one body) situation.

"Let's take the example of Karl saying, 'I'm going to bring the tape recorder next week.' He said that, but of course 'I' is many 'I's'. What is the likelihood that the 'I' that says *I'm going to ...* will come back next week. So when Karl comes back, and I ask for the tape recorder, he uses those famous words, *I forgot*. Of course the 'I', the person here with us this week saying this to me, never forgot; he never heard and never knew about the promise in the first place. But since he has to present himself as one thing, and because he thinks I'm requiring that he present himself as one thing, he says those famous words, *I forgot*. By using this convenient phrase, a person effectively cloaks the actuality of the situation with a deception, one that he actually believes."

"Could you go over that one more time," Barnett asked, screwing up his face to convince Ray that he was lost and it was necessary.

Ray said the whole thing again. "Let's take the example of Karl saying, 'I'm going to bring the tape recorder next week.' He said that, but of course 'I' is many 'I's'. What is the likelihood that the 'I' that says *I'm going to ...* will come back next week. So when Karl comes back, and I ask for the tape recorder, he uses those famous words, *I forgot*. Of course the 'I', the person here with us this week saying this to me, never forgot; he never heard and never knew about the promise in the first place. But since he has to present himself as one thing, and because he thinks I'm requiring that he present himself as one thing, he says those famous words, *I forgot*. By using this convenient phrase, a person

261

effectively cloaks the actuality of the situation with a deception, one that he actually believes."

"I think I get that one," Karl said. "Can you give us some more examples."

Ray laughed and said, "That's your job. There are numerous small ways in which a person can see this phenomenon in themselves, and maybe you can discover some as well, if it interests you to do that. I'm presenting this as sort of a game, and an interesting one. But I can tell you this -- some of you will be entertained by these ideas, some will be curiously interested in them, some will be very interested, some will become students of these ideas and discover things about them. Then some few, very few, will do all that, and put what they learn into action.

"This point of view of many selves in one person is a revolutionary idea. You may think that you've thought about it before, or you've read it somewhere. But as I said, of this iceberg you've seen only the minuscule tip, and even that, you will forget within the hour. You will proceed like this distortion doesn't exist. No matter what you think now, you will proceed in that way. You will be called on to respond as though you are one thing and your first words will be, 'I' was, 'I' did. They won't be, 'Well, it depends on which me you're asking.' That isn't what you'll say, and more importantly, that isn't what you'll think or feel. Always, always in everything, you will present yourself as one thing."

I liked to think of myself as being one of the few that would put what I learned into action, but I wasn't sure yet. I guess I needed some reassurance that it was possible for someone like me to get free of all this. I asked, "If all that chaos is going on inside me, how am I going to get something going?" It wasn't as complete as the question in my guts, but it's what came out.

So much had been said already that Ray just added a few finishing touches. "Politicians sometimes have grandiose ideas for sweeping change. They have to make super-human efforts to convince thousands of people that these changes are worthwhile. Similarly, we have ideas to change ourselves. We also have a lot of convincing to do, but the people that we have to convince all live within us.

"There are a lot of exciting times ahead, if you can see this kind of exploration as exciting. Now of course, it's different than video games and movies. It's a different kind of excitement. It's tough to consider this exciting when you've been fed so much of that other kind of excitement.

"But sometimes even the people who study ordinary science can appreciate subtlety. A scientist identifies a teeny microbe, and all the specialists in that field just go nuts. Or an astronomer discovers a star, and astronomers around the world are on the phone all night. And you say, 'Big deal,' then turn on the T.V. or read a book where seventeen civilizations rise and fall in an hour. We're spoiled by all that high rev business."

Shortly thereafter we left the restaurant.

Ray declined when we asked to do a farewell scene with him on his day of departure. Now we were seven.

EPILOGUE

You gotta learn how to fall
if you're gonna learn to fly.

Paul Simon

In a way the story is over, and in a way it's not. So if you feel the empty feeling that sometimes goes with endings, you can at least postpone it by reading on. I have saved some juicy tidbits for those of you that have become family.

Writing this book has been a very curious undertaking. The ideas that I've been writing about, and that you've been reading about could hardly be considered casual. This lack of casualness would, in a face-to-face relationship between people, result in extreme intimacy. Our relationship is, however, far from intimate. In fact, we are not only unknown to each other, but might also be considered totally unaccountable to one another.

I say 'considered' totally unaccountable because I intend to cross the line of what you would normally be entitled to expect of me, and make an attempt at what I imagine you would *like* to expect of me, even though I certainly don't have to do that. My actions are inspired by the words of someone who lived long before my gyrations began: *Do unto others as you would have others do unto you.*

265

I have a long history of being an enthusiastic film-goer and television watcher. Because of that history, I have learned about certain human sensitivities, one of those being, that no matter how profound a story is and regardless of where and when it took place, we as human beings are always, to some degree, curious about what happened after -- "The End."

The following is the letter received by Patricia shortly after Ray's departure:

March 19, Berkeley, CA

Dear Patricia et.al.:
    I read your letter last night in the bathtub. A few words bled to death, but the ones that remained seemed compelling enough to require a response. The day after tomorrow I am off on my journey to the West. As you know, my daughter is coming with me, so I have had to take care of numerous additional details. Since this will be my last opportunity to meddle, I've decided to take it.
    In answer to your question: you're not the only person who wants more; everyone wants more. No one wants less. The only reason a person would want less, is because they thought that less was going to be more. But here's a bulletin for you: THERE IS NO MORE! So what you want is not going to happen.
    When you go to a store, you want something that you don't have, but you're willing to give something that you do have. You give them the money, they give you the food. You have less of something that you had, and you have more of something new. That's the way it works.
    If you want less youth, you get more age. If you want to lay back and let your body relax, you can't run and jog. If you run and jog, you can't do the other. Maybe you know the song about the guy who wants to have a family and also wants to go sailing around the world. Well, if you have a family, you can't sail around the world, and if you sail around the world, it's hard to have a family. But still, everybody wants more. From your letter, I can see that wanting more has now even extended into the world of consciousness for you.
    How often have you had the attitude when getting together with your teammates: I wonder what I could give?

266

No, I don't mean give to them, I mean, I wonder what I could dispense with, what I could leave behind, what I could give up?

When you go to the store, you know that when you take the food away, you're going to have to give up something, $$$. Well, it's the same in this world of freedom seeking, you understand? If you're going to take something away, you're going to have to leave something there.

But you're not thinking what can I leave? You want to keep your whole thing together and get something more on top of it. Of course then, there's no place for expansion. It is possible for extraordinary things to happen, but something has got to give. Something has got to be left behind.

Let's say that you're in a position of losing something that you've known to be valuable in the past -- like in your case, your affinity for being insincere. That has been a precious commodity for you, as it has been for so many others. So when you see that you're going to have to give up your old act, you balk, because your phony performance is what has gotten you through life. You haven't gotten by on your essential qualities, on your vulnerability and simplicity. You've gotten by on your ability to shuck and jive. Yes, it has worked to get you to this point, but it's not going to get you any further. Sooner or later, if you ever do move on, you're going to have to leave something behind.

Regards to you and the rest of the team,
Ray

In addition, it might interest you, the reader, that I have, sometime between then and now, given up playing poker. Both the time and concentration that it took to write this book and a curious aversion that crept over me are what (as far as I can see) are responsible. This aversion to which I refer is one that denied me the sense of satisfaction in winning that always ran concurrent with my disdain for losing. When I began to realize the 'cost' paid by others for my pleasure, it fell from its position of sweetness.

For the past year or so I have been living near the ocean with a few people that were and are on my team. During the summer we have a business together -- teaching windsurfing and renting and selling sailboard equipment. For those of you who are interested in my present comings and goings, I will include a few paragraphs about my current activities. My involvement with this present vocation began some time ago. I'll tell you how it started.

It can be fantastic to do something so simple and pleasurable as windsurfing, even though going through the learning process can be so completely and absolutely challenging and humiliating. In the beginning, learning to windsurf is an incredible process of looking totally uncoordinated. I consider myself to be somewhat athletic, but when I tried to stand up on a sailboard, it felt totally impossible. I was like a person with pressure on the brain, you know, no balance whatsoever. One little rock or roll, and splash, I was off the edge.

The first time I ever tried to windsurf was on a trip to Mexico a few years ago. I had never even been curious about it before; there was no magnetism there. Three of us rented a board and sail after convincing the man with our assurance, "Oh yeah, no problem, we've done it before." After all, how hard could it be, we thought.

We paddled out there and after a while we were laughing so hard over our inability to get this thing up straight, that it was exhausting. We never even got close to standing up on it. All the principles that we used were completely against aerodynamics and wind direction, so we'd just keep falling in the water.

I had so much fun that even though I never got up and sailing, when I got back to the U.S. I took some lessons, and as time went by I progressed from one stage to another. After a year or so, I recognized a pattern that occurred throughout my progressions to each new level.

What I recognized was that toward the end of one stage and at the beginning of the next, there is a required payment, and it is always the same: You must give up whatever competency you've achieved in order to take on the next step, knowing that once again you'll be falling in the water, looking clumsy, and being frustrated.

What I also recognized was that towards the end of each stage things became repetitious. I was doing the same moves over and over again, and to some degree was even enjoying the repetitions, but there was no exploration there. It was more like building self-confidence, I guess.

There was this resistance against going ahead with the exploration and looking like a fool, falling in the water, not feeling in control, not having it together. But sooner or later I would break through, and then boom, splash, boom, splash, boom, splash, it would be happening again. I would be learning again, taking chances, being excited, and feeling danger. All those wonderful feelings would be there again.

This sequence happened enough times for me to recognize that not only is this the case for windsurfing or sports, but probably it is analogous to life, that at each stage some requirement is made of us in order to once again tap that vitality. The point at which some payment is due is most easily recognized by signs that life starts to feel stale and dry, and we begin wondering what it's all for.

In addition to a sailboard business, Linda and I live with some friends, two of whom are a lady and her one year old boy. Over this past year I've gotten to see him learning to walk. He has definitely recognized that the process of learning to walk involves falling down, and he's okay with that part of it. He doesn't think, *Damn!* every time he falls down.

I recognize how superior he is to the rest of us, because we're not willing to accept the falling down part of learning. We think there's something wrong with falling down -- he doesn't. He falls like it's all part of the process.

He really doesn't have to learn to walk, but there is a force in him that wants walking to happen. He crawls far better than he walks at this stage. He can crawl pretty fast; he can retrieve things and get where he wants to go. When he gets to where he's going, he'll try to stand up, then boom, he falls down. It's really just like when I started to learn how to windsurf, you know, fall

down-splash-boom, fall down-splash-boom, but still he keeps getting up and trying to walk.

Why does he do that? You might think, "Hey, kid -- take it
easy, crawl around, you do that much better," but the kid's going
to keep trying to walk. It's a certain strength that's in him that's
going to keep doing it. With that strength he can accept falling
down as part of learning to walk.

These days I often think of my own life and of how much
falling down I'm willing to accept. Many of us seem to have developed the idea that the path of life should be smooth, and that
smoother is better. 'Smoother is better' is very different than this
little kid's attitude. Insisting that smoother is better has meant that
basically we've lost the thread that falling down is part of the
process, because falling down is certainly not smoother. So we
spend our lives trying to find ways to avoid the falling down, and
we pay for that avoiding, because we never learn how to take the
next step.

Yes, I am still deep in the midst of the process that I was
introduced to by Ray.

It has now been several years since I've seen him. Since, from
an ordinary point of view, we had no reason to separate -- no
falling out, no parting of the ways, no growing bored with each
other -- it has been different from any separation that I have
previously known. I also recognize its importance, because it has
allowed me to either put into action what he taught me, or to proceed in some other way. The fact that I've persevered sufficiently
to write this book has been for me the most tangible evidence of
my choice.

Throughout this period of separation, though not maintaining
contact with Ray in person, I have tried to keep track of his
whereabouts on the planet, and from time to time I write a letter
and mail it in the way that a quarterback would lead a wide
receiver with a forward pass.

Aside from the comments that he sent me concerning the ade-
quacy of this book (which I would not have had published until he

approved), I have also received several postcards sent, I suspect, out of compassion for my situation.

I recently confirmed, by means of a mutual acquaintance, a rumor that Ray had been spotted somewhere in South East Asia, Singapore, I think. When I can faithfully adhere to the guidelines he suggested in those days that we went to the Special Olympics together, I suspect and hope that our paths will cross again.

...and since that moment no one can truly claim to have seen Reepicheep the Mouse. But my belief is that he came safe to Aslan's country and is alive there to this day.

Voyage of the Dawn Treader, **C.S. Lewis**

Postface

Into a dancer you have grown
From a seed somebody else has thrown
Go on ahead and throw some seeds of your own
And somewhere between the time you arrive and the time you go
May lie a reason you were alive but you'll never know.

Jackson Browne

Over the past several years, I have tried to fulfill an obligation by putting words on these pages. I wonder if you, by having read this far, and to the extent that you have been capable of absorbing these ideas, have not also accumulated a debt?

Acknowledgements

EPIGRAPHS

Chap. **2.** Doris Lessing, *The Making of theRepresentative for Planet 8*
   (New York: Alfred A. Knopf, Inc.,1982, Canopus in Argos-archives)
   3. Paul Simon, *Slip Slidin' Away* (Copyright © 1977 Paul Simon)
   4. Leonard Cohen, *Sisters of Mercy* (Copyright 1967 Leonard Cohen Stranger
   Music, Inc.) Used by Permission. All Rights Reserved.
   5. Carlos Castaneda, *Tales Of Power* (New York: Simon & Schuster, 1974)
   6. Bob Dylan, *It's Alright Ma, (I'm Only Bleeding)* (Copyright 1965 by Warner
   Bros. Music - Copyright renewed 1993 by Special Rider Music)
   7. Olive Schreiner, *Dreams* (Boston: Little, Brown, & Co., 1929)
   8. The Bhagavad Gita
   9. Peter S. Beagle, *The Last Unicorn* (New York: The Viking Press, 1968)
   10. Laurens van der Post, *A Story Like The Wind* (New York: Morrow, 1972)
   11. Peter Matthiessen, *The Snow Leopard* (New York: Viking Penguin,Inc.1978)
   12. Laurens van der Post, *A Far-Off Place* (New York: Morrow, 1974)
   13. Hermann Hesse, *Demian* (New York: Harper & Row, Inc., 1965)
   14. Rene Daumal, *Mount Analogue* (New York: Pantheon Books, 1959)
   15. Kathryn Hulme, *The Nun's Story* (Boston: Little, Brown, & Co., 1956)
   16. Hermann Hesse, *The Glass Bead Game* (New York: Holt, R. & W., 1969)
   17. G. I. Gurdjieff, *Meetings with Remarkable Men* (New York: Dutton, 1969)
   18. James Hilton, *Lost Horizon* (New York: William Morrow & Co., Inc.,1933)
   19. Arthur C. Clarke, *2001 A Space Odyssey* (New York: Dutton, 1968)
   20. Richard Brautigan, *In Watermelon Sugar* (New York: Dell, 1973)
   21. Robert A. Heinlein, *Stranger In A Strange Land* (New York: Putnam, 1961)
   22. Peter S. Beagle, *The Last Unicorn* (New York: The Viking Press, 1968)
   23. (Also in Postface.) Jackson Browne, *For A Dancer* (© 1974 Swallow Turn
   Music, All Rights Reserved. Used By Permission.)
Epilogue. Paul Simon, *Learn How To Fall* (Copyright © 1973 Paul Simon)

REFERENCES IN TEXT

Page **14.** Leonard Cohen, *Diamonds In The Mine* (Copyright 1971 Leonard Cohen
   Stranger Music, Inc.) Used by Permission. All Rights Reserved.
   24. Rene Daumal, *Mount Analogue* (New York: Pantheon Books, 1959)
   43. Barbet Shroeder, *The Valley*, (© 1972 Films du Losange)
   54. Carlos Castaneda, *Tales Of Power* (New York: Simon & Schuster, 1974)
   68. Ibid., Page 61
   138. Bob Dylan, *Stuck Inside Of Mobile With The Memphis Blues Again*
   (Copyright1966, Dwarf Music)
   146. Hermann Hesse, *The Glass Bead Game* (New York: Holt, R. & W., 1969)
   173. Olive Schreiner, *Dreams* (Boston: Little, Brown, & Co., 1929)
   209. Ibid., Page 146
   244. Bob Dylan, *One Of Us Must Know(Sooner or Later)* (© 1966 Dwarf Music)
   244. Leonard Cohen, *The Story of Isaac* (Copyright 1968 Leonard Cohen Stranger
   Music, Inc.) Used by Permission. All Rights Reserved.
   252. Hermann Hesse, *Steppenwolf* (New York: Holt, Rinehart & Winston, 1963)
   271. C.S. Lewis, *The Voyage of the Dawn Treader* (New York: Macmillan, 1970)

My deep appreciation to the people who wrote the precious words referred to
above, and to my mom and Ray, and the others who have tried to encourage
me, and especially to Jack, who I suspect had something to do with all this.

Index

I wish to express my appreciation to the following people who directly participated in the coming into being of this book.

Amalthea, Annette, Arnie, Bob G.,
Crystal, Dan, David, Donna, Jeff,
Jon R., Karl, Kim, Lisa, Patrick C.,
Patsy, Terry, Tim, & Tish